W9-BGL-745

Chinatown Gangs

STUDIES IN CRIME AND PUBLIC POLICY
Michael Tonry and Norval Morris, *General Editors*

Police for the Future
David H. Bayley

Incapacitation: Penal Confinement and the Restraint of Crime
Franklin E. Zimring and Gordon Hawkins

The American Street Gang: Its Nature, Prevalence, and Control
Malcolm W. Klein

Sentencing Matters
Michael Tonry

The Habits of Legality: Criminal Justice and the Rule of Law
Francis A. Allen

Chinatown Gangs: Extortion, Enterprise, and Ethnicity
Ko-lin Chin

Responding to Troubled Youth
Cheryl L. Maxson and Malcolm W. Klein

Making Crime Pay:
Law and Order in Contemporary American Politics
Katherine Beckett

Community Policing, Chicago Style
Wesley G. Skogan and Susan M. Hartnett

Crime Is Not the Problem: Lethal Violence in America
Franklin E. Zimring and Gordon Hawkins

Hate Crimes: Criminal Law and Identity Politics
James B. Jacobs and Kimberly Potter

Politics, Punishment, and Populism
Lord Windlesham

American Youth Violence
Franklin E. Zimring

Bad Kids: Race and the Transformation of the Juvenile Court
Barry C. Feld

CHINATOWN GANGS

Extortion, Enterprise, and Ethnicity

Ko-lin Chin

OXFORD UNIVERSITY PRESS
New York   Oxford

0017999

Oxford University Press

Oxford   New York
Athens   Auckland   Bangkok   Bogotá   Buenos Aires   Calcutta
Cape Town   Chennai   Dar es Salaam   Delhi   Florence   Hong Kong   Istanbul
Karachi   Kuala Lumpur   Madrid   Melbourne   Mexico City   Mumbai
Nairobi   Paris   São Paulo   Singapore   Taipei   Tokyo   Toronto   Warsaw

and associated companies in
Berlin   Ibadan

Copyright © 1996 by Oxford University Press, Inc.

First published in 1996 by Oxford University Press, Inc.
198 Madison Avenue, New York, New York 10016

First issued as an Oxford University Press paperback, 2000

Oxford is a registered trademark of Oxford University Press

All rights reserved. No part of this publication may be reproduced,
stored in a retrieval system, or transmitted, in any form or by any means,
electronic, mechanical, photocopying, recording, or otherwise,
without the prior permission of Oxford University Press.

Library of Congress Cataloging-in-Publication Data
Chin, Ko-lin.
Chinatown gangs : extortion, enterprise, and ethnicity / Ko-lin Chin.
p. cm.
Includes bibliographical references and index.
ISBN 0–19–510238-X; 0–19–513627-6 (pbk.)
1. Gangs—New York (N.Y.)   2. Chinese American teenagers—New York
(N.Y.)   3. Chinese American criminals—New York (N.Y.)   4. Extortion—New
York (N.Y.)   5. Chinatown (New York, N.Y.)—Social life and
customs.   I. Title.
HV6439.U7N433   1996
364.1'06'608995107471—dc20   95-37331

Earlier versions of portions of this book have appeared in various books and
journals. Portions of chapter 1 appeared in Ko-lin Chin and Jeffrey Fagan,
"Social Order and Gang Formation in Chinatown," in *The Legacy of Anomie
Theory*, vol. 6 of *Advances in Criminological Theory*, ed. Freda Adler and
William Laufer (New Brunswick, N.J.: Transaction, 1995): 228–246; reprinted
by permission of Transaction Publishers. Portions of chapter 2 appeared in
"Methodological Issues in Studying Chinese Gang Extortion," *Gang Journal*
1(2) 1993: 25–36; reprinted by permission. Portions of chapter 4 appeared in
Ko-lin Chin, Jeffrey Fagan, and Robert J. Kelly, "Patterns of Chinese Gang
Extortion," *Justice Quarterly* 9(4): 1992: 625–646; reprinted with permission
of the Academy of Criminal Justice Sciences.

1 3 5 7 9 8 6 4 2

Printed in the United States of America
on acid-free paper

To Marvin E. Wolfgang,

whose work, teaching, and guidance
inspired this undertaking

PREFACE

Gang researchers, from Frederick Thrasher to contemporary scholars, have rarely discussed the role of adult organizations in the processes of gang formation. Theory and research on gangs have typically attributed gang formation to the structural characteristics of communities and to the processes that develop when poor people congregate in destitute communities (A. Cohen, 1955; Cloward and Ohlin, 1960; Short and Strodtbeck, 1965; Moore, 1978; J. McLeod, 1987; Hagedorn, 1988; Vigil, 1988; Taylor, 1990). While researchers such as Whyte (1943) and Suttles (1968) recognized the importance of social order in poor and socially isolated neighborhoods, they assumed that the social order in these neighborhoods reflected the social organization among adults and that youth and adult groups were disconnected. Accordingly, early conceptions of youth gang formation assumed either that influential adult organizations were not present in the community or that adult organizations played no significant role in the socialization and formation of adolescent delinquent groups. The youth gangs portrayed in the bulk of the literature were seen primarily as an adolescent phenomenon, formed spontaneously or purposefully by youths and removed from larger community influences.

In the early twentieth century, for youth gangs in European immigrant communities, ties with adult criminal organizations were situational and nonsystematic (O'Kane, 1992); legal avenues to success competed with the excitement and perceived status of organized criminal activity for the hearts and minds of young people. Most adolescents usually abandoned delinquent behavior and gang ties as they approached adulthood. A small number continued their criminal activity into their adult lives, often as part of adult crime groups. However, the transition appeared to be a journey navigated by young men who chose to associate with older criminals. It usually took place without any active recruitment or formal organizational ties between the youth gangs and the adult crime groups. When adolescents were incorporated or drafted into adult crime groups, it was usually when young gang members sought out the older groups. Rarely in the gang literature is it mentioned that formal ties between adult organized crime groups and adolescent youth gangs existed.

The emergence of youth gangs within Chinese communities in contemporary American cities challenges these classical theories on youth gang formation and their various socialization functions. As discussed in this volume, Chinese gang members describe their social world as secretive, highly structured, and disciplined. More important, Chinese gangs have close ties with criminally influenced adult organizations that are active in Chinatown. The gangs are extensively involved in extortion, which is usually carried out under the strict supervision of gang leaders, who negotiate their territory with members of adult crime groups. Gang recruitment activities in Chinatown are less spontaneous than they are deliberate, symbolically ritualized, and calculated strategies designed to attract individuals with the presumed characteristics and backgrounds suitable for gang activities. Except in Vietnamese gangs, elaborate initiation ceremonies are conducted by a member of the sponsoring adult organization. This person is referred to as "uncle," and he is the link between the gang leader and the adult organization.

There also appear to be functional economic relationships between youth gangs and adult organizations. Chinese youth gangs often are hired by adult organizations for lucrative work, such as protecting gambling and prostitution houses, collecting debts, and working as "street soldiers" in economic and territorial affairs. Their involvement in these enterprises, under the influence of adult crime groups, provides them with income and access to a career ladder within the illegal organizations, which decreases their dependence on extortion and other forms of business exploitation. The adult groups also exert considerable control over the gangs and discourage their involvement in nonsanctioned extortion and violent activities that might jeopardize the adult organizations' enterprises. Social control is maintained by the implicit threat of exclusion of gang members from this more lucrative work. The adult organizations also provide mechanisms for the resolution of petty disputes and conflicts that for nonaffiliated gangs would escalate into lethal intergang violence. These adult groups play a central role in the Chinese community's affairs by resolving conflicts, providing jobs, financial help, loans, protection, recreational activities, and business opportunities to members of the community, and offering economic assistance to the poor.

This study examines the dynamic relationships between social order and gang formation and the patterns and seriousness of victimization of Chinese business people by Chinese gangs. It seeks to describe the social processes in Chinese communities that may contribute to or mitigate against these offenses. It also investigates how business owners and law enforcement authorities react to gang activities in American Chinatowns. Moreover, this book explores the individual and group characteristics of Chinese gangs, and their involvement in violence and a variety of profit-generating crimes.

Two theoretical frameworks—victimology and organized crime—are relevant to this investigation. From the victimology perspective, I have sought to learn as much as possible about the interactive processes involved in extortion attempts. The context and setting in which criminal behavior occurs, the duration of victimization, its escalation or de-escalation, the range of reactions of victims and offenders, the conditions under which violence occurs, the methods used by victims and offenders to terminate extortion, and the role of law enforcement agents in controlling and containing it are all different facets of the process and therefore are part of the research.

Generally, organized crime literature depicts criminal activity in economic and social terms. From the criminology perspective, the extortion activities conducted in Chinese communities may be assumed to serve particular social and economic functions. From the standpoint of the predatory gangs, communities are transformed into "markets" for criminal exploitation, and power over these markets varies according to the composition of the community/market and the criminal resources and capacities of gangs.

The connection between organized criminal activities and enervated social institutions, together with the improved criminal opportunities occasioned by inadequate crime-control policies in a population poorly equipped to exploit favorable occupational conditions, forms the conceptual framework of this study. Thus, the study is governed by a focus on three interrelated aspects of gang criminal behavior in the community: the criminal offenders, the dynamic processes of their offenses, and the organizations in which the offenses occur.

The perspective emphasizes the organized nature of the criminal activities of street gangs. The problem of crime for the Chinese community lies, of course, in the pattern of substantive criminal offenses that the gangs commit; also important, however, are the special features of the gangs and the social contexts in which they formulate and conduct criminal behavior. Chinese criminal gangs appear to gather strength from the inherent weaknesses in the social and economic fabric of the communities in which they operate and are able to resist law enforcement efforts that are enfeebled by a subcultural community ravaged by poverty. The street gangs pose additional threats in that they are able to extend and expand their criminal activities (insofar as their current behaviors are tolerable) to the Chinese community at large.

Chapter 1 offers a theoretical framework of gang formation in the Chinese community. It is based on theoretical concepts of conflict and the web of group affiliations developed by Simmel (1955) and empirically utilized by Whyte (1943) and Suttles (1968) in their studies on the social order in the slum, Aldrich's (1979) concepts of inter-organization relationships and resource dependency, and extensions of Cloward and Ohlin's (1960) concept of "criminal subculture."

Chapter 2 describes the methods used in the study. It presents methodology for sampling, questionnaire construction, pretesting, interviewer recruitment and training, securing support from the community, subject recruitment, building rapport with the subjects, and ensuring the validity and reliability of the data. The practical and unusual problems of doing field interviews in the Chinese community and ways of coping with these problems are also examined.

Extortion is considered to be one of the major activities of Chinese gangs. Accordingly, chapters 3–5 concentrate on this phenomenon. In chapter 3, I evaluate the prevalence, frequency, and seriousness of extortion in New York City's Chinese communities, focusing on quantitative questions that measure the percentage of subjects who were victimized, how often were they exploited, along with the financial, psychological, and physical damages suffered by victims. The key question in organizing the data and in analyzing it is, What characterizes a vulnerable victim?

Chapter 4 describes the patterns or social processes of extortion. It explains the ways Chinese offenders extort money, food, and services from business owners, the methods used by offenders in approaching their victims, the interactions between offenders and victims after the initial victimization, and the social organization of extortion.

Chapter 5 focuses on how victims and the Chinese community in general react to the extortion in their midst. Specifically, I examine the justifications and rationales for complying with demands, the reasons for resistance, the prevalence of reporting crime to law enforcement authorities, the reasons businesspeople either approach or shy away from the criminal justice system, and the patterns of adaptation to extortion.

In chapter 6, I look at the individual and group characteristics of Chinese gangs and offer a picture of gang members in terms of age, sex, country of origin, education, family background, and so on. Group characteristics such as size, turf, structure, the division of labor in Chinese gangs, the rules and norms of the gangs, and the nature of the affiliation between gangs and other Chinese crime groups are analyzed. The chapter also depicts and delineates the social processes of joining and leaving the gangs.

Chinese gangs are believed to be extremely violent. In chapter 7, I discuss the participation rate in; the frequency, typology, and causes of; and the restraining mechanisms on gang violence. The chapter examines how and why Chinese gang members direct their aggression toward members of rival gangs, members of their own gang, and victims who are not gang members. Gang mechanisms to control aggression are also investigated. Finally, hypothetical explanations of Chinese gang violence are presented and assessed in light of the findings.

Besides extortion and violence, Chinese gangs are reportedly involved in other profit-generating criminal activities such as prostitution, gambling, robbery, drug trafficking, and human smuggling. Chapter 8 looks into the involvement of gangs and other crime groups in these activities. In addition, this chapter presents some data on gang involvement in legitimate businesses.

How local and federal law enforcement authorities cope with Chinese gangs and other Chinese crime groups in the United States is the substance of chapter 9. I describe the activity and structure of local and federal units established to combat Chinese crime groups, local and federal policies against Chinese criminal organizations, prosecution of major Chinese crime groups, and some of the problems encountered by the law enforcement community in dealing with crime in the Chinese community.

A glossary, explaining all the Chinese words mentioned here, is located at the end of the book.

Newark   K-l. C.
March 1995

ACKNOWLEDGMENTS

Every book is a communal effort even though it is also a personal matter. This work has grown out of many conversations, discussions, and arguments, and it is accordingly a cooperative venture.

First and foremost, I would like to thank Jeffrey Fagan of Rutgers University and Robert Kelly of Brooklyn College, City University of New York, for their critical contributions to this endeavor. Jeff was the principal investigator, and Bob and the author were the co-principal investigators of this project. Both of them have guided me from the very beginning to the very end of this study. They were instrumental in all phases of the project, including proposal writing, grant management, questionnaire development, sampling, interviewer training, and data analysis and presentation. Both Jeff and Bob's suggestions and reactions over the course of the research helped shape the study's scientific and scholarly contours, and the two of them played a critical role in guiding the research along unprecedented paths from a focus on gang extortion activities to a more comprehensive exploration of the community contexts of gang organization and organized crime. Without their assistance, insights, and encouragement, this book would not have been written.

I was fortunate to have recruited a very special group of interviewers and research assistants who were, despite the personal risk of potential harm and danger, completely dedicated to the project. It is they who made this study come to life, and I owe them a great deal. My debt of gratitude is to Lai I Man, Jade Wong, Elain Lam, Hai Shan Liu, Suk Kam Chan, and Julie Han for conducting the interviews and to Yurong Zhang, Jessica Chan, and Kai S. Yum for managing the project in its various stages.

I also wish to thank those who participated in the study as subjects and informants and those who influenced my understanding of the shape and character of the community and its problems. I owe thanks to the business owners, community leaders, and gang members who agreed to be interviewed. Special thanks must go to Paul Yew, former president of the Chinese Consolidated Benevolent Association; M. B. Lee, chairman of the Lee Family Association; and Alan Mansin Lau, former president of the Fukien American Association.

The information, advice, and generous assistance of law enforcement specialists made my work a satisfying and enriching experience. I wish to take special note of the efforts of Catherine Palmer, former Assistant U.S. Attorney, Eastern District of New York; Tom Rynne, Department of Defense; Robert Perito and Mark Taylor, Department of State; Jeannette Chu, Kenny Lin, and Bruce Nicholl, Immigration and Naturalization Service; Sergeant Michael Collins, Detectives Agnes Chan and Robert Chu, Intelligence Division, New York City Police Department; Lloyd Hutchinson, Investigator, Queens District Attorney's Office; Eric Kruss, Federal Bureau of Investigation; Nicholas Caruso and Wayne McDonnell, Drug Enforcement Administration; Steven Rackmill, Chief Probation Officer, Eastern District of New York; and Luke Rettler, Manhattan District Attorney's Office.

Alex Peng, one of the most knowledgeable journalists on the issue of crime in New York City's Chinatown, helped us in many ways. He played a major role in arranging contacts with community leaders and gang members. I would also like to thank Tamryn Etten of Auburn University, who spent countless hours editing the manuscript and providing many valuable comments.

Institutions and their representatives have been no less vital to this project than the persons mentioned above. In the foreground of support were Lois Mock, project liaison and program director at the National Institute of Justice; Deans Ronald Clarke and Allan Futernick of the School of Criminal Justice at Rutgers University; Clayton Hartjen, Chair of the Department of Sociology, Anthropology, and Criminal Justice at Rutgers University; and Dr. Mary Eckert, Director of Research of the New York City Criminal Justice Agency, a pretrial service agency I was affiliated with during the data-collection stage of this study.

Thanks to Gioia Stevens, Helen McInnis, and Cynthia Garver of Oxford University Press and Caroline Herrick, whose support and excellent editorial help made this endeavor a pleasant and rewarding experience. I want to thank Rumoldo Arriolla of the New York City Criminal Justice Agency for his assistance in computer programming. I would like to express my sincere gratitude to Betty Lee Sung of City College of New York and an anonymous reviewer for their helpful critiques. I also want to recognize Shirley Parker and Jean Webster of the School of Criminal Justice, who provided me administrative help throughout this project. My wife, Catherine, deserves a special note of appreciation. Without her constant encouragement and enduring care, this work would not have been possible.

It is hardly necessary to absolve others from responsibility for the views set forth, but I do so anyway, to resolve any doubt that those acknowledged necessarily share my assessments of the problems. Support for this research was provided by Grant 89–IJ–CX–0021 and a supplemental grant from the National Institute of Justice. The opinions in this book are those of the author and do not necessarily represent the official positions or policies of the U.S. Department of Justice.

CONTENTS

0017999

Chinatown Gangs

1

Introduction

In the past decade, the confluence of gangs and violence has fueled political perceptions of American crime problems. Since 1985, adolescent homicide rates have risen sharply in cities such as Los Angeles, San Diego, and Chicago where gangs are prevalent. The crack crisis of the mid–1980s and the violence that accompanied it further contributed to perceptions that there were more gangs, more teenagers in gangs, and more violent gangs in urban centers throughout the United States than there had been before. These concerns were amplified in the popular culture through movies and hip-hop music that depicted gang life as a stew of violence, guns, drug money, police repression, and exploitation of women.

Gangs have always provided an organizational context that leads to elevated rates of violence. Studies comparing gang and nongang members show that gang members engage in more violent crimes than do nongang delinquent youths (Tracy, 1987; Fagan, 1990). Adolescents have higher rates of violence during periods of gang membership than they do either before joining or after leaving a gang (Thornberry et al., 1993). Gang participation during adolescence also appears to increase the proclivity toward and seriousness of adult violent crime, especially among core gang members who have leadership roles in their gangs (Spergel, 1990). Accordingly, whether they are called "sets," "klikas," or "nations," gangs evidently provide a fertile organizational context for individual and collective acts of violence.

Much of what we know about gangs and gang organization comes from research on African American, Puerto Rican, and Chicano gangs. However, Chinese gangs are an increasingly visible part of the landscape in American cities on both coasts (Chin, 1990; Joe, 1994). Many participants in Chinese gangs, like those in other gangs, are involved in violence (Emch, 1973; Daly, 1983; Meskil, 1989; U.S. Senate, 1992). Yet research on Chinese gangs is limited. Most information about Chinese gangs comes from journalists, freelance writers, and law enforcement authorities. Although some researchers (J. Chan, 1975; Sung, 1977; Chin, 1990; Toy, 1992a; Joe, 1993, 1994) have been able to interview small numbers of neighborhood leaders and gang members, in no systematic study has detailed information on the dynamic relationships between Chinese gangs and their victims and communities been collected.

While extortion and other racketeering activities appear to be quite prevalent in Chinese communities (Penn, 1980; Bresler, 1981; Butterfield, 1986; Meskil, 1989), no comprehensive data are available so that an evaluation of claims about its patterns and an assessment of the scope and persistence of extortion-related problems can be made. We do not know what proportion of Chinese merchants are subjected to extortion regularly or even occasionally, or how much they are paying, or the impact of these crimes on the economic and social life of Chinese communities. Nor do we know much about the responses and resistance of Chinese businesspeople to extortion. The proportion of Chinese business owners who are intimidated but who nonetheless resist paying has not been estimated, nor is it clear how they manage to avoid gang shakedowns. The decision of some victims to report the crime and of others not to has not been examined empirically, and the responses of gangs to victim resistance or reporting have not been documented systematically. Whether resistance is helpful or dangerous to victims has been a matter of speculation.

Even though gangs are deeply involved in crimes against businesses in Chinese neighborhoods, there is no information about the types of Chinese youths who become involved in gangs, the reasons for their participation in gangs, the processes of recruitment, the structure of gangs, the causes of gang aggression, and gang involvement in transnational crimes such as heroin trafficking and human smuggling.

Even though Chinese gangs are not well understood, their emergence has prompted local and federal law enforcement officials to suggest that Chinese gangs will soon become the major organized crime problem in the United States (President's Commission on Organized Crime, 1984; Butterfield, 1986; Seper, 1986). To deal effectively with the problem of Chinese gangs, it is necessary to understand how they operate within the Chinese community—especially how their reciprocal and symbiotic relationships with adult organizations[1] in the community develop, how they operate in both legitimate and illegitimate activities, and how they support themselves through extortion activities.

Since the term gang can mean many things (Spergel, 1995), I should make it clear at the outset what I mean by Chinese gangs and how I distinguish gangs from other crime-involved youth groups. According to Klein, a gang is "any denotable group of youngsters who (a) are generally perceived as a distinct aggregation by others in the neighborhood, (b) recognize themselves as a denotable group (almost invariably with a group name), and (c) have been involved in a sufficient number of delinquent incidents to call forth a consistent negative response from neighborhood residents and/or law enforcement agencies" (1971: 111). In the Chinese communities of American urban centers, such as New York City and San Francisco, most street crimes, especially extortion and violent activities, are committed by members of youth groups that meet all the criteria proposed by Klein in his definition of gang. In the American Chinatowns, rarely has any nongang delinquent or group of nongang delinquents been charged with serious crimes or observed to have been involved in delinquent activities. As a result, this study did not make an attempt to deal with nongang delinquents, assuming that, in the Chinese American communities, other crime-involved youth groups do not exist.

Moreover, in the Chinese American communities, adolescent and adult groups that are involved in criminal activities include street gangs, tongs, triads, heroin trafficking groups, and human smuggling rings (Chin, 1990; U.S. Senate, 1992). Although these groups are unique in terms of their structures and criminal activities, the law enforcement community tends to view all these crime groups as racketeering enterprises or organized crime groups. Likewise, Chinese gangs and other crime groups are often referred to as the Chinese mafia in the press and popular books. However, it is important to understand that many groups are often indiscriminately described as mafia. The term *mafia* is employed in a generic sense in discussions about minority organized crime and used loosely to refer to any clandestine group engaged in criminal or quasi-criminal activities. Lacking precision, the term invites misunderstanding and obscures the historical, cultural, social, and economic conditions and antecedents that give rise to organized criminal conduct. Thus, an underlying theme of this work is the distinction and relationship among gangs, tongs, triads, heroin trafficking groups, and human smuggling rings.

Concern over Chinese Gangs in America

During the mid-nineteenth century, tens of thousands of Chinese males came to the United States to work in the gold mines and on railroads (Barth, 1964). The first major Chinese community was established in San Francisco by these so-called sojourners (Nee and Nee, 1986). Activities such as gambling, prostitution, and opium smoking were reported to be rampant in San Francisco's Chinese community (Seward, 1881; M. Martin, 1977). Local media and law enforcement agencies alleged that Chinese fraternal associations known as *tongs*[2] were in control of vice activity in Chinatown[3] and that these adult organizations hired young thugs known as *boo how doy*, or "hatchetmen," to protect their illegal operations (North, 1944). The *boo how doy* were often involved in group conflicts, and these bloody battles came to be known as tong wars (Dillon, 1962; C. Y. Lee, 1974).

The issue of crime in the Chinese community was often exploited by various interest groups in their efforts to urge Congress to prohibit the immigration of Chinese into the United States (S. Miller, 1960). Dramatic public hearings were held in San Francisco in 1876, and scores of politicians, labor union leaders, and public officials testified that Chinese women were imported to work as prostitutes, that American women were lured into the sex trade to service Chinese men, that gambling establishments were controlled by tongs, and that opium-smoking habits among the Chinese were spreading into the larger society (U.S. Senate, [1877] 1978).

Although San Franciscans were well-informed about the crime problem in the so-called Chinese quarter, fighting crime in the Chinese community was not a priority for the city's law enforcement community. Crime control in the Chinese community was basically under the auspices of police officers hired by Chinatown merchants, and these officers were often bribed by the tongs to look the other way when disputes occurred (Liu, 1981). Community residents had to protect themselves because they were virtually abandoned by the regular police force. Consequently, the community was reported to be infested with hundreds of prostitution houses, gambling establishments, and opium dens (Seward, 1881).

In 1882, the Chinese Exclusion Act was enacted, and most Chinese were banned from entering the United States (S. Miller, 1960; Saxton, 1971). Since there was a drastic curtailment of immigration, the demand for illicit services and goods diminished, and the tongs' illegal operations were significantly reduced (Liu, 1981). However, tong conflicts continued unabated until the establishment of the Wo Ping Huey (Peace Committee) in San Francisco in 1913. It brought temporary peace to the warring groups (R. H. Lee, 1960).

Because of restrictive immigration policies, between 1882 and 1964 there were few young Chinese in the United States. During that long stretch, which included the two world wars, Chinese youths in America were reported to be mostly law-abiding and hard-working students (Beach, 1932). Accordingly, social researchers began to wonder why Chinese American communities had such low delinquency rates (Sollenberger, 1968).

The repeal of the Exclusion Act in 1943 and passage of the War Brides Act in 1946 allowed Chinese males who had served in the United States armed forces during World War II to apply for immigration visas for family members in China, and it allowed Chinese bachelors residing in the United States to travel to Hong Kong or Taiwan to find a bride without losing their residency status (Sung, 1967, 1979).[4] These two measures, along with the liberalization of immigration laws in the mid–1960s, which allowed many women from Hong Kong and Taiwan to immigrate here, resulted in a dramatic increase in the number of young Chinese in America (Tsai, 1986).

Two other developments increased the number of young Chinese in America. First, with the fall of Saigon in 1975, tens of thousands of youths from Southeast Asia were allowed entry into the United States as refugees, and many of them were of Chinese ethnic origin (Vigil and Yun, 1990). Second, in 1978, the U.S. government established diplomatic relations with China. Since then, people from China have immigrated to the United States (Zhou, 1992).

In the late 1960s and early 1970s, journalistic accounts on the rise of Chinese delinquency began to appear in newspapers in San Francisco and New York City (C. Howe, 1972; Pak, 1972; Bryan, 1973; Chernow, 1973). The media reported that there were a substantial number of disenchanted young immigrants who were terrorizing merchants and residents in the Chinese community (Kneeland, 1971; Howe and Pak, 1972; Ching, 1974a). Street fights among these groups were reported in the media (Egan, 1971; Hudson, 1972). There was an uneasy sense of an emerging Chinese delinquent subculture in American Chinatowns, which, despite initial anxieties, was viewed as nothing unusual for a community that was coping with large numbers of newly arrived youths who were unfamiliar with American customs and values. Since there was little extraordinary violence associated with the reported delinquency patterns, police intervention was minimal. Nevertheless, the media continued to report on the seriousness of gang extortion in Chinese communities and to show that Chinese communities were intimidated into virtual silence by gang members (Penn, 1980). They also reported the existence of shadowy organizations in Chinese American communities and accused these clandestine associations of heavy involvement in illegal activities. The media characterized Chinese gangs as "street muscle" for the adult criminal underworld active in the Chinese communities (Meskil, 1989).

Chinese gangs began to form in various American urban centers in the mid–1960s and rapidly expanded in the 1970s (U.S. Department of Justice, 1988). During their emergent stage, Chinese youth groups or gangs were, in essence, martial arts clubs headed by masters who were also tong members. Gang members were mainly involved in practicing martial arts, in driving away American-born young Chinese from Chinatown, and in protecting the community from rowdy visitors. In the late 1960s and early 1970s, the youth groups transformed themselves completely from self-help, transient groups to predatory gangs. They terrorized the community by demanding food and money from businesses and robbing illegal gambling establishments. But when the youth gangs started to shake down merchants and gamblers who were tong members, the tongs finally decided to hire the gangs as their street soldiers to protect themselves from robbery and extortion and to solidify their position within the community (Spataro, 1978).

By the mid–1970s, some gangs in Chinatown had become inseparable from certain tongs. Gang members lived in apartments rented to them by the tongs and ate in restaurants owned by tong members. Although gang members were offered membership and jobs by the tongs, they were too powerful to be fully controlled. Predictably, the community continued to experience an increase in extortion and robbery (Ching, 1974b). After many fierce power struggles that finally crystallized internal power relationships, the gangs settled down in their respective territories or turfs. The least powerful gangs either dissolved or left the Chinatown area to find new territories of their own (Chin, 1990).

In the late 1980s, diffusion occurred on three dimensions: ethnicity, space, and activity. First, besides the Toisanese and Cantonese, other ethnic Chinese youths such as the Vietnamese Chinese, Fujianese, Hakka, and Taiwanese began to join Chinese gangs.[5] Second, Chinese gang activities spread out to the newly established Chinese communities in New York City, or to Chinese communities in Asia. Third, perhaps due to better links with criminal individuals or groups in China, Hong Kong, and Taiwan, Chinese gangs extended their activities from extortion to other type of criminal operations, especially transnational crimes such as heroin trafficking, human smuggling, money laundering, and credit card fraud. Table 1.1 illustrates the name, starting year, affiliation, dominant ethnicity, and turf of the active Chinese gangs in New York City. Figure 1.1 shows the area in Manhattan that is controlled by the major gangs.

The American public did not pay much attention to the Chinese gang problem until serious gang shootouts erupted in Chinese communities. The first incident occurred in September 1977, in San Francisco's Chinatown. Three heavily armed Chinese gang members walked into the Golden Dragon Restaurant and opened fire on customers, killing five and wounding eleven (Ludlow, 1987). The fact that none of the victims were members of a rival gang made the incident all the more horrifying.

Table 1.1. Active Chinese Gangs in New York City

Name	Year Started	Affiliation	Dominant Ethnicity	Gang Turf
Ghost Shadows	1966	On Leong	Cantonese, Toisanese	Canal, Mulberry, Mott, Bayard
Flying Dragons	1967	Hip Sing	Cantonese, Toisanese	Doyer, Pell, Bowery, Grand, Hester
Tung On	1974	Tung On and Tsung Tsin	Hakka	Division, E. Broadway, Catherine
White Tigers	1980	None	Cantonese, Toisanese	Flushing (in Queens)
Hung Ching	1980	Chih Kung	Cantonese, Toisanese	Mott
Golden Star	1980	None	Vietnamese, Vietnamese Chinese	Eighth Avenue (in Brooklyn)
Born-to-Kill or Canal Boys	1983	None	Vietnamese, Vietnamese Chinese	Canal, Baxter, Center, Lafayette, Broadway
Fuk Ching	1983	Fukien American	Fujianese[b]	E. Broadway, Chrystie, Forsyth, Eldridge, Allen
Green Dragons	1986	None	Fujianese	Jackson Heights, Elmhurst (in Queens)
Taiwan Brotherhood	1989	None	Taiwanese	Flushing (in Queens)

a. The Hakka are the descendants of a group of people who emigrated from northern China to Guangdong Province many generations ago.

b. The Fujianese come from Fujian Province and constitute the fastest-growing group in New York's Chinatown.

In New York City, on Christmas Eve in 1982, three masked gunmen randomly shot at customers inside a Chinatown bar (Blumenthal, 1982). Three were killed and several wounded. In February 1983, three young offenders robbed the Wah Mee Club, a gambling house, in Seattle's Chinatown and, in the process, hogtied all 14 victims inside the house and shot them in the head at point blank range (Emery, 1990). Only one person survived the attack. And if this was not enough, in the wake of these murders, more Chinese gang-related violence broke out in Los Angeles, Houston, Boston, Chicago, Vancouver, and Toronto (Daly, 1983; Dubro, 1992). In some cases, innocent non-Chinese bystanders were wounded or killed (Steinberg, 1991; Dannen, 1992). Reactions were predictable: Chinatowns in the United States came to be described in the media and in Hollywood films such as *The Year of the Dragon* and *China Girl* as places where gun-wielding gang members roamed and ruled.

Between the late 1970s and early 1980s, because of widely reported media accounts of the killings in the Golden Dragon Restaurant in San Francisco and the

Wah Mee Club in Seattle, Chinese gang violence gained national attention (Ludlow, 1987; Emery, 1990). In reaction to the Golden Dragon shootout, San Francisco established the first Chinese gang task force in the United States (Bresler, 1981). Likewise, when a prominent community leader in New York City's Chinatown was viciously attacked by an assailant in 1977, the New York City Police Department

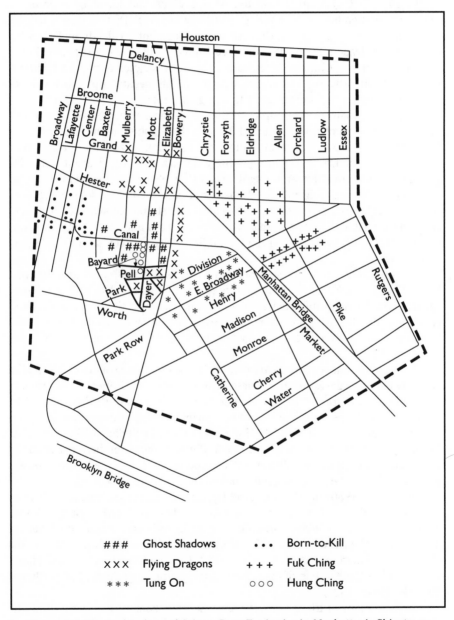

Figure 1.1 The Archipelago of Crime: Gang Territories in Manhattan's Chinatown

(NYPD) responded by forming the Special Task Force (Hetchman, 1977). Throughout the early 1970s, despite the fact that gang extortion and violence in the Chinatowns of San Francisco and New York City were often reported in the local media, little action was taken by the local police departments, and it was not until the late 1970s and early 1980s that the viciousness of gang violence shocked the entire nation.

In 1982, a Caucasian female tourist was raped and killed by a group of Chinese gang members in New York City's Chinatown (U.S. District Court, 1985b). Two years later, an American-Chinese writer was shot to death in Daly City, California, by leaders of the Taiwan-based United Bamboo gang (Kaplan, 1992). Since the victims of Chinese gangs were no longer restricted to politically powerless Chinatown residents and merchants, the public began to pressure law enforcement officials to confront the Chinese gang problem.

In the aftermath of the murder of the Caucasian female tourist, the NYPD, the Federal Bureau of Investigation (FBI), and the Manhattan District Attorney's Office conducted a two-year investigation into the criminal activities of the Ghost Shadows, a major Chinatown gang. Ninety detectives and FBI agents were involved in the investigation, and several former Ghost Shadows members worked as informers in the case. Twenty-five leaders and core members of the gang were eventually indicted under a federal antiracketeering statute known as RICO (Racketeer Influenced and Corrupt Organizations Act) (Faso and Meskil, 1985). It was the first time a Chinese gang in the United States was indicted as a racketeering enterprise.

Likewise, after the Chinese American writer was assassinated in California, the NYPD and the FBI infiltrated the United Bamboo gang—two FBI undercover agents were formally inducted into the group. As a result of the undercover operation, nine key gang members were arrested in New York City, Los Angeles, Houston, and Las Vegas and charged with violation of the federal RICO Act (Lubasch, 1985).

Even though the media began to report on the prevalence of extortion and the brutality of gang aggression in Chinese communities, the Chinese gang problem did not become a priority for law enforcement authorities until the mid–1980s, when Chinese gangs were reported to be heavily involved in international heroin trafficking (Seper, 1986; Kerr, 1987a; Buder, 1988; DeStefano, 1988; Douglas, 1988). The conviction of leaders of major Chinese gangs for heroin trafficking finally compelled the law enforcement community in the United States to take serious notice of the Chinese gang problem (U.S. Senate, 1992).

In the late 1980s, as Chinese drug traffickers became increasingly active in the heroin trade, the Drug Enforcement Administration (DEA) in New York City established the Asian Heroin Group to deal exclusively with heroin importers of Asian origin. The DEA's special task force, commonly known as Group 41, worked closely with federal prosecutors in New York City, and their cooperative efforts culminated in the breakup of many heroin smuggling rings (Kerr, 1987b; Buder, 1988; M. Howe, 1989).

Since in many of these cases, the Chinese traffickers were either visiting the United States on temporary visas or were illegal aliens, the law enforcement community sought help from the Immigration and Naturalization Service (INS) in dealing with Chinese crime groups (U.S. Immigration and Naturalization Service, 1989). Typically, the INS screens Chinese visa applicants and deports those convicted of serious crimes. In the late 1980s and early 1990s, the role of the INS became more crucial as many Chinese were active in two types of transnational crime—heroin trafficking and human smuggling.

In the early 1990s, the unprecedented murders of federal witnesses by gang members led the NYPD and the FBI to successfully crack down on two notoriously violent gangs, the Born-to-Kill and the Green Dragons (Faison, 1991; Dannen, 1992). Also, in the aftermath of a Chinese human smuggling ship running aground in New York City in 1993, because Chinese gangs were alleged to be increasingly involved in human smuggling, federal law enforcement agencies became extremely aggressive in investigating crimes committed by Chinese gangs (Gladwell and Stassen-Berger, 1993; Treaster, 1993b). Within a year and a half after the incident, seven major Chinese gangs and two adult organizations in New York City, San Francisco, and Boston were indicted by federal authorities on RICO charges (Faison, 1993c; *World Journal*, 1993b, 1993c). By the end of 1994, with the exception of the Wah Ching in San Francisco, all major Chinese gangs in the United States had been indicted on racketeering enterprise charges.

In sum, before the eruption of major gang turbulence in the late 1970s, law enforcement authorities generally took a hands-off approach toward crime in Chinese communities. Although gang task forces were established in the late 1970s and early 1980s in response to several rather sensational incidents, the principal responsibility of these groups was to contain reckless violence against innocent bystanders. Only after nongang victims were intentionally killed by gangs did local law enforcement authorities become actively involved in investigating Chinese gangs: when the gangs assaulted or murdered court witnesses and were alleged to be on the verge of forming alliances with foreign-based organized crime groups in heroin trafficking and human smuggling, the various federal authorities eventually began the attempt to combat Chinese gangs.

Social Order in Chinatown

Explaining the formation of youth gangs in Chinese communities requires an examination of the social and political environment in which adult crime groups develop and grow. This involves understanding the hierarchy, the sources of group conflict, and the way in which social order is negotiated and maintained among disparate and competing groups within the Chinese community.

Chinatowns in America are social, cultural, political, and economic centers of Chinese immigration (Nee and Nee, 1986; Kwong, 1987; Loo, 1991). Most Chinese communities have many voluntary associations, and in the well-established Chinatowns of New York, San Francisco, and Vancouver, there are hundreds of community associations (Kuo, 1977; Liu, 1981; Lai, 1988). Four major types of associations are dominant: family, district, tong, and professional. Family or clan associations are established mainly by people with the same family name. Some family associations are built up by more than one surname group. A district association is usually composed of people who came from the same district of China or whose fathers or grandfathers were born in that district. Within the overseas Chinese communities, family and district associations are the two most important sources of identification for most people. The third type of organization, the tong, recruits members without regard to their surname or district affiliation. Tongs usually dominate illegal activities in Chinatowns (U.S. Senate, 1992). Professional associations are established by businessmen, workers, or social service providers (R. Lee, 1960). All four types of associations play an important role in the establishment and maintenance of social order within the Chinese community (Liu, 1981).

Legitimate Sources of Social Order

There are two layers of social order in Chinatown: legitimate and illegitimate (Lyman, 1986). The legitimate social order regulates political, economic, and social behavior, while the illegitimate social order dictates territorial rights for the operation of gambling places, and the level and intensity of involvement in other illegal activities such as heroin trafficking, loansharking, and human smuggling. Most community associations play a role only in the maintenance of the legitimate social order, but a few are influential in both the legitimate and illegitimate worlds. It is the latter groups that are closely affiliated with Chinese gangs (Chin, 1990).

Political struggles among community organizations have a long tradition in American Chinatowns (Ching, 1971; Kwong, 1979). In the early stages of Chinese immigration, American Chinatowns tended to be divided into at least two political factions—one in support of Sun Yat-sen's revolution, and the other in favor of the Manchu Qing regime (Ma, 1990).[6] During the civil war in China (1927–49), Chinese immigrants were politically polarized into pro-Kuomintang or pro-Communist groups (R. Lee, 1960). Currently, community associations may be divided into two political groups. The first, which is led by the Chinese Consolidated Benevolent Association (CCBA), consists of many pro-Taiwan traditional groups.[7] The second includes a number of old and new associations that are sympathetic to and supportive of the Communist government in China.

The economy of American Chinatowns is sustained by the large number of restaurants, retail stores, wholesale suppliers, and garment factories located in them. Most of these businesses are owned and operated by Chinese and cater to Asian customers and tourists. Commercial rents in most Chinatowns are extremely high, and business competition is fierce.[8] Many Chinatown businesses operate within the informal economy—an economy that is based largely on cash or barter, that is unregulated by licensing or other administrative law (such as child labor laws or health standards for workers), and that is outside the formal system of taxation and accounting (Kinkead, 1992). Furthermore, some community associations own many commercial properties within their territories and dictate the business activity within them (Kwong, 1987). Certain businesses are controlled by a specific group, for example, the preponderance of take-out restaurant businesses is controlled by the Fujianese.

The popularity of cash transactions, the existence of a large number of illegal businesses, the widespread use of illegal practices, the dominance of certain businesses by particular ethnic groups, and the control of commercial properties by community associations all contribute to the precarious nature of the Chinese communities' economic order. That is, business activities often involve other, noneconomic issues such as territorial rights, ethnicity, and legality. Consequently, not only do business-related conflicts frequently occur, but they are unlikely to be settled in court. This is because the discord that lays at the heart of the conflict may not be, strictly speaking, a business issue, and legitimate courts, which would ordinarily adjudicate such problems in mainstream society, would not be able to comprehend the intricate nature of the conflicts (Butterfield, 1989).

The communal order in New York City's Chinatown is maintained by four major ethnic groups: the Toisanese, the Cantonese, the Hakka, and the Fujianese. All four groups speak their own dialects (although they all speak Mandarin, the national language, too), are different subculturally, and tend to dominate certain types of business enterprises (Zhou, 1992).[9] Historically, these ethnic groups were at odds over trivial matters (Lipman and Harrell, 1990).

Illegitimate Order in Chinatown

In addition to the legitimate order, there is also an illegitimate underside to business and social life in Chinatown (Leong, 1936; Glick, 1941). It determines which streets belong to which association or group and who is permitted to operate what types of illegal operations (Kwong, 1987; Kinkead, 1992). The core areas of Chinatown are dominated by six adult organizations, the Chih Kung Tong,[10] the On Leong Merchant Association,[11] the Hip Sing Association,[12] the Tung On Association,[13] the Tsung Tsin Association,[14] and the Fukien American Association[15] (Chin, 1990). By claiming a certain area as its turf, a community organization is able to demand respect and financial contributions from business owners within that designated territory. For protection, most owners join the organization that controls the area in which their business establishments are located. As members, store owners are obliged to pay a membership fee (a few hundred dollars a year) to the adult organization. For the gangs associated with the adult organizations, the territories become the area in which the gangs can generate protection money from the business owners.

The illegitimate order also dictates the rules governing participation in illegal activities such as gambling and prostitution (Kinkead, 1992). In the late nineteenth century, San Francisco's Chinatown was transformed into a battleground for tongs that were vying for control of opium dens, gambling places, and prostitution houses (M. Martin, 1977; U.S. Senate, [1877] 1978). Street battles were fought not by members of the associations, but by their hired gunmen (Gong and Grant, 1930; North, 1944; Dillon, 1962; C. Lee, 1974). Currently, although most associations are allowed by the more powerful community organizations to operate their own small gambling places, only certain specified organizations or their members are permitted to manage large gambling establishments (Daly, 1983).

In short, Chinatown has its own legitimate and illegitimate social order that regulates community resident involvement in political, economic, communal, and illegal activities. Most associations also need to maintain order within their own organizations. When individuals or groups challenge the existing order, there are repercussions from the well-established associations. In order to maintain external and internal order, be it legitimate or illegitimate, the adult organizations must have access to individuals who are willing to use threats and violence as a means of resolving disputes within the community as such disputes are unlikely to be settled through the American court system. The absence of one powerful community organization to handle individual or group conflicts obliges community associations to adopt unconventional, sometimes violent, methods to protect their interests. Because of these social circumstances, the formation of youth gangs has been encouraged by adult groups as a means of maintaining or challenging the existing legitimate and illegitimate social order.

Social Processes of Gang Formation

In New York City, Chinese gangs began to form in the mid–1960s (H. Chang, 1972). Many immigrant children who entered the United States after the liberalization of the immigration law in 1965 had trouble adjusting to school because of language and cultural barriers (Chernow, 1973). Those who were ridiculed by students from other ethnic groups and heckled by American-born Chinese often joined together for self-protection (Pak, 1972). A number of them eventually dropped out of school and hung out in the Chinese community. Thus the initial processes of Chinese gang formation in many ways reflected the patterns of youth gang formation among ethnic European and Mexican American adolescents.[16] However, the unique role of adult organizations, which themselves had ambiguous status in both the legal and illegal order of the Chinese community, suggests that some distinctive factors were at work in shaping and molding the formation and behaviors of Chinese youth gangs in their later stages of development. The adult groups offer legitimacy, organization, and purpose to already loosely knit groups of youths.

Interdependence among Adolescent Gangs and Adult Crime Groups

Figure 1.2 shows the social process of gang formation in New York City's Chinatown. In this framework, the emergence of a new, powerful adult organization is prerequisite to the formation of youth gangs in the community. The expansion of existing adult organizations or the appearance of new ones produces social tensions and instability in the relative positions of the existing organizations, compelling some groups to seek monopoly control over important territories and resources (English, 1991). Conflicts may reflect the organizational strategies of these groups to defend their positions, and the development of ties with youth gangs may be seen as a strategic use of resources to avoid interorganizational

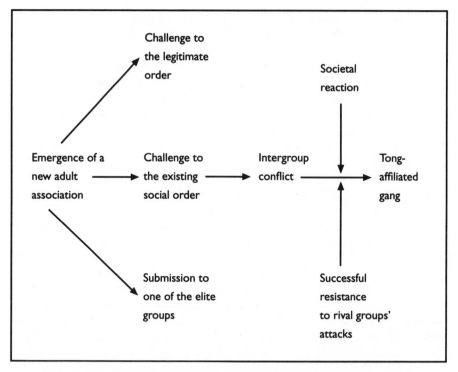

Figure 1.2 Social Process of Gang Formation in New York City's Chinatown

dependencies among adult groups that are striving for autonomy and independence.

Generally, an association achieves some influence in the community when new immigration swells its ranks and there is a dramatic increase in its membership. More members mean more income and power. The history of the Fukien American Association illustrates the process. It was established more than 50 years ago, but became prominent only recently, as many Chinese newcomers to the United States are now Fujianese. With donations from wealthy members, the Fukien American Association recently bought a huge building at the corner of East Broadway and Pike Street and established its headquarters there. Ownership of expensive real estate signifies the association's intention of and capability to settle within the community permanently, and it also shows the affluence of its members and the loyalty to the organization.

Nevertheless, the emergence of a new organization is not always accompanied by the formation of a new street gang. A new organization may only be concerned with certain aspects of the legitimate social order. So when a new organization finds itself in conflict with tongs and other traditional associations, it may turn to the American courts to resolve its problems. For example, when the Chinese American Planning Council (CAPC), a multipurpose social service agency, evolved into a powerful community organization and inadvertently challenged the legitimate order of Manhattan's Chinatown, many traditional associations were infuriated. The conflict between CAPC and the tongs reached its peak when CAPC attempted to exclude tong members from the board of a residential project for the elderly by accusing them of organized crime activities (M. Howe, 1986). Throughout the conflict, CAPC never developed a gang of its own, nor did the tongs threaten CAPC with their gangs. Eventually, the tongs withdrew their candidates.

Only those organizations that seek to challenge *both* the legitimate and the illegitimate order seem destined to develop their own gangs. Some associations interested in both legal and illegal activities may avoid forming their own gangs; they may decide to subordinate themselves to one of the existing groups and thus avoid violent confrontations with other groups. For example, when the Tsung Tsin Association became very active in gambling activities, it established a close relationship with the Tung On Association, located in the same street, and hired the Tung On gang to protect its gambling establishments. This avoided a confrontation between the two.

Any of the following steps taken by a new organization presents a challenge to the existing legitimate and illegitimate order: a claim to a certain area (normally the street where its headquarters are located) as its territory; a disclosure of political orientations; a request to business owners within its territory to join it; and the establishment of its own gambling places. Whenever a new organization claims a certain area as its territory or attempts to become involved in gambling, other organizations may react strongly, especially when the territory in question is geographically contiguous to one of the established groups' turf or when the new gambling establishment may compete with well-established gambling clubs.

In 1982, a Hip Sing member formed a new association, the Kam Lun Association, and established its headquarters on East Broadway, where he operated a gambling establishment. Not only did he claim East Broadway as the Kam Lun's territory, but also he solicited businesspeople in the area to join his association. Members of the Flying Dragons, a gang affiliated with the Hip Sing, were recruited by the Kam Lun to guard its gambling den and protect its territory. Within a few months, the Kam Lun appeared to be on the verge of becoming a powerful organization within the community. However, in December 1982, three gunmen alleged to be affiliated with the Hip Sing walked into a bar on East Broadway that the young Kam Lun members frequented and opened fire. Three were killed and eight were seriously wounded (Daly, 1983). After the shootout, which was named the Golden Star Massacre, the Kam Lun disappeared from Chinatown, and the youth group associated with it never developed into a powerful street gang.

Through conflicts and tensions among adult organizations, the young members of these organizations are able to integrate into cohesive units. Leaders of the adult organizations may provide young members with a place to congregate, usually a room within the headquarters that is close to the organization's gambling establishment. Although the leaders of an adult organization may or may not intend to form a gang affiliated with their organization, the regular appearance of a large number of young people within the organization's headquarters is always welcomed and naturally helps the adult organization by providing a means of protection for its gambling establishment and by strengthening its claims over a certain area as its territory.

Two vital intervening factors must be examined to understand the mechanics of social transformation in Chinatown through which youth groups evolve into gangs. Moore (1978), in her study of gangs, observed that negative societal reaction is a crucial factor in the process of gang formation. In the Chinatown context, the congregation of large numbers of young people within an association's headquarters or outside its major gambling establishment may attract the attention of law enforcement authorities. Whenever these adolescents are arrested for violating the law, police will, if only for the sake of identification, label the offenders as members of a street gang. For example, the group of youths associated with the Tung On Association is labeled the Tung On gang, and the young Fujianese who convene at the headquarters of the Fukien American Association are referred to as the Fuk Ching (meaning Fujianese youth) gang. Soon, the names adopted by the police are endorsed by gang members or community residents to identify certain youth groups in the community.

In addition to the dynamics of societal reaction, the ability of the affiliated adult organization to successfully sustain itself and remain in existence is also important in the formation of a youth gang and in its ability to thrive. Consider the example of the Kam Lun Association. It was unable to regroup after the Golden Star Massacre, and the youth group formed by the association dissolved along with the association. Youth groups can be transformed into more permanent gangs only if the sponsoring groups are capable of growing and maintaining themselves amidst adversity. Any new adolescent criminal organization that forms will immediately face conflict and challenges not only from other youth gangs but also from the adult associations that sponsor them.

Thus, the second intervening factor has to do with the expansion of an association's influence. As the power of an adult group consolidates, its associated youth group also expands its influence. With the support of the adult group, gang members are able to extort money from business owners within their territory, collect payment from the adult organization for protecting its gambling establishments, and legitimize their existence within the community. The adult organization usually assigns one of its senior members (who is often called euphemistically "youth activity coordinator" or "uncle") to act as a liaison officer between the association and the leader of the gang. Younger gang members never interact directly with the youth activity coordinator. The style here is reminiscent of a Cosa Nostra crime family in which organizational structure insulates the leadership from the criminal activities of subordinates.

Accordingly, the relationship between youth gangs and their sponsoring groups may be seen as one of interorganizational dependence and resource dependence (Aldrich, 1979; Burt, 1987). By themselves, the adult organizations may be unable to marshal the resources necessary to achieve their goals, and this necessitates a cluster of transactions that effect exchanges with street gangs and inevitably link the two types of organizations. The structure of these relationships may be determined by the shared interests of the youth gangs and their sponsoring groups as criminal enterprises. Because the adult organizations themselves vary in terms of their access to resources and their capacities to pursue instrumental goals, however, these relationships will vary in terms of their intensity, complexity, and prominence.

Functional Relationships between Youth Gangs and Adult Crime Groups

Gangs have been active in the Chinese community for almost three decades, and there is no evidence to indicate that they are likely to disappear in the foreseeable future. The isolation of the Chinese community, the inability of American law enforcement authorities to penetrate the Chinese criminal underworld, and the reluctance of Chinese victims to come forward for help all conspire to enable Chinese gangs to endure. The persistence of Chinese gangs may also result from the multiple functions that they serve in the community. Thus, it is important to understand the social functions of Chinese gangs.

For adult organizations involved in providing illegal services, gangs are effective devices for protecting gambling establishments and prostitution houses from police interdictions and the intrusions of other gangs. They ensure order and client safety within the premises of these illegal establishments. Gangs also play an important role in maintaining the integrity of adult criminal territories. Simply put, an adult group that lacks a street gang to back up its territorial rights cannot maintain them. The existence of a gang within a territory thus works to the advantage of the adult group. Business owners within the adult organization's territory will be intimidated by the gang and will therefore join the organization and make donations to it in order to obtain the organization's blessing and protection from gang intimidation tactics.

Also, individual members of adult organizations may use the gangs to solidify their positions within the organization and the community. Most community organizations experience chronic internal power struggles, and the ability to establish a good relationship with an affiliated gang offers some guarantee that when a person needs street muscle, the gang will be there to provide it. A leader of a community association may use a gang to promote his position within the community. Finally, the gang may be exploited to build up the reputation of a community association leader so that anyone who wishes to do business within the community association's territory will need to obtain the leader's support by offering either money or partnerships.

Gang leaders, who often have close ties to the adult crime groups, use their gangs to create situations whereby merchants feel compelled to pay protection money. They also use the gangs for local crime activities, such as gambling, or even in international criminal conspiracies, including heroin trafficking and human smuggling, and to position themselves so that they can leverage advantageously for power within the adult organization. Street gangs may also be used in gang leaders' legitimate business operations. Even legitimate merchants make use of gangs to protect themselves against the threat of gang extortion or robbery attempts and to serve as mediators in business conflicts (Kwong, 1987).

Summary

According to Thrasher (1927), gangs are primary organizations formed by youths in response to social and economic conditions. That is, gangs establish themselves to create order when there is none. They are developed consciously and intentionally by teenagers for specific goals. But unlike youth gangs in other ethnic neighborhoods, Chinese youth gangs are not simply expressions of adolescent mischief or young adulthood. In Chinatown, order emerges from behavioral rules articulated by adult community organizations. Youth gangs develop their orientations in response to the existent social order of adult crime groups and community organizations. Although the community is not socially disorganized, its social order is precarious and constantly being realigned. The gangs become primary tools in the negotiation process.

Accordingly, the gangs are not merely spontaneous primary organizations established by young people to create a sense of order within a disorganized community. Rather, gangs are the product of inter- and intragroup conflicts among larger forces within Chinatown. The factors that allow well-organized adolescent gangs to emerge are functions of adult organizations. That is, adult groups (1) provide gangs with a place to gather, (2) allow gangs to operate within their territory, and thus legitimize the gangs' existence within the community, (3) provide criminal opportunities for gangs, such as the protection of gambling establishments, and (4) support gangs with money and guns. Youth group affiliations with adult groups provide some refuge from law enforcement authorities, who seem largely unconcerned about nonlethal crimes in Chinese communities (Kelly et al., 1993). And, like their adult sponsors, Chinese gangs exhibit many of the characteristics that Maltz (1985) identified as characteristics of organized crime groups: multiple enterprises, the doubling up of legal and illegal businesses, hierarchy, discipline, bonding, continuity, and the use of violence as a tool to maintain control and settle disputes.

Gangs are intricately associated with the maintenance of the legitimate and illegitimate social order in Chinatown. When new adult organizations emerge and plan to challenge the existing social order, they generally equip themselves with a gang of their own to act as "street soldiers" who help carve out their territory and protect both their legitimate and illegitimate enterprises.

The adult group and the youth group reciprocally support each other and become, in the process, mutually involved in each other's survival. The adult group will put up a legitimate front, the youth group a potentially violent, illegal one. For the adult group, the gang provides aid in the intermingling of legal and illegal activities and in the establishment and maintenance of territory that both groups require.

The explanatory framework for formation of Chinese gangs departs from the classical social disorganization and cultural deviance perspectives found in much of the gang literature. Adolescent gangs in Chinatown form not because the Chinese community is utterly disorganized or because they are just a reaction to a disorganized community. Neither are they play groups, merely mimicking the functions and roles of adult crime groups or symbolically ritualizing and antici-pating the roles and behaviors of esteemed adults. Gangs do not just crystallize their structures and dynamics through conflicts among competing youth groups or between adolescents and formal social institutions. They are consciously formed by adults (within Chinatown) or by former gang members (outside of Chinatown) rather than by noncriminal adolescents. Although they are similar to the criminal gangs described in Cloward and Ohlin's (1960) study of New York, Chinese youth gangs are subordinate to, but not completely controlled by, adult organizations.

The long history of conflict and shadow government that predates the social order of contemporary Chinatown (Chin, 1990) illustrates the existence of vener-able and respected community organizations that mix legal and illegal activities. It affords the special context in which youth gangs mature and play a critical role. This ambiguous legal context suggests that sociocultural processes interact close-ly with social structure in the formation of adolescent gangs within Chinese immigrant neighborhoods. Chinese youth gangs exist within the unique political economy of Chinatown, where resources and power are concentrated among elite community groups and where formal government is at best merely a secondary source of social control.

2

Research Strategies and Methods

In order to examine as comprehensively as possible the many aspects of Chinese gangs, this study used multiple research methods to collect data from subjects with diverse backgrounds. Overall, five research strategies were involved, each designed to achieve one or more specific aims. Table 2.1 illustrates the subjects, the sample size, and the goals of the research components of the study reported here.

In the following sections, I describe the five components in detail. Specific methodological issues encountered—including sampling, questionnaire construction, pretesting, interviewer recruitment and training, securing support from the community, and building rapport with the subjects—are discussed in depth. Unique problems in doing field interviews in the Chinese community and ways of coping with these problems are also considered.

The Business Survey

As discussed in the first chapter, the allegations of widespread and costly extortion by Chinese gangs have not been substantiated by research. No comprehensive data are available to validate claims about the process and scope of extortion by Chinese gangs. Because public awareness of the phenomenon of Chinese gang extortion is relatively recent, there have been few opportunities to develop methods for studying the phenomenon or to accumulate empirical knowledge about it. Extortion by youth gangs began in earnest twenty-five years ago, and only within the past ten years has it attracted the attention of legal and academic institutions. More importantly perhaps, the major data sources for the study of crime and victimization have limited use in the study of commercial victimization in Chinese communities.[1]

The study of extortion and commercial victimization is also made difficult by the social dynamics of the crimes themselves and the milieus in which they occur. The economically, culturally, and socially closed Chinese communities in the United States are hard to penetrate, even by Chinese social scientists, to say nothing of the problems faced by non-Chinese researchers. There are cultural sanctions against frank dialogue with people from outside the neighborhood and,

Table 2.1. An Overview of Five Research Components[a]

Component	Subjects	N	Research Focuses
Business survey	Asian business owners	603	Patterns, prevalence, and seriousness of gang victimization; victims' reaction to crime
Follow-up study	Sample of respondents from the business survey	50	Social processes of gang victimization
Gang study[b]	Chinese gang members	70	Social organization and criminal patterns of Chinese gangs and tongs
Law enforcement agents as key informants	Local and federal law enforcement authorities	23	Containment and prosecution of Chinese crime groups
Community leaders as key informants	Leaders of community associations	15	History, social organization, and activities of tongs and other community organizations

a. All interviews were conducted face-to-face, and a standardized questionnaire was used in each research component.
b. Includes eight female subjects who were associated with gangs.

for some, taboos against talking with non-Chinese (Kinkead, 1992). Data collection using systematic measures such as the National Crime Victimization Survey (NCVS) or self-reported items are circumscribed by language in two ways. First, some items are difficult to translate and have no analogue in any of the Chinese dialects. Second, conducting research in English is difficult because of the large number of non-English speakers.

To assess the extent and severity of extortion and other crimes against businesses in the Chinese community in New York City, a commercial version of the NCVS was used to collect data from business owners in 1990–91. From the data, patterns and methods of extortion, along with the victims' reactions, were examined. Since this is the first systematic study of Chinese gang extortion, it is important to provide some insights into the methodological issues encountered to assist other researchers who may wish to replicate or independently examine the same phenomenon in other American or Canadian Chinese communities where similar problems have been reported.

Site Selection and Sampling

The research strategy focused on three socioeconomically different Chinatowns situated in Manhattan, Queens, and Brooklyn in New York City.[2] In order to compare the victimization rates of Chinese entrepreneurs in Chinatowns with those of Chinese who do business elsewhere in New York City, Chinese merchants in other areas of Manhattan, Queens, and Brooklyn were also interviewed.

The economic, social, and spatial concentration of the Chinese communities in their respective, rapidly changing neighborhoods complicated the use of probability sampling strategies (such as household enumeration or block samples). Therefore, a target sample was generated from the *Chinese Business Guide and Directory*.[3] Businesses from the *Directory* were classified into ten categories, which incorporated the whole range of commercial business activities in the Chinese community. They included restaurants, retail food stores, retail nonfood businesses, professional offices (e.g., the offices of accountants, architects, attorneys), manufacturing industries (e.g., garment factories), entertainment businesses, services (e.g., plumbers), wholesale/retail business suppliers, vocational schools (e.g., driving schools, beautician schools), and cultural or recreational centers.

A purposive, targeted sampling method was adopted to ensure adequate representation of the different types of businesses that are reported in the media to be the most vulnerable to extortion by Chinese gangs. Since heavily guarded businesses, such as banks, were rarely reported to be victimized by Chinese gangs, they were excluded from the sample. Because of concern about risks to interviewers, businesses defined as extremely vulnerable to gang extortion, such as massage parlors and gambling dens, were also excluded from the sample.

Otherwise, sampling quotas were designed to ensure adequate representation of highly vulnerable categories of businesses in order to permit comparisons of categories across neighborhoods. The sampling quotas for the various business types were as follows: 200 restaurants, 100 retail food stores, 100 retail nonfood stores, 100 service-oriented firms, and 100 other businesses (mainly garment factories and wholesale supply firms) that did not belong to any of the other categories. A large number of restaurants were sampled because restaurants are the most common type of Chinese business in New York City.

In addition to oversampling by business type, there was also oversampling by locale. Since the main focus of this study is extortion in Manhattan's Chinatown, businesses in this community were oversampled. Furthermore, similar businesses from non-Chinatown neighborhoods were included in the sample for comparison.

Originally, 888 business establishments from the *Directory* were included in the sample. Stratified random sampling methods were used to select these businesses from the 4,290 businesses listed under the ten business categories in the *Directory*. Of the 888 business establishments chosen, 678 were contacted. The remaining 210 businesses could not be found or could not be interviewed for the following reasons: the businesses had moved or closed ($N = 93$); the addresses given were wrong ($N = 27$); the owners had been misidentified as Chinese ($N = 38$);[4] or the business could not be reached by telephone ($N = 52$).

Response Rates

The response rate was high: 580 out of the 678 subjects (85.5%) contacted by interviewers completed the interview. To supplement the relatively small number of business owners on the sample list from Brooklyn's Chinatown, 23 business owners in that area who were not originally part of the target sample were solicited and interviewed. Interviewers went door-to-door along Eighth Avenue in

Brooklyn and interviewed owners whose business fit the ten categories selected for the study.[5] The final sample thus included 603 businesses.

Concept Development and Questionnaire Construction

The problem of extortion in the Chinese community is difficult to measure because extortion is intrinsically hard to define, and because it involves the application of a Western legal definition to a culturally unique social situation in which distributing cash on certain occasions denotes good luck or celebration. Paying protection money to local thugs has long been an accepted norm in Chinese social circles (Zhang, 1984; Chi, 1985; Seagrave, 1985). In order to achieve a better understanding of extortion and the contexts in which extortion occurs, I asked the survey respondents to recount the history of their interactions with visitors to their stores or offices whom they sometimes paid, willingly or under threat. Because I knew that Western legal conceptions of and distinctions about extortion are much too broad and, in a sense, too crude to capture the essence of "lucky money" and other nonreciprocal gratuities and gifts of cash, the interview protocol distinguished the social patterns and contexts within which monies are exchanged between businesspeople and gang members.

From the perspective of symbolic interaction, social problems are products of a process of collective definition (Blumer, 1971; Spector and Kitsuse, 1977; Gusfield, 1981). A "social problem exists primarily in terms of how it is defined and conceived in society" (Blumer, 1971: 300). Hilgartner and Bosk (1988: 70) further propose that a social problem "is a putative condition or situation that (at least some) actors label a 'problem' in the arenas of public discourse and action, defining it as harmful and framing its definition in particular ways." This perspective is especially relevant to the explanations for extortion in the Chinese community. A few business owners interviewed said they did not perceive the gangs' practice of asking for money as criminal or as a technical act of extortion.[6] Owing to the subjective perception of extortion activities among business owners in the Chinese community, I could not accept a survey respondent's definition of activities as extortionistic or criminal as a gauge of such activities. To do so would compromise the validity and reliability of the research. Instead, based on previous studies (Kwong, 1987; Chin, 1990) and from prior discussions with business owners, I devised my own culturally sensitive categories and developed victimization types that are unique to the intimidation of businesses in the Chinese community.

The questionnaire was first tested with ten store owners in their own dialect. Based on the pilot test results, a more concise interview protocol was developed.[7] Certain questions that pertained to the respondent's personal and business characteristics were eliminated, and interviewers were instructed to conduct the interviews in a less formal manner.[8] Items related to other forms of victimization, such as robbery and burglary, were added to the interview schedule.

The final protocol consisted of 107 questions, which were mostly closed-ended items with categorical responses. The questions were organized into three major sections. The first asked the respondents about their personal and business characteristics, such as their age, country of origin, and education, and whether they were the sole owners of their business. The second section dealt with the processes and patterns of victimization. Respondents were asked whether they had reported any victimizations to the police and what their attitudes toward the police were. The third section asked the subjects about their feelings, reactions, and attitudes toward crime in the community and toward the criminal justice system in general. An interviewer's report section was appended to the questionnaire so that interviewers could describe the size of the business and the subject's sex and include their impressions and subjective evaluations of the respondent's honesty and cooperativeness. Interviewers were instructed to complete this section immediately following the interview, but out of sight of the respondent.

Recruiting and Training the Interviewers

Of the seven interviewers hired, six were female. I preferred females because it was apparent that female interviewers would be seen as less threatening to the business owners and would not be suspected of being gang members. All of the field workers were familiar with the Chinese community and were fluent in either Cantonese or Mandarin. It was found that speaking the respondent's dialect was extremely important, not only in persuading a respondent to cooperate but also in acquiring culturally sensitive information that might be overlooked by those unfamiliar with specific ethnic customs or ethnic gang slang.

The interviewers received two days of training. During the training sessions, interviewers were instructed on the development of Chinese youth gangs in New York City, the political and economic aspects of the Chinese community, the nature and purpose of the study, and the specific purpose of each item in the interview schedule as it related to the hypotheses of the study. The interviewers also were trained to follow certain guidelines and to use proper wording and phrasing for each item in both Mandarin and Cantonese.[9] They observed the author demonstrate the interview technique in both Mandarin and Cantonese. The training sessions also included simulated interviews and pretests that served as role models for the actual interview process.

Securing Support from the Community

Approaching suspicious or fearful respondents often requires permission not only from the subjects themselves but also from influential community members who can affect the outcome of the study (Marshall and Rossman, 1989). It is almost impossible to do fieldwork in the Chinese community without drawing the attention of community associations and their leaders (Chin, 1990). Had the community leaders chosen to do so, they could have mobilized the community to boycott the study if they decided it would hurt the community's image. Thus, it was important that key community leaders were made aware of the project. Had I failed to do this, or if I had ignored them, the community leaders could have interpreted my behavior as disrespectful of their authority and power within the community.[10]

The most important community leader in Chinatown is the president of the

Chinese Consolidated Benevolent Association (CCBA), who is known as the mayor of Chinatown. Through arrangements by a third party, I met the CCBA president and briefed him about the project's objectives. He listened carefully, but did not express any approval. He said he would raise the issue at the CCBA monthly meeting and ask whether any of its member organizations opposed such a study. Although I wanted to inform the CCBA about the research before I began the field interviews, I did not want the 60 major community associations that are members of the CCBA to become involved in a debate about the merits of the research. I speculated that it was likely that some of the associations would not support this research and that if the issue became a matter in the CCBA public agenda, I would lose the initiative. Therefore, I decided to ask for the president's personal approval without going through the formal process of obtaining the larger community board's support. I expressed concern about raising the issue at the CCBA monthly meeting. Fortunately, the president was sympathetic to my reservations and apprehensions and suggested that I start my work. He promised his support should any community leader attempt to boycott the research. The leaders of the major family and district associations and the captain of the local police precinct were duly informed about the study, and their support was obtained.

After I had obtained endorsements from leaders in the community, I sent a letter written in English and Chinese to the business owners selected for my sample. The letter was prepared on Rutgers University stationery. It described the nature and purpose of the study, the method of sample selection, the confidentiality of the study, and the voluntariness of participation. It emphasized that an interviewer would conduct the survey at the respondent's place of business at a convenient time and in the dialect with which the respondent was most comfortable. The letter indicated further that a stipend of $20 would be paid to the interviewee on completing the interview.[11] Sensitive words such as "extortion" and "gangs" were not mentioned in the letter.

To convince the business owners that the study was officially supported by the United States government, a letter of support from James Stewart, then director of the funding agency (the National Institute of Justice), was attached. This letter was also written in both English and Chinese. Pretest results showed that individuals were more likely to cooperate if they believed that the study was supported by the government.

Field Contact

Once the solicitation letters had been mailed, the names, addresses, and phone numbers of the businesses were provided to the interviewers. Store owners were contacted by phone; they were reminded of the letter and asked for an interview appointment.[12] Interviewers were issued identification cards that indicated their affiliation with Rutgers University. These were to be shown on request.

In the initial stages of the fieldwork, interviewers encountered many problems locating owners or persuading them to be interviewed. First, the person who answered the phone often would say that the owner was not in and would refuse to say when the owner would return. In view of the pervasiveness of extortion problems in the Chinese community, it was not surprising that many owners were reluctant to identify themselves as owners, even over the phone. Indeed, interviews later revealed that Chinese merchants did this to protect themselves from victimization by gang members.

Second, although the *Chinese Business Guide and Directory* is updated annually, a substantial percentage of the phone numbers (about 15%) had been either disconnected or changed. As a result, the interviewers were unable to contact many businesses.

Third, even when the interviewers managed to talk to the owners over the phone, convincing them to participate in the study was not always easy. Owners would often come up with questions: Why were they selected? How were the names, addresses, and phone numbers of their businesses obtained? How could we assure them of confidentiality? Why did we wish to collect data from them instead of from the police? Finally, Who was sponsoring the study? They often asked interviewers personal questions such as whether they were students, whether they were American-born or immigrant, and what their country of origin was. It became tiresome for the interviewers to spend at least half an hour over the phone answering a business owner's queries. Respondent anxieties and resistance disenchanted some interviewers, who thought seriously about resigning.

During weekly debriefing meetings, interviewers would describe the problems they were encountering in the field. When it became clear that finding some subjects and persuading them to participate in the study over the phone was a frustrating and often futile experience, an alternative approach was adopted. Since most of the subjects were located in one of the three Chinese communities, it was more effective and quicker to have the interviewers simply visit the stores after the notification letters were mailed.

This alternative approach worked well with restaurants and retail stores, but was not especially successful with professional offices or large business firms. Store owners were available most of the time, and they were less suspicious and more approachable when their first encounter with the interviewers was face-to-face. Nonetheless, some business owners were still wary, even after meeting interviewers, and preferred to be called "manager" or "worker" instead of owner even though they agreed to be interviewed. Some owners simply refused to participate. Owners of professional offices, however, had tighter schedules and thus preferred to be called prior to being visited. Since subjects in professional offices were cooperative over the phone, the interviewers were instructed to employ the new approach with restaurants and retail stores while retaining the original over-the-phone approach with professional offices.

Conducting the Interview

Prior to the initiation of the survey, I obtained approval from the Institutional Review Board of Rutgers University for conducting research involving human subjects. I also obtained a federal certificate of confidentiality from the Department of Justice. Finally, before conducting the interview, the interviewer asked each subject to read and sign an informed consent form.

After the interviews began, two major problems arose. Most respondents were owners of small restaurants or retail stores that did not have offices; thus interviews could not be conducted in private. Some of the businesses did have an office, but the owners were often unable to retreat to the office because they had to attend to their business. Thus, most interviews were conducted in the dining area, kitchen, or basement or at the counter of the business establishment. Whenever a customer walked in or the phone rang, the interview was interrupted. On some occasions, the interview had to be terminated; if an unusually large number of customers interrupted the conversation, another trip was necessitated.

The other problem was the subjects' anxiety and concern about safety. Since the interview was about Chinese gangs and extortion, the subjects were often uncomfortable with some questions. According to the interviewers, a small number of subjects warily kept an eye on the entrance during the entire interview, as if they expected gang members to walk in at any moment. On one occasion, the parents of a subject asked the interviewer to end the questioning because they feared that their son might be compromised with the gangs. Some subjects were distrustful and worried that their participation would somehow be discovered by gang members. Nevertheless, many saw the interview as an opportunity to reveal their fears and problems to someone who was willing to listen. Despite their apprehensions, most subjects were very appreciative and felt relieved to know that their problem was finally being recognized by the larger society.

In this type of sociological research, fear is often experienced not just by the subjects. In conducting field research with deviant groups, many researchers have expressed concern for their own safety (Adler, 1985; Hagedorn, 1988; Bourgois, 1989; Taylor, 1990). During the fieldwork, gang members walked in on a few interviews. In one case, an interviewer saw several teenagers walk in. The gang members surrounded the interviewer and the owner, and one of the youths asked the interviewer, "Little Sister, what are you doing here?" The youths then told her to get lost and turned their attention to the owner. One of the gang members appeared to be carrying a gun. The youths asked the owner for $70 protection money a month, and the owner tried to negotiate. After being punched by the gang members, the owner paid the gang and they left. The interview was terminated after the incident.

On some occasions, when they arrived to conduct the interview, the interviewers bumped into teenagers who appeared to be gang members. Following fieldwork instructions, the interviewers left the premises immediately and later stopped by to set up another interview appointment. One interviewer was warned by a subject to be careful: "You could be hit and killed by a car as though it was an accident."

Data Management

A bilingual research assistant coded the answers to the closed-ended questions before the data in the questionnaire were entered into a computer. Answers to the open-ended questions were translated into English from Chinese by the author and installed in a word-processing file.

Validity and Reliability

The measurement of gang victimization appeared to have high validity. Gang victimization was measured by four types of gang extortion: demands for protection money, demands for lucky money, the forced selling of items, and the theft of goods or services. In addition, the frequency of extortion, the amount of payment, and the prevalence of extortion-related threats were also measured. The author consistently checked the completed questionnaires for discrepancies when they were received from the interviewers.

The interviewers were asked to evaluate (based on their gut feelings) the subjects' honesty and memory. Interviewer ratings thus provided assessments of the respondents' honesty in answering the questions. The interviewers thought that most subjects were either "very honest" or "simply honest" in answering questions and that they appeared to have a good memory. According to the interviewers, many owners kept records of extortion payments or received a receipt from the gang members for each payment. These records or receipts helped the owners keep track of their payments and, for the purpose of this study, their victimization. Thus, estimates of the prevalence, frequency, and the financial costs of gang victimization have high validity.[13]

The data show no association between the respondents' personal/business characteristics and the honesty/accuracy of their responses except that (1) businesses located in Queens' Chinatown and in other parts of Manhattan were evaluated by the interviewers to be more honest in answering questions about personal information and to have a better memory than respondents in Manhattan's and Brooklyn's Chinatowns; (2) male respondents were evaluated to be more honest than female respondents in answering questions about their attitudes toward the criminal justice system and crime reporting behaviors; and (3) younger respondents, owners of relatively new businesses, and more recent immigrants were evaluated to have a better memory than older subjects, owners of older firms, and subjects who have lived in the United States for a long time.

The Follow-up Study

One year after the business survey was completed, 50 subjects who participated in the survey were selected for the follow-up study.[14] The process of soliciting respondents for in-depth interviews was part of the original research design. When the first phase interviews of the study were completed, respondents were asked if they would participate in a second, more concentrated interview, which would explore more carefully their experiences with extortion in their business activities.

The creation of a subpopulation for the follow-up study required field interviewers to evaluate the responsiveness of interviewees during the initial contacts and interviews. Each field-worker was asked for an assessment of the respondents' candor, truthfulness, cooperation, and willingness to participate in a follow-up study.

I decided for several reasons that one year should elapse before a group of

0017999

respondents from the initial sample should be approached for another interview. First, the follow-up study was designed to chart changes in respondent reactions toward extortion over time. Second, a period of a year encompasses holidays, festive occasions, and seasonal ups and downs in business activity. Getting reactions from business owners after one year enabled me to determine whether the extortion was systematic and routinized or spontaneous and episodic. Third, by going back into the field, I could assess the reliability of the data and thus become more confident about the data's generalizability. Fourth, it was possible that the second wave of interviews would turn up unexpected data and refinements that the initial interviews glossed over or ignored.

The questionnaire for the follow-up study was divided into several sections that built on items presented in the original interview protocol. It reflected some of the results of the first survey and explored in more detail the interactions between gang members and their victims.

The questionnaire for the follow-up study was written in English and translated into Chinese. It included 89 questions, mostly open-ended, which focused on such issues as the social process and dynamics of various types of victimization, the drama of negotiation between victims and offenders, the subjects' perception of the Chinese subculture of paying extortion money, the natural history of victimization, the roles of adult organizations in the business of intimidation, and the subjects' attitudes toward local law enforcement authorities.

The Gang Study

One major obstacle that faces researchers (even those with appropriate language skills) is that many of the areas or scenes in which gangs are active are too dangerous for nonpatrons of vice activities. For example, gambling dens are closely guarded by gang members and are virtually closed to would-be participant observers. The close relationship between gangs and adult organizations poses numerous barriers for those who wish to contact gang members. Consequently, only one previous study attempted and partially succeeded in collecting data directly from a relatively substantial number of Chinese gang members (Toy, 1992a).

I was aware that for me to reach and obtain cooperation from Chinese gang members would be a major challenge. It was my conviction that gang members were not likely to be honest in answering questions if they felt even indirectly coerced by the criminal justice system. As a result, I ruled out the possibility of asking police officers in Chinatown to refer gang subjects to me. The thought of recruiting gang members through social workers was also dropped because, at that time, there was no social service agency in Chinatown that provides services to gang members. I decided that the best way to recruit Chinese gang members as subjects was through someone who was an active or former gang member. An interviewer who worked for me on the business survey introduced me to a former gang member with whom she was acquainted. The interviewer, a school counselor by profession, had provided help to the former gang member when he was a high school student.

Sample

The targeted sample for the gang study consisted of 62 male subjects who were former or active members of New York City's Chinese gangs and 8 female subjects who hung out with male gang members. Most male participants ($N = 58$) were recruited by a former gang member.[15] Others were referred by a Chinatown journalist. The sampling goals for the study were (1) to interview at least one subject from each of the active Chinese gangs; (2) to interview gang members from all ranks; and (3) to interview a proportionately representative number of subjects from each active gang.

The sample achieved most of the goals. First, it included at least one respondent from every Chinese gang. Second, it included ordinary (lowest level) gang members, street leaders, and faction leaders.[16] I was unable, however, to interview the top gang leaders. Third, with the exception of one gang (the Fuk Ching gang), the sample included, proportionately, more members from the larger and more active Chinese gangs and provided a close approximation of the actual distribution of gang members in the neighborhood.

This part of my study has some limitations. First, the use of nonrandom sampling techniques may limit the generalizability of this study's results to the Chinese gang population in New York City at large. However, because of the lack of concrete, reliable information about the number of Chinese gang members in New York City, random sampling was simply not feasible. Second, the findings of this study may not be applicable to Chinese gangs in other cities or to non-Chinese Asian gangs. Compared to Chinese gangs in other urban centers such as San Francisco (Toy, 1992a, 1992b), Los Angeles (Dombrink and Song, 1992), Vancouver (Dubro, 1992), and Toronto (Lavigne, 1991), Chinese gangs in New York City are considered to be more stable, better organized, more entrenched in the Chinese community, and more involved in profit-generating criminal activities (Bresler, 1981; Chin, 1990; Kinkead, 1992). Also, Chinese gangs are uniquely different from the gangs formed exclusively by other young Asian immigrants such as the Vietnamese, Cambodians, Laotians, and Koreans (Badey, 1988; Vigil and Yun, 1990; Knox, 1992). Third, my inability to interview top gang leaders may have resulted in the underestimation of certain types of aggression, especially the premeditated violence associated with drug trafficking, human smuggling, and turf expansion (Daly, 1983; Meskil, 1989).

Data Collection

Face-to-face interviews with gang members were conducted in the summer of 1992 by a female Chinese interviewer in an office located near Manhattan's Chinatown. The recruiter (the former gang member) arranged for two to three subjects who belonged to the same gang to be interviewed in the field office every day. While one subject was being interviewed in a separate room, the recruiter and the other subjects played cards in an adjacent room. A third room served as the field office for the researcher who positioned himself in the office to monitor the interviews. At the end of the day, after all the subjects had been interviewed, the recruiter would escort the subjects out of the office building. Each subject was paid $50 for the interview.

A standardized questionnaire with both closed and opened-ended questions was used for the interviews. The questionnaire had both English and Chinese versions. Prior to the interview, subjects were asked to read and sign an informed consent letter and to choose the language with which they were most comfortable. The interviewer would use the language selected to conduct the interview.[17] Most interviews were conducted in either English or Cantonese, and a few were conducted in Mandarin. Information was collected about the subjects' socioeconomic status, the stages they went through in becoming a gang member, the structure of their gangs, and patterns of gang activities.

Validity and Reliability

Efforts were made to ensure the validity and reliability of the data. The recruiter and the interviewer had known each other for more than six years, and the recruiter had complete trust in the interviewer, who was his high school counselor.[18] Also, most subjects were acquaintances of the recruiter and appeared to trust him. The interviews were conducted in a private office inside an office building located on neutral turf. The subjects were relaxed and seemed to be candid in their answers to most of the questions. Most subjects appeared to be uneasy when asked about their involvement in burglaries, the number of members in their gangs, and the amount of money they earned from their criminal activities.[19]

At the end of each session, the interviewer was asked to evaluate the subject's honesty based on her subjective perceptions. The interviewer's ratings thus provided some assessment of the respondents' honesty in answering the questions. According to the interviewer's evaluations, most subjects were perceived as being either "very honest" or "honest" in answering the questions.

Data Management

The management of data for the gang study was similar to the management of data for the business survey. Data from the questionnaire was coded by a bilingual coder, and the coded data was entered into a computer. Certain open-ended questions were not coded, but the information was arranged according its issue relevance. And if the answers were in Chinese, they were translated into English.

Law Enforcement Authorities as Key Informants

To supplement and cross-check data collected from victims of gang extortion, 23 in-depth interviews were conducted with law enforcement authorities in the New York metropolitan area. The interviews were conducted for the purpose of assessing the views of law enforcement officials about the Chinese communities and the problems law enforcement officials encounter with Chinese street gangs. The interviews focused on four major areas: (1) the structure of Chinese street gangs; (2) law enforcement perceptions of extortion and other gang activities in Chinatown; (3) law enforcement responses, both local and federal, to crimes committed by Chinese offenders; and (4) the problems encountered by criminal justice agencies in preventing and combating crimes in Chinese communities.

Research Instruments and Data Collection

Interviews were conducted with New York City Police Department (NYPD) precinct police officers and commanding officers, Intelligence Division specialists in community anticrime units, members of the Manhattan Detective Task Force, and the Jade Squad—the Oriental Gang Unit of the NYPD that operates out of the Manhattan District Attorney's Office and has had experience with extortion cases and Chinese gang members. In addition, federal officers from the Federal Bureau of Investigation (FBI), the Drug Enforcement Administration (DEA), and the Immigration and Naturalization Service (INS) were interviewed. Interviews were also arranged with specialists outside the immediate area of the research in order to develop a more comprehensive picture of the street gang phenomenon. Altogether, 23 law enforcement officials in the New York metropolitan area were interviewed.[20]

I relied on my personal knowledge of the law enforcement divisions, a local crime reporter's knowledge, and scholarly articles on crime in Chinese communities in deciding whom to interview. The author not only knew who the important figures were in combating Chinese crime but also personally knew most of them. To assure that the sample represented the organizational complexity of the law enforcement community, at least one subject from each of the several types of law enforcement units, both local and federal, was interviewed. These units are considered by journalists and Chinatown researchers to be representative of the American criminal justice system in dealing with crime in Chinatown (Kwong, 1987; Chin, 1990; Kinkead, 1992).

The interview schedule was pretested on three law enforcement officers. The schedule that emerged was significantly altered and shortened. The final version of the schedule contained 62 predominantly open-ended questions. Several respondents wished to examine the protocols in advance of the interview and chose to prepare written responses to the questions. Only three respondents permitted tape recording of the interview session. The interviews were conducted by Robert Kelly, one of the co-principal investigators of this study.

Since the sample for law enforcement officers was relatively small and the questions contained in the interview protocol were predominantly open-ended, I did not code the answers. Rather, information from law enforcement subjects was sorted and typed into a word-processing file that contained various topics and issues.

Community Leaders as Key Informants

In addition to collecting information from law enforcement authorities, my interviewers also interviewed leaders of 15 community organizations. The purpose of the interviews was to collect data on how certain leaders of adult organizations, especially those who are influential in the community, view the Chinese gang problem and the roles their associations play in the prevention or escalation of gang extortion.

I purposively selected twenty community organizations,[21] however, out of the initial sample of 20, five were not interviewed. In order to avoid any potential risks to my interviewers, four of the organizations (all alleged to be affiliated with Chinese gangs) were dropped after one was prosecuted as a racketeering enterprise during the time of this study, and one could not be reached after several phone calls.

Of the 15 organizations interviewed, two were alleged to be associated with Chinese gangs. The rest were family (3), district (2), commercial (3), social service (4), and political (1) associations located in the Chinatowns of Manhattan, Queens, and Brooklyn.[22]

After the organizations were selected, a notification letter was sent to each one. A week later, an interviewer called the organization and asked for the president or the chairman. After the connection with the president or the chairman was made, the interviewer explained the purpose of the call and the nature of the study. Most community leaders were receptive and granted an interview on the first phone call. However, there were three organizations in which the interviewer had difficulty finding the president or the chairman, and, as a result, the interviews were conducted with a senior member of the organization.

The face-to-face interviews were conducted between May and September of 1990, following the completion of the business survey, by two female interviewers who were also involved in the business survey. All the interviews were conducted in either Cantonese or Mandarin and a standardized questionnaire was used. As with the data collected from the law enforcement interviews, the data collected from the community leaders was not coded, but was entered into a word-processing file of topics and issues.

3

Severity of Gang Victimization

One of the most prevalent forms of crime committed by Chinese gang members is extortion (Penn, 1980; Kerber and Gentile, 1982; Louttit, 1982; President's Commission on Organized Crime, 1984). Sensational newspaper headlines such as "Street Crime Casts a Pall of Fear over Chinatown," "The Tongs' Hammer Lock: Merchants Silent in Face of Extortion," "How Gangs Are Terrorizing S.F. China-town," and "Young Hoodlums, Scorning Tradition of Hard Work, Plague San Francisco Chinatown" underscore the pervasiveness of extortion in the Chinese American community.

The term extortion requires some explanation. In the context of the Chinese communities, it must be understood in its broadest connotations: it refers not just to the demand under threat of violence for money on either a regular or irregular basis, but to other forms of intimidation specific to the Chinese community. These include the forced sale of items to merchants, and the coercion of free meals and goods or services from local businesses (Chin, 1990). Accordingly, extortion in Chinatown may be classified into four types. The first is "protection." Protection denotes a demand for a fixed amount of money from a business to ensure that the business will not be disturbed by a gang or by other predators. The amount of money is negotiated between the business owner and the gang member; the money then is paid fairly regularly, for example, monthly. This type of extortion is closely related to territorial rights because theoretically only members of a gang that controls the area where the victim operates his or her business are supposed to ask for protection money.

The second type of extortion is sporadic and spontaneous demands for money from business owners by gang members. Although it has various names, I will refer to this form of extortion by its most common name—lucky money.[1] Unlike protection payments, the amount of lucky money payments is negotiated on each occasion, and the perpetrators do not promise to provide any service in return. Victimization here is a manifestation of the parasitic relationship between the offender and the victim, which transcends gang turf. Gang members prey on any member of the business community for lucky money, regardless of where he or she operates.

In the third type of extortion, gang members sell commodities to business owners at prices higher than their market value. The Chinese norm of ensuring harmony at all costs on major holidays, coupled with the custom of consuming or displaying certain items on these occasions, offers gang members culturally reinforced opportunities for criminally exploiting the community's commercial sector.[2]

In the fourth type of extortion, gang members may refuse to pay for goods or services, or may ask for heavy discounts. Although this type of behavior could be legally called theft of goods or services, it is often culturally regarded as reciprocal face giving behavior between the offender and the victim.[3]

How widespread is gang extortion in Chinese communities in the United States? The police in New York City believe that over 90 percent of the businesses in Manhattan's Chinatown are subject to extortion by Chinese gangs (U.S. Department of Justice, 1988). Our interviews with officials in New York City suggest that there is a consensus among local and federal authorities that gang extortion in Chinese areas is widespread and serious. Police in Toronto concur that Chinese gangs victimize nearly 90 percent of the Chinese businesses there (Allen and Thomas, 1987).

Authorities also estimate that Chinese gangs generate large incomes from extortion activities. A police officer in New York City disclosed that a leader of the Flying Dragons received $3,400 a week from a gambling house on Pell Street (Bresler, 1981). Another gang leader, Nickey Louie, formerly of the Ghost Shadows, told a reporter in the mid-1970s that his gang made $10,000 a week from extortion (*Canal Magazine,* 1978). A federal prosecutor in New York City charged that the Tung On gang received $10,000 to $15,000 a month in extortion payments from Chinese businesses (Bowles, 1993).

Although there is a widespread consensus that gang extortion is prevalent in Chinese American communities, there has been little systematic research to validate claims about its prevalence or severity. We do not know what percentage of the Chinese business community is approached by gangs for money, how many of those approached are actually victimized, how often they are subjected to extortion, how much money they pay, how often they are expected to pay, and what the consequences of these crimes are for the economic and social life of Chinese communities. The limited research efforts of prior victimization studies have resulted in a paucity of knowledge about the characteristics of victims and offenders, their interactions with each other, and the extortion activities themselves.

To describe and analyze patterns of commercial victimization of Chinese businesses, I use the paradigm of a victimization career, which is similar to the concept of a criminal career. The concept of a criminal career includes several dimensions of criminal behavior: participation and specialization in, and continuation and desistance of crime or drug use (Blumstein et al., 1985). Like other professional careers, a criminal career involves certain career patterns. It begins with the social process of initiation, which is followed by the persistence and routinization of criminal activity, periods of peak activity within an age "window," stabilization of behavior, periods of decline or disruption as the criminal ages or is incarcerated, and a process of desistance after a number of years of criminal activity. Moreover, the career patterns differ for individuals who avoid criminality, for those who desist early after brief careers, and for those who persist for lengthy periods (Blumstein et al., 1985). These concepts may also be adapted and applied to victimization. That is, like criminals, victims may also have careers patterns. Thus, the natural history of victimization may involve the processes of initial victimization or avoidance, escalation of the process, its truncation due to the resistance of the victims or incarceration of the offenders, and finally desistance. In this chapter, I use these concepts to examine the vulnerabilities to and avoidance of victimization among Chinese business owners.

Career parameters of victimization were used to estimate the seriousness of gang extortion during the lifetime of a business.[4] As in research on offender careers (Blumstein et al., 1985), the prevalence and frequency of victimization careers were estimated. Also, because extortion and other victimization of Chinese businesses is primarily an instrumental crime involving monetary loss, the seriousness of victimization was estimated by the amount of money paid or the value of the goods or services stolen. Because different types of businesses present varying opportunities for victimization, victimization estimates were disaggregated by business type.

Sample Characteristics

Table 3.1 shows the personal and business characteristics of the respondents in this study. Most respondents were male. The mean age for respondents was 43. Most were immigrants from Hong Kong. All but 19 (97%) were born abroad (data not shown in table 3.1). Most had at least attended high school. The average number of years they had resided in the United States was 16 years.[5]

The businesses in the sample were mostly restaurants, retail food stores, and retail nonfood stores (shoe stores, bookstores, and so forth) located in the Chinatowns of Manhattan, Brooklyn, and Queens. Most business establishments were relatively new, and the mean age of the firms was eight years in business. Interviewers classified most businesses as small or medium-sized on the basis of their physical size and reported volume of activity. Fifty-two percent of the business firms in the sample had more than one owner.[6] Only 14 percent of the subjects indicated that they owned the properties in which their businesses were located.

The data suggest that female respondents, many of whom were from Taiwan, were involved predominantly in service-oriented businesses or in the garment industry. The Chinatowns of Manhattan and Brooklyn were dominated by entrepreneurs from Hong Kong, whereas merchants from Taiwan were most active in the Chinatown in Queens and in midtown or upper Manhattan. Respondents from China tended to congregate in areas of Brooklyn outside the borough's Chinatown. All the factories in the sample were located in Manhattan's Chinatown. Many service-oriented firms were situated in the Chinatown in Queens.

Because of their large number, restaurants ($N = 212$) were assigned an exclusive category. The retail food store category ($N = 130$) included 13 types of businesses, although most were bakery shops (24%), grocery stores (14%), liquor stores (10%), and supermarkets (10%). There were 37 types of business firms in

Table 3.1. Business Survey Respondents' Personal and Business Characteristics ($N = 603$)[a]

Personal[b]	N	%	Business[c]	N	%
Sex			Type of business		
Male	472	78	Restaurant	212	35
Female	131	22	Retail food store	130	22
Country of origin			Retail nonfood store	108	18
Hong Kong	324	54	Service	117	19
Taiwan	104	17	Factory	36	6
China	85	14	Neighborhood		
Other	89	15	Manhattan's Chinatown	335	55
Ethnicity[d]			Queen's Chinatown	129	21
Cantonese	332	56	Brooklyn's Chinatown	42	7
Fujianese	44	7	Manhattan non-Chinatown	34	6
Chiu Chao/Hakka	29	5	Queens non-Chinatown	22	4
Taiwanese	44	7	Brooklyn non-Chinatown	41	7
Shanghainese	45	8	Size of firm		
Other Chinese	73	12	Very small	55	9
Others	28	5	Small	172	29
Education			Medium	253	43
No schooling	8	1	Large	111	19
6th grade or less	55	9	Sole owner of business?		
7th to 9th grade	68	12	Yes	283	48
10th to 12th grade	198	33	No	305	52
College	230	39	Also own the property?		
Graduate school	34	6	Yes	80	14
			No	508	86

a. Number of missing observations: Country of origin = 1; Ethnicity = 8; Education = 10; Size of firm = 12; Sole owner of business = 15; Also own the property = 15. Percentages have been adjusted to account for this.

b. Age in years: mean, 43; median, 42; mode, 41.

c. Age of firm in years: mean 8; median, 5; mode, 3.

d. Number of years in the United States: mean, 16; median, 14; mode, 10.

the retail nonfood store category ($N = 108$), and no particular type was predominant. In the service category ($N = 117$), there were 29 types of businesses, and accounting offices (11%), beauty salons (15%), travel agencies (13%), and real estate companies (15%) were the most common types. Factories ($N = 36$), invariably garment factories, were also included in the survey.

The Severity of Gang Extortion

Severity of gang extortion may be measured by seven criteria: (1) the prevalence of attempted and completed victimization; (2) the annual incidence of completed extortion; (3) the monetary costs; (4) the extent of threats and violence associated with extortion; (5) the degree of multiple exploitation; (6) the level of persistence; and (7) the victims' perception of its seriousness.

Prevalence of Attempted and Completed Victimization

Table 3.2 shows the lifetime prevalence of gang extortion for businesses.[7] The assessment of the severity of gang extortion based on the prevalence rate should take into consideration (1) that most businesses in the sample existed only for a relatively short period of time (three to eight years); (2) that there could be underestimation, but not overestimation (respondents have little reason to exaggerate their victimization but every reason to deny it); and (3) that some of the businesses included in the sample were situated in obscure places unlikely to be noticed by the gangs.

The table indicates that forced sales was reported to be the most prevalent type of both attempted and completed extortion, followed by demands for lucky money. Protection demands were reported to be more commonly attempted than theft of goods or services, but the subjects were less likely to be victims of protection demands than of theft of goods or services because business owners were more likely to resist paying protection money on a regular basis than they were to resist occasionally offering free goods or services.

Table 3.2 suggests that Chinese gangs have diversified their patterns of victimization from the more overt forms of extortion to subtler means—namely, selling items to business owners. Before 1980, selling items to business owners was relatively rare among gang members (Chin, 1990), but it now appears to be the most common form of extortion. The reason for the gang members' increased involvement in forced sales may be the business owners' relative lack of resistance.

Although merchants are less likely to defy gang demands for free or discounted goods and services than they are to defy other sorts of gang demands, many businesses are spared this form of victimization. Either these businesses do not carry goods (such as real estate agencies), or their goods are not easily portable (as in garment factories), or their services are needed only occasionally (as in barbershops). Consequently, it is fair to say that certain businesses are unlikely to be the targets of theft of goods and services.

The table also indicates that law enforcement authorities may have overestimated the prevalence of Chinese gang extortion. My data show that 69 percent of the sample experienced attempted extortion and 55 percent submitted to gang

Table 3.2. Lifetime Prevalence of Gang Extortion
per Business ($N = 603$)

Types of Victimization	Attempted		Completed	
	N	%	N	%
Protection	130	22	70	12
Lucky money	246	41	164	27
Forced sales	308	51	246	41
Theft of goods or services	103	17	94	16
At least one of the four types	416	69	330	55

demands. Even if we consider the possibility that certain respondents might have denied their victimization, it is highly unlikely that 90 percent or more of the Chinese-owned legitimate businesses were subjected to extortion by gangs. It is possible, as the later discussions in this chapter suggest, that 90 percent or more of a particular type of business within a particular block may have been targeted for extortion. Although these data suggest that police generally overestimate the prevalence of extortion in the Chinese business community, the findings substantiate the claim that extortion in the Chinese communities is widespread.

Since there is no research on the prevalence of gang extortion in other ethnic communities, I am unable to assess the relative severity of gang extortion in the Chinese business community. Nevertheless, it is fair to conclude that, when almost 70 percent of the members of a business community admit that they have been approached by gangs for money, goods, or services, the business of intimidation may be considered pervasive.

Frequency of Completed Victimization

There is little data on precisely how often incidents of extortion in the Chinese community occur. Law enforcement agencies tend to assume that Chinese business owners are frequently subjected to extortion by gang members; however, few incidents of extortion are reported to the police in Manhattan's Chinatown each year. For example, between September 1989 and August 1990, the Fifth Police Precinct that covers the core areas of Manhattan's Chinatown, received only 17 complaints of gang extortion.

Table 3.3 shows that the incidence of completed victimization varies by type of extortion. Most victims of protection demands (42%) paid the gangs monthly. Many (22%) offered only one lump-sum payment and thus avoided unpleasant encounters with the perpetrators on a regular basis. Others (16%) were forced to pay weekly. On average, victims of protection demands paid the gangs 14 times annually, but most paid 12 times a year.

Lucky money payments occurred infrequently, either four times a year (54%) or once a year (39%). Only 7 percent were subjected to extortion in this manner once a month or more. Lucky money payments occurred five times a year on average, but for most victims, the occurrence was not more than three times a year.

Although forced sales was the most prevalent type of gang extortion, victims were exploited only once or twice a year, during the Chinese New Year or the Mid-Autumn (Moon) Festival.[8] The average annual frequency of completed forced sales was two times, and the mode was only once.

Theft of goods or services happened more often than forced sales and demands for lucky money, but slightly less often than protection demands. The average annual frequency for theft of goods and services was 17 times, and the mode, three times. The average annual incidence of completed thefts of goods or services was higher than the incidence of any other type of gang extortion. This is probably because of the almost daily victimization of certain businesses, such as videotape rental stores, retail food stores, and movie theaters.

Table 3.3. Frequency of Completed Gang Extortion of Businesses Admitting Victimization

	Protection (N = 70)	Lucky Money (N = 164)	Forced Sales (N = 246)	Theft of Goods or Services (N = 94)
Businesses admitting victimization (% of completion)				
2–3 times a week, or about 130 times a year	0%	0%	0%	8%
Weekly, or about 52 times a year	16	1	0	4
Biweekly, or about 26 times a year	0	1	0	12
Monthly, or about 12 times a year	42	5	1	6
Several times a year	0	0	5	23
Quarterly, or about 4 times a year	6	54	26	27
Semiannually, or twice a year	5	0	27	0
Annually, or once a year	9	39	41	15
Once/lump-sum payment	22	0	0	5
Annual frequency (number of incidents)[b]				
Mean	14	5	2	17
Median	3	2	2	7
Mode	12	3	1	3

a. N = number of businesses admitting this type of completed victimization.

b. The annual mean, median, and mode are approximate figures calculated from the frequency.

In sum, victim encounters with perpetrators varied by type of extortion. Protection demands involved more frequent interaction between victims and perpetrators: 58 percent of the protection victims encountered the perpetrators once each month or more, compared to 30 percent of the theft victims and 7 percent of the lucky money victims. Forced sales involved infrequent contact since these incidents are usually structured around specific cultural events such as the Chinese New Year.

In general, most victims were exploited no more than three or four times a year. The actual attempts at victimization, however, were more frequent. Most merchants refused to satisfy all the demands of the gangs during the initial encounters and adopted a variety of ruses to deflect gang members. Store owners may ask gang members to come back another time, or they may pretend that they are not the owners and, therefore, cannot agree to pay. Thus, although table 3.3 suggests relatively low rates of completed victimizations, gang members may have attempted harassment more often. I estimate that for every completed victimization at least three to four attempts (or encounters between the victim and the offender) may have occurred. Even victims who agreed to pay a gang monthly or weekly may have interacted with gang members more than once before a payment was made because the victims often do not pay on time. The frequent encounters between victims and offenders may have led the authorities to conclude that merchants in Chinatown are frequently the victims of completed extortion rather than attempted extortion.

Financial Costs

The financial costs of extortion to Chinese businesses provide an additional dimension to the severity of Chinese gang activity. Table 3.4 illustrates the financial costs of gang extortion per incident and per year. For protection and lucky money payments and the forced purchase of unsolicited items, the monetary costs are the dollar amounts reported to us by the respondents. For theft of goods or services, the monetary value of the goods or services was estimated by the business owner.

Table 3.4 purports that in a normal extortion incident, a victim may experience a loss of as little as $1 (a cup of coffee and a piece of cake) or as much as $3,000.[9] On average, the victims paid $129 for each protection payment, $75 for each lucky money payment, and $51 for forced purchases, and they lost $119 worth of goods or services. Respondents reported that the typical payments or loss per incident (the mode) were $100 for protection, $20 for lucky money, $50 for forced purchases, and $30 when gang members demanded free or discount goods or services.

The annual costs for gang extortion per business were as little as $3 or as much as $31,220. The average annual costs for subjects who had been victimized at least once, regardless of the type of extortion, was $688. The annual payment to gangs for most subjects was $50. Half of the respondents paid not more than $120 a year to the gangs (data not shown in table 3.4).

For protection, a subject may have needed to pay as little as $5 or as much as

Table 3.4. Financial Costs of Gang Extortion (in Dollars)[a]

	Protection (N = 70)	Lucky Money (N = 164)	Forced Sales (N = 246)	Theft of Goods or Services (N = 94)
Per incident				
Minimum	$ 3	$ 2	$ 5	$ 1
Maximum	1,000	1,300	200	3,000
Mean	129	75	51	119
Median	65	30	40	45
Mode	100	20	50	30
Per year				
Minimum	$ 5	$ 3	$ 5	$ 4
Maximum	12,000	9,100	1,250	31,200
Mean	1,294	313	117	1,532
Median	480	90	80	210
Mode	100	20	30	210

a. N = number of businesses admitting this type of completed victimization. Monetary amounts were estimated by business owners.

$12,000 a year. The maximum annual costs for lucky money and forced purchases were lower than for protection, but the maximum annual costs for theft of goods and services was higher than for protection.

In sum, for most victims, the annual financial loss from gang victimization was estimated at less than $1,000. Relative to the other costs of doing business, the costs Chinese entrepreneurs attribute to gang extortion are not significant in strictly financial terms. For most businesses in the Chinese communities, where rent may run tens of thousands of dollars a year (Scardino, 1986), an annual loss of less than $1,000 to gangs cannot be considered a serious threat to their financial well-being. Among small businesses, annual losses due to gang extortion were less than $200. Yet there is a small group of business owners who pay dearly for operating businesses in the Chinese community. For example, a large restaurant owner indicated that he paid several hundred dollars a month for protection to one gang, was subject to extortion for a few hundred dollars more a month by individual members of the gang and other gangs, and was left with the unpaid bills of gang members that added up to over $1,000 per month. His total gang bill added up to about $25,000 per year.

These data challenge allegations by police that most Chinese merchants are forced to pay gangs thousands of dollars a year (Bresler, 1981; Posner, 1988). The discrepancy between police estimates and these results may reflect the social process of *kong so* (negotiation) between gang members and business owners. Police estimates may reflect the asking price, but business owners rarely pay this.

Extortion-Related Threats

Extortion-related violence has been reported occasionally in the media. In a few incidents, merchants have been wounded or killed by Chinese gangs for refusing to meet their demands. In 1976, a couple who owned a restaurant in midtown Manhattan were believed to have been murdered because they resisted a gang's demand for protection money (*China Tribune*, 1976). In 1983, a female manager of a restaurant in Philadelphia's Chinatown was shot to death by three gang members from New York City after she declined to pay them lucky money (Chin, 1990). In yet other incidents, gang members were shot and killed or wounded by furious merchants (Ruffini and Cotter, 1980; Scilla and Locksley, 1985; McFadden, 1988).

There have been no systematic data on the prevalence of extortion-related aggression committed by Chinese gang members or Chinese business owners, however. To assess the severity of gang extortion, the respondents in my survey were asked to report whether they had been threatened by gang members, what types of threats were made, and whether they or their businesses were attacked when they refused to pay.

Table 3.5 illustrates the prevalence of threats associated with gang extortion. When gang members approach business owners for money, they may threaten to harm the owners' family, assault the owners, damage property, or disrupt the business. Gang members may also flash a gun or intimidate the owners with the threat of sending their *dai lo* (gang leader).[10] Respondents targeted by gang

Table 3.5. Prevalence of Extortion-Related Threats[a]

	Protection (N = 130)	Lucky Money (N = 246)	Forced Sales (N = 308)	Theft of Goods or Services (N = 103)
Threatened to hurt your family?	3%	0%	0%	1%
Threatened to hurt you?	11	5	1	2
Showed weapons?	2	1	1	0
Threatened to harass you?	33	20	10	16
Threatened to damage property?	11	8	2	2
Threatened to disrupt business?	15	9	4	4
Said their boss will get angry?	5	3	1	4
Other threats?	12	3	3	6

a. N = number of businesses admitting this type of attempted victimization. Percentage of respondents who answered "yes" to the question.

members for protection money indicated that the most prevalent form of threats were harassment against them (33%), followed by threats to disrupt their businesses (15%) or to damage their property (11%). Rarely did the gang members display a weapon or threaten to hurt the victim's family. Table 3.5 shows that the patterns of threats associated with other types of extortion were similar to those associated with protection, except that victims were most likely to be subjected to threats when they were approached for protection money and least likely to be intimidated when gang members asked them to purchase certain items. Gang members were most persistent when asking for protection money from the business owners.

In sum, Chinese gang members tend to use verbal threats rather than physical violence to coerce business owners. Only two subjects reported having been physically assaulted by gang members. One business owner disclosed that he had been beaten by gang members when he refused to pay protection money. Another store owner revealed that her store was shot at when she did not meet gang demands for money. More often than not, offenders harassed the owners with threats against their property or businesses. Most of the threats were verbal threats such as "We will disrupt your business," "We will damage your property," or "We will hurt you." In a few unusual cases, owners were subjected to more dire warnings such as "You might not live for long" or "You will be shot to death tonight." Many respondents indicated that very often the offenders were polite and unassuming. For example, the extortionists might ask merchants to pay whatever they could, but even when they were dissatisfied with the amount, they rarely complained.

The absence of violence reflects several features of Chinese gang extortion. It may be that those who ask for protection money have a widely acknowledged reputation for violence. No threats need be made in such circumstances. Also, younger gang members' threats of retaliation if refused may not be credible.

Evidently, the willingness of victims to pay gang members was not the result of explicit coercion, intimidation, violence, or threats. Instead, the high compliance rates in the absence of threats perhaps reflects an expectation that violence or other unfortunate problems may befall the businessperson who fails to comply with extortion demands. Or possibly, high compliance rates may be a cultural adaptation to the giving face norm practiced by Chinese. Finally, if, as this survey shows, the demands do not seem too unreasonable and are anticipated, high compliance rates may be due to the fact that paying extortionists does not seem all that unusual or bothersome.

Multiple Victimization

The seriousness of gang extortion can also be measured by the diversity of attempted and completed victimization. Table 3.6 shows that, for those who were approached by gang members ($N = 416$), a substantial proportion (41%) experienced only one form of attempted exploitation. Only 23 percent reported three or more types of attempted victimization. Of victims who experienced at least one form of completed victimization, more than half (55%) were exploited in only one way; and 17 percent admitted they had experienced three or more different forms of completed victimization.

Data (not shown in the table) indicate that 45 percent of the lucky money victims and 19 percent of the protection victims were victimized by more than one gang.[11] The division of subareas of Manhattan's Chinatown and other Chinese neighborhoods into gang territories appears to limit the interactions of victims with more than one gang, because, as noted above, in Manhattan at least, most businesses are tong-affiliated, as are the gangs. The tong connections of both victims and victimizers tends to organize extortion and circumscribe its frequency and its participants.

Table 3.6. Multiple Attempted and
Completed Victimizations

	N	%
Attempted victimizations per business ($N = 416$)		
Only one form	170	41
Two forms	149	36
Three forms	69	16
All four forms	28	7
Completed victimizations per business ($N = 330$)		
Only one form	182	55
Two forms	92	28
Three forms	42	13
All four forms	14	4

Persistence of Gang Extortion

How persistent are gang members in exploiting Chinese merchants? Is there an escalation over time in the frequency or severity of gang extortion? Are the victims able to resist or avoid gang extortion after a short period of exploitation? What happens to those who take the initiative in closing down their victimization careers? These questions are relevant to the evaluation of the severity of gang extortion.

Data (not shown in the tables) suggest that 74 percent of the victims of protection reported no change after their initial episode with gang demands. That is, they were asked to pay the same amount of money with the same regularity. The rest (26%) indicated that there were changes over time. Some were asked to pay slightly more or more often, but others were allowed to decrease the amount or frequency of payments. According to data collected from those who paid the gangs protection money, some had been victimized as recently as two months prior to this survey or as long ago as 20 years prior. Among the victims of protection, only 28 percent had tried to stop payments. These owners had adopted many tactics to rid themselves of the gangs, including joining tongs, hiring non-Chinese employees, asking powerful community figures to talk to the gangs, paying the *dai lo* a large sum of money, or moving the business to another location. Interestingly, none of them experienced any type of retaliation from the gangs.

Data on the length of victimization were not collected for the other three forms of victimization. However, the subjects were asked what happened when they refused to meet the continuous requirements of the gang members after their first encounter. In most cases, the offenders refused to leave the business premises or created a scene by yelling and cursing at the owners. In a few incidents, gang members damaged furniture or goods inside the store. In one particular incident, a group of gang members smashed the windows of a store when the owner refused to purchase items from them. In another incident, a gang member pulled out a gun, placed it on the counter, and said, "Don't force me to do something I don't want to." When he released the safety on the gun, the owner threatened to call the police. The gang member left the store abruptly.

The data suggest that most victims did not experience an escalating frequency or severity of victimization after their initial experience. Indeed, some were even able to resist the gangs without any serious repercussions.

Victim Perceptions of Gang Extortion

Subjects were asked to evaluate the severity of gang extortion, the seriousness of the Chinese gang problem in their communities, and the impact of gangs on their business activities. Armed robbery was ranked by the subjects as the most serious crime, followed by gang extortion, shoplifting, and drug sales. The majority of the subjects viewed the Chinese gang problem as either "very serious" (51%) or "somewhat serious" (25%). However, almost 70 percent of them thought that the existence of Chinese gangs had no effect on their business activities (data not shown). Most of those who said the gangs did affect their commercial activities blamed the gangs for decreases in business volume and profits and for the negative psychological impact they had on the subjects themselves and their employees. The data show that the perceptions of those who were subject to extortion attempts ($N = 416$) and those who were the victims of completed extortion ($N = 330$) on the severity of the Chinese gang problem were almost identical to those of the sample as a whole ($N = 603$).

Summary

The estimates in this study are circumscribed by sampling decisions and ignore extortion within the commercial sex and gambling industries for the reasons given in chapter 2. Because owners of certain businesses (i.e., gambling clubs and prostitution houses) were not sampled, the data may underestimate gang involvement in extortion activities and the extent of violence associated with it. Moreover, since some respondents may have denied or minimized the severity of their victimization, the results should be viewed as conservative estimates of the prevalence and seriousness of the gang problem. While this study is an important step in developing methods to assess nonpersonal commercial forms of victimization, further research should include businesses that operate in the informal economy, as well as in the illicit economy, so that the full measure of the extent of exploitation of business activity by Chinese gangs can be assessed.

How serious is gang extortion in the Chinese communities in New York City? There is no straightforward answer to this question. Gang extortion is indeed prevalent. The majority of the respondents were approached by gangs, and more than half were victimized. Further, for reasons cited here, I believe that the prevalence of extortion is likely to be significantly higher for semilegitimate and illegitimate businesses. However, regardless of the frequent encounters between victims and offenders, the incidence of completed victimization is relatively low. This is probably due to the process of *kong so* and to the cultural restraints on normal extortion.

The financial costs of extortion rarely overwhelmed most victims. Store owners were rarely physically assaulted by the offenders in the process of extortion. Moreover, demands and threats did not significantly escalate after the initial approach, and some merchants were able to evade the gangs. Nevertheless, business owners see gang extortion as the second most serious crime in their community and the gang problem as rather severe, although the gangs had little impact on their actual business activities and profits.

In short, we may conclude that most business owners are not crushed financially by the costs of gang extortion but find being constantly involved in negotiating with gang members an annoying or even a traumatic experience. While businesses manage to absorb the costs of extortion and other victimization easily, the returns to gangs and gang members appear to be quite substantial.

Vulnerability to Gang Demands

Police assume that certain business owners are more vulnerable to Chinese gangs than others (U.S. Senate, 1992). The authorities believe that recently arrived entrepreneurs, owners of restaurants or retail stores, and businesspeople in the gang turfs are most vulnerable. In this section, I shall examine the relationships between subjects' personal and business characteristics and their vulnerability to gang extortion. I will then assess vulnerability according to the prevalence of attempted and completed victimization, frequency and financial cost of victimization, and the occurrence of multiple victimization.

Vulnerability to Attempted Extortion

Table 3.7 illustrates the association between the subjects' personal and business characteristics and their vulnerability to attempted extortion. The dependent variable is the percentage of respondents who were approached by gang members at least once, regardless of the form of gang extortion or whether they were victimized or not. For the whole sample ($N = 603$), the percentage of subjects who experienced at least one form of attempted extortion was 69 percent ($N = 416$).

Table 3.7 suggests that the subjects' sex and country of origin were not related to the likelihood of being approached by gangs. Gang members appeared to pay little attention to gender or country of origin in selecting their targets.

Many people in the Chinese community, including the police, assume that business owners who are affiliated with one or more community organizations are less vulnerable than others to gang extortion. The organizations are believed to be powerful enough to shield their members from the gangs. My data do not support this assumption. Table 3.7 shows that whether they are affiliated with a community organization or not, merchants have the same chance of being approached by the gangs. There is also no evidence to support the view that recent immigrants are more vulnerable to gang extortion than those who are well established here. Neither is a subject's age of any significance. The data show that respondents across various age groups were approached indiscriminately by gang members. Briefly, personal characteristics such as sex, age, country of origin, length of stay in the United States, and affiliation with community associations were not associated with vulnerability to extortion attempts. It is likely that many of these factors may be unknown to gangs at the outset or start of an extortion attempt.

Of all the personal attributes, only educational attainment and English proficiency were associated with vulnerability. Subjects who had more education were less likely to be approached by gangs. Table 3.7 shows that for those who had attended graduate school the likelihood of being approached by gang members was almost half that of those who had only a sixth-grade educational level or less. Also, subjects who spoke fluent English were substantially less likely to have encounters with the gangs. The cultural characteristics may be construed by gang members to be indicative of a businessperson's degree of assimilation and famil-

Table 3.7. Association between Subjects' Personal and Business
Characteristics and Attempted Extortion ($N = 603$)

Personal	%[a]	Business	%[a]
Sex		Type of business***	
Male	69	Restaurant	84
Female	68	Retail food store	75
Country of origin		Retail nonfood store	65
Hong Kong	71	Service	47
Taiwan	65	Factory	47
China	71	Neighborhood*	
Other	65	Manhattan's Chinatown	72
Education*		Queen's Chinatown	59
No schooling	75	Brooklyn's Chinatown	76
6th grade or less	80	Manhattan non-Chinatown	79
7th to 9th grade	72	Queens non-Chinatown	55
10th to 12th grade	72	Brooklyn non-Chinatown	71
College	67	Sole owner of business?*	
Graduate school	47	Yes	64
English proficiency***		No	74
Poor	80	Estimated profitability*	
Average	75	Good	75
Fluent	60	Average	67
Affiliation with		Poor	61
community organization?		Manhattan's Chinatown**	
Yes	69	Vietnamese zone (Born-to-Kill)	58
No	69	Italian zone (Ghost Shadows)	80
		On Leong zone (Ghost Shadows)	77
		Hip Sing zone (Flying Dragons)	70
		Tung On and Tsung Tsin zones (Tong On)	82
		Fujianese zone (Fuk Ching)	76
		Other core zone (No dominant gang)	59
		Outskirts (No dominant gang)	29

$*p < .05; **p < .01; ***p < .001$

a. Percentage of respondents who were approached at least once for extortion by gang
members.

iarity with law enforcement; Americanized business owners might be more inclined to summon the police.

Restaurants and retail food stores were most likely to be approached by gang
members, while service-oriented businesses and factories were the least likely
targets. The rates of attempted extortion reported by the respondents in my survey
are many times greater than the rates of personal or property victimization
reported in the National Crime Victimization Survey or in the commercial crime
surveys of the 1970s (Garofalo, 1990). Factories were least likely to be approached
because most were located on the second story or above in buildings where there
were no elevators. The offenders may have found it not only tiresome to climb the
stairs but also difficult to leave the crime scene expeditiously if warranted. More-

over, most factories have little cash handy most of the time; and these business establishments have no goods or consumer-services that might appeal to gang members.

Table 3.7 shows that Chinese merchants in midtown and upper Manhattan, followed by store owners in the Chinatowns of Brooklyn and Manhattan, were more vulnerable than Chinese business owners in other locations. Since there are no Chinese gang turfs in Manhattan other than in Chinatown, it may well be that gang members are more aggressive in victimizing store owners away from their turfs than merchants within their territories. A saturation point may have been reached, and the gangs may have felt compelled to stake out new territory. Also, the recently established Chinese community along Eighth Avenue in Brooklyn is becoming a major target for Chinese gangs. Consistent with this is the finding shown in table 3.7 that business owners in Brooklyn's Chinatown reported a higher level of attempted gang extortion than merchants in Manhattan's Chinatown. Even those who operated businesses in Brooklyn outside of the periphery of its Chinatown experienced almost similar levels of attempted gang extortion as merchants in Manhattan's Chinatown. Of the three boroughs, Queens appeared to be the safest for Chinese business owners. The data clearly suggest that Chinese gangs are expanding their extortion activities to areas some distance away from their power bases in Manhattan's Chinatown.

Gangs appeared to approach businesses owned by more than one person more often than businesses with a sole owner. At least one reason for this may be that when a business establishment has more than one owner, the owners may be reluctant to stand up and resist the gangs. Because the costs of the extortion will be equally distributed among all the owners, for them submitting to gang demands is less of a nuisance than resisting. Sole proprietors of businesses, on the other hand, may be more willing to resist because they cannot easily absorb the full costs should they yield to the gangs.

Not surprisingly, profitability and vulnerability appear to be linked. Table 3.7 shows that stores considered by the interviewers as good businesses were more likely to be approached than stores that seemed not to be doing well.

Vulnerability also varied by specific subneighborhood within Manhattan's Chinatown. About 82 percent of businesses within the territory of the Tung On Association (Division Street, Catherine Street, and East Broadway) were targeted by the gangs affiliated with that association, but only 24 percent of the businesses on the outskirts of Chinatown were shaken down (see figure 1.1, the map of Chinatown). The second most risky area was the On Leong's territory, which includes the Italian zone.[12] Although the Vietnamese gang Born-to-Kill has often been assumed to be more active in extortion than the other Chinese gangs, business owners within Born-to-Kill's turf were less likely to be approached than were those in other core areas of Manhattan's Chinatown.

Table 3.8 illustrates the association between street location in Manhattan's Chinatown and vulnerability to extortion. Attempted victimization rates for merchants in Manhattan's Chinatown, with the exception of protection, are slightly higher than the attempted victimization rates for the sample as a whole. Businesses located on Catherine Street (the Tung On gang's turf) were most vulnerable to protection, followed by business establishments on Bayard Street (the Ghost Shadows' territory) and East Broadway (the Tung On gang's turf). Interestingly, none of the stores located in the heart of the Flying Dragons' turf (Pell Street) were solicited for protection money. Merchants on other streets in the Flying Dragons' turf (the Bowery and Hester Street) were also unlikely to be approached for protection money, but not those on Grand Street. The streets controlled by the Fuk Ching (Eldridge and Chrystie) and the Born-to-Kill (Center, Lafayette, and Broadway) were also less vulnerable to the protection racket. Thus, I assume that the Tung On and the Ghost Shadows attempt to ask for protection money from merchants more actively than do the other gangs.[13]

Merchants on Eldridge, Hester, and Chrystie appeared to be most vulnerable to gang demands for lucky money, whereas store owners on Pell Street were least likely to be asked for lucky money. None of the three blocks most vulnerable to

Table 3.8. Association between Streets in Manhattan's Chinatown and Vulnerability to Gang Victimization ($N = 335$)[a]

Streets in Manhattan's Chinatown	Protection	Lucky Money	Forced Sales	Theft of Goods or Services	Extortion in General
Attempted victimization rate for the entire Manhattan's Chinatown	22%	44%	56%	19%	72%
Ghost Shadows					
Mott	23	40	76	21	81
Bayard	39	31	92	46	92
Mulberry	17	58	42	25	58
Elizabeth	27	55	73	18	82
Canal	11	34	43	11	63
Flying Dragons					
Pell	0	8	58	17	58
Bowery	8	17	67	25	75
Hester	9	82	91	0	100
Grand	27	64	55	27	73
Tung On					
East Broadway	35	38	62	35	76
Division	14	71	43	21	71
Catherine	42	58	75	25	83
Fuk Ching					
Eldridge	0	88	75	13	88
Chrystie	9	73	55	27	91
Born-to-Kill					
Center	20	30	20	0	50
Lafayette	33	25	25	25	50
Broadway	20	70	40	0	70
Elsewhere	25	16	36	10	59

a. Percentage who responded yes to this type of attempted victimization.

Table 3.9. Association between Type of Business and Type of Attempted Victimization ($N = 603$)[a]

		Attempted Victimization			
	Protection	Lucky Money	Forced Sales	Theft of Goods or Services	At Least One of the 4 Types
Total ($N = 603$)	22%	41%	51%	17%	69%
Type of business					
Restaurant ($N = 212$)	25	51	67	29	84
Retail food store ($N = 130$)	27	45	58	12	75
Retail nonfood store ($N = 108$)	22	33	43	13	65
Service ($N = 117$)	13	27	33	10	47
Factory ($N = 36$)	8	36	22	0	47
Chi square	12.7	20.6	53.8	58.0	58.0
p	.013	.000	.000	.000	.000

a. Percentage who responded yes to this type of attempted victimization.

demands for protection ranked high on the vulnerability scale for being asked for lucky money. This suggests that demands for protection and lucky money are two parallel but not complementary crimes. Merchants in a particular street are unlikely to be approached by gang members for both protection and lucky money simultaneously.

Bayard, Hester, and Mott were the three streets reported to be highly vulnerable to forced sales, whereas Center and Lafayette were least vulnerable to this type of extortion activity. Merchants on Bayard, East Broadway, Grand, and Chyrstie were most vulnerable to theft of goods and services. Business owners on Hester, Center, and Broadway were highly unlikely to be asked to provide free or discounted goods or services.

Among the major streets of Manhattan's Chinatown, Hester appeared to be most attractive to the gangs: all the respondents from that street reported they had experienced some form of attempted extortion. More than 90 percent of the business owners on Bayard and Chrystie had been approached by gangs, compared to only 50 percent of the business owners on Center and Lafayette. Other streets that were comparatively vulnerable included Mott, Elizabeth, Catherine, and Eldridge.

An examination of the association between personal and business attributes and specific types of attempted extortion shows that those personal and business characteristics that were significant in determining vulnerability to any type of extortion were also critical in enhancing (or diminishing) a subject's vulnerability to attempted protection, asking for lucky money, forced sales, and theft of goods or services. For example, table 3.9 shows the association between type of business and type of attempted victimization. Table 3.9 illustrates that, regardless of type of attempted victimization, restaurants were the most vulnerable, followed by retail food stores, retail nonfood stores, service-oriented businesses, and factories, except that factories were more likely to be approached for lucky money than were retail nonfood stores and service-oriented businesses, and retail nonfood stores were slightly more likely to be asked for free or discounted goods or services than were retail food stores.

Vulnerability to Completed Victimization and Other Severity Measures

Table 3.10 shows the relationship between type of business and type of completed victimization. It clearly indicates that type of business is significantly associated with vulnerability to completed victimization, regardless of the type of victimization. Also, the patterns of association between type of business and type of *completed* victimization are similar to the patterns of association between type of business and type of *attempted* victimization.

I further explored whether certain personal and business characteristics were associated with two measures of the severity of completed victimization—frequency and financial loss. An analysis of variance was conducted to determine whether completed incident rates of gang victimization vary by type of business. Rates were computed for those businesses which had been subjected to extortion at least one time. The influence of business owner and business characteristics were also introduced to determine the effects of business type independent of the business owner's characteristics.

Overall, completed extortion rates were greatest for retail nonfood stores and lowest for factories (data not shown). However, these differences were not statistically significant. There were significant differences in rates of completed victimization only for theft of goods or services ($p[F] = .012$). Factories were the least

Table 3.10. Association between Type of Business and Type of Completed Victimization ($N = 603$)[a]

	Completed Victimization				
	Protection ($N = 70$)	Lucky Money ($N = 164$)	Forced Sales ($N = 246$)	Theft of Goods or Services ($N = 194$)	At Least One of the 4 Types ($N = 330$)
Total ($N = 603$)	12%	27%	41%	16%	55%
Type of business					
Restaurant ($N = 212$)	15	36	59	28	73
Retail food store ($N = 130$)	15	26	39	10	55
Retail nonfood store ($N = 108$)	8	18	32	11	46
Service ($N = 117$)	8	19	25	9	37
Factory ($N = 36$)	3	25	14	0	31
Chi square	8.7	15.5	57.0	39.7	55.8
p	.068	.002	.000	.000	.000

a. Percentage who responded yes to this type of completed victimization.

frequently victimized type of business for this type of crime. Statistical significance was approached ($p[F] < .10$) for lucky money and forced sales, but did not
meet the conventional threshold of $p < .05$ for large samples. Since the data were
highly skewed, analysis of variance was completed for the natural log of the
frequency of each type of victimization. The results remained the same. Also, none
of the covariates was significant for any of the crime types, which suggests that the
backgrounds of the business owners or their businesses (e.g., age, business volume, business size) were unrelated to the frequency of completed victimization.

The highest rates overall were found for forced sales in retail nonfood stores.
Although the prevalence rates for victimization were highest among restaurants,
the incidence rates were highest among retail nonfood stores (e.g., beauty shops).
Only for theft of goods and services were incidence rates highest among restaurants. Other businesses forced to provide free or discounted goods or services were
bakery shops, barbershops, videotape rental stores, and other retail stores, such as
grocery stores and optical stores. Protection was most frequent among retail food
stores, and lucky money rates were highest for service establishments. Forced
sales rates were highest among retail nonfood stores such as retail hardware
stores or clothing stores.

I also conducted an analysis of variance to determine whether the monetary
costs of gang victimization varied by type of business. Rates were computed for
businesses that had been victimized at least one time. The influence of business
owner and business characteristics were also introduced as control variables to
determine the effects of business type independent of business owner characteristics.

Monetary costs differed significantly by business type only for thefts of goods
or services; for other types of extortion, and for all types added together, there
were no significant differences in the amounts lost by type of business (data not
shown). As in the analyses of the incidence of completed victimization, these
results were unchanged after log transformations to adjust for the skewness in the
estimates of monetary costs. And also as in the analyses of the frequency of
completed victimization, losses were mediated by neither the characteristics of
the business owners nor the business itself.

Location plays a big role in the use of intimidation. Gang members were more
likely to intimidate merchants in Queens' Chinatown than in Manhattan's Chinatown (data not shown). Because Chinese gangs in Queens are not affiliated with
adult organizations there, Queens gangs need not consider any repercussions if
they offend local merchants who are part of an association or a tong. Business
owners within the tongs' territories in Manhattan's Chinatown were less likely to
be crudely harassed than were merchants outside the tongs' turfs, in such areas as
the Vietnamese territory on the west side of Manhattan's Chinatown.

Gang Extortion as an Institution

Over the past 10 years, it has become evident that Chinese gangs have been
shifting their patterns of victimization from overt extortion to subtler means of

illegally obtaining money—namely, selling items to business owners at unreasonably high prices. Before 1980, selling items to business owners was a relatively rare occurrence among gang members (Chin, 1990); however, it now appears to be their most popular form of extortion. In the past few years, in addition to selling plants or firecrackers for the Chinese New Year and cakes for the Mid-Autumn Festival, gang members have become more active in selling Christmas cards and tickets to popular music concerts and in providing (under implied or explicit threat) any items whenever they feel so inclined. This shows that certain gang members have intuitively decided to expand their criminal operations and are quite sensitive to the laws about extortion itself.

The seriousness of extortion in the Chinese community may be examined from a broader perspective than the legal criminological paradigm. We need to understand how gang victimization may have eroded the informal controls and social capital of the Chinese community and created instead an environment in which an organization or an individual's ability to take care of (meaning "to be in control of") the gangs can became a passage to power and money.

Because of the tongs' influence with and control over gangs, merchants may be compelled to join the tongs and pay money to them on a regular or irregular basis. Because of the tong leaders' reputations as mediators, as individuals who can talk to the gang leaders, merchants within a tong's territory may be persuaded to obtain the tong leaders' "blessings" either through monetary rewards or business partnerships. Because of the gang leaders' reputation as caretakers of the younger gang members, they can exploit their gang connections in several ways: by demanding protection money from business owners, by seeking positions in the tong hierarchy, and by infiltrating legitimate businesses as partners. Indeed, many merchants in the community would welcome the opportunity to have tong or gang leaders on their list of friends. From a purely economic perspective, merchants are content to deal with one powerful tong or gang rather than face shakedowns from every erstwhile street hoodlum.

Furthermore, although merchants are rarely assaulted by gang members in the process of extortion, this does not mean that the phenomenon of gang intimidation is unrelated to the escalation of street violence in the community. Rather, extortion plays a major role in the promotion of inter- and intragang violence (to be discussed in chapter 7). Violence is used to regulate gang interactions. The motives for many intergang killings among Chinese gangs appear to be related to territorial conflicts, and the struggle for territory is basically a fight for market share, for control of territory in order to extort money from merchants within that territory.

The distribution of the proceeds from extortion has always been a major issue within gangs. Intragang violence has often erupted because one or more gang members did not handle fairly or distribute equitably the money gained from extortion. While extortion may not be as pervasive as believed, its psychological stress on the community is significant, and it does play a pivotal role in the eruption of violence among gang members.

I assumed that three social and economic factors caused and sustained the pervasiveness of extortion in the Chinese community. First, the communities reflect a unique political economy: they are small, congested, and isolated from the dominant mainstream American culture. Interactions take place within a small, congested physical space. There are language barriers that exclude English speakers, cultural rituals that are distinct from those of the surrounding society, and preferences for doing business with other Chinese. All of these contribute to a physically, socially, and economically isolated and self-contained community. Routine social and economic interactions are concentrated among community members, who call on the community's social and economic institutions for social regulation and control (Kuo, 1977; Kwong, 1987). Interaction between offenders and victims is not restricted to rule-breaking behavior, but also involves day-to-day routines in which gang members patronize the business premises without criminal intent. Thus the social distinction between offenders and victims is often blurred.

Because business competition within the community is fierce, and because the family networks of most Chinese immigrants are truncated by immigration and numerous other social factors (Sung, 1987), business owners have an enormous workload. When threatened by a gang, few merchants have the inclination, time, knowledge, or presence of mind to seek help from formal social control agencies such as the police or the district attorney's office. Compounding the difficulties in reaching out to such agencies are powerful adult organizations within the community, such as tongs, that somehow discourage local people from contacting the authorities. The extent of the cultural self-containment of the Chinese community is evident in references to the authorities as "outsiders" (Kinkead, 1992). Because outsiders are distrusted, contacting them is considered a betrayal of the community (Kuo, 1977). And some of the adult organizations tend to condone rather than deplore or oppose extortionate activities. Under such circumstances, extortion can become institutionalized.

Second, community cultural norms may facilitate the spread and pervasiveness of extortion in the community and provide gang members with opportunities to engage in predatory acts that are unique to the social context of Chinese communities. For example, certain items are necessary for most Chinese celebrations and holidays (Mano, 1988). The gangs take advantage of this fact and sell these items to business owners at inflated prices. During the Chinese New Year, custom dictates that adults give *hung bao* (red envelopes containing cash) to family members, relatives, and even strangers (Henican, 1987). Gang members seize the opportunity to exploit the custom by asking business owners for *hung bao* during the holiday. Thus the gangs manage to use customs as a shield against police and legal sanctions.

Third, a symbiotic relationship exists between the gangs and the adult organizations that provide the community with illegal services (e.g., gambling, prostitution, and loan-sharking) (Meskil, 1989). Despite the illicit nature of their services, these organizations are viewed by many community residents as acceptable and as important parts of the social and economic networks that make up the community. Association with these organizations enables the gangs to present themselves as the organizations' "youth groups." Thus the gangs manipulate their image and attempt to "legitimize" themselves by associating with the adult organizations.

These patterns are relevant to efforts to develop criminological theories that can more adequately explain the formation of Chinese youth gangs and their often ambiguous status in specific communities. A theory that is limited to constructs such as the presence or absence of gangs or adult criminal groups, the level of isolation of the community, and the personal characteristics of the residents may not be sufficient to explain why the patterns and processes of gang victimization differ across ethnic communities. Certain processes sustain youth gangs; they result from the interaction of physical space, routine economic activities, the social organization of adult groups engaged in both legal and illegal activities, and the rules and organizing principles fostered by language and culture. Although the intentions of gangs or gang members to generate gains by illegal means may be similar across ethnic groups, spatial, social, economic, and cultural differences among communities may contribute to quite varied patterns and processes of gang activity.

Summary

Victimization of Chinese store owners by local street gangs is pervasive but rarely occurs more than a few times per year. There is little violence, and rarely are threats made explicit. Victimization seems to affect most types of businesses, and there is little evidence that there are vulnerabilities to victimization beyond such characteristics as the type of business and its dollar volume. Through a complex web of rationales, victimization has been integrated into the cultural and commercial life of the Chinese business community in New York. Moreover, since dollar losses due to extortion are a small fraction of the overall volume of business costs and are relatively easily absorbed by most businesses, extortion seems to be more of an inconvenience than a serious threat to the integrity of most business operations.

Victimization appears to be a systemic process that is deeply ingrained in both cultural and business practices. Furthermore, it is a process of continuous interaction between victims and offenders who negotiate the extent of the payment to a gang. Although most merchants reported three or four payments or episodes of extortion per year, the frequency of attempted extortion was much higher than the number of completed victimizations. In other words, in many instances, gang members made repeated visits to find owners or to persuade them that they intended to persist unless and until they were paid. Thus, estimations of victimization careers for Chinese businesses involve parameters for measuring the number of attempted and completed victimizations, as well as the amount of actual monetary loss.

Monetary loss attributable to gang extortion activity may seem less serious to business owners than to law enforcement agencies and the media. In most instances, merchants were able to satisfy the gangs by paying from $30 to $40. In some extortion cases, young gang members were content to receive only a few dollars.[14] Law enforcement authorities have tended to overestimate the amount of money gang members derive from extortion. Of course, there are some unusual cases in which Chinese merchants have lost thousands of dollars because of extortion, but such cases seem to be rare. In most cases, there is a substantial discrepancy between the amount of money demanded and the amount actually paid. Accordingly, caution is needed in estimating the seriousness of gang extortion. It should not be predicated on the extortionists' demands alone.

Since type of business is associated with type and seriousness of victimization, I would like to make it clear that the prevalence and seriousness estimates of gang extortion discussed here are influenced by the sampling design. Since certain types of businesses located in certain areas were overrepresented in the business survey sample, my findings may not be applicable to the entire, legitimate Chinese business sector of New York City. Also, since illegitimate businesses such as gambling establishments and prostitution houses were not included in the sample, my estimates of the prevalence and seriousness of gang extortion are not applicable to the underground economy of New York's Chinatowns.

4

Patterns of Gang Extortion

This chapter focuses on two issues related to extortion—its social processes and its social organization—in order to provide a detailed account of how gang members approach business owners for money or goods, how offenders and victims interact, and how gangs are organized to carry out extortion activity.

Social Processes of Gang Extortion

Protection

In the Chinese American community, protection money is known as *po oo fai* (protection fees) or *gai so* (street money). The money is paid regularly by merchants to an individual, a gang, or an association that controls the area in which the merchants conduct their business; they pay to obtain the "blessing" of those who are in a position to disrupt commercial activities or do damage to business property. The practice of paying protection money to gang members is pervasive in Hong Kong and Taiwan, the areas from which most Chinese businessmen in New York City emigrated from (Zhang, 1984; Chi, 1985; Chin, 1986).[1]

The process of asking for protection money often begins when a businessperson is accosted by gang members prior to or at the opening ceremony of the business premises. Data from the business survey indicate that at least 52 percent of the protection incidents for the survey respondents occurred during the first day of business. Most Chinese retail businesses that are about to open place large advertisements in the Chinese newspapers, informing the public of the time and place of the grand opening ceremony. Two gang members revealed that their gangs often looked through the local newspapers for potential victims. In the words of one gang member:

> We check the advertisements in the Chinese newspapers. If there are new stores or large advertisements, these are our targets. We go to the store and ask for the manager. If we can't find the manager, we go back again. We will tell him to pay and warn him to bear any responsibility if he refuses.

Another member put it this way: "We read the newspapers for new businesses. These stores normally are willing to pay us at the grand opening ceremony."

Some businesses may not advertise in the media but may observe some form of ritual, such as exploding firecrackers, during the first day of business. In fact, some participants in the business survey indicated that they did not publicize their businesses' grand opening ceremonies precisely because they did not want to attract gang members. Even if new businesses fail to promote themselves in the media or to follow traditional customs, gang members in the neighborhood are sure to learn of their existence, sooner or later. One business owner disclosed that a gang leader became very upset when he discovered that a business establishment had been operating for some time without his knowledge. A few business owners, convinced that they will never elude the gangs, take the initiative and inform gang leaders in their neighborhood of their grand opening celebrations. One merchant explained how he dealt with the problem:

> We like the idea of "open the door and see the mountain" [meaning "being straightforward"]. We open our door to do business, so we view protection payments as expenses for public relations. We approached them [gang members] before we started our business. If you wait for them to come, it's too late. We sent someone to talk with leaders of the XX [unnamed] gang and asked them to make it very clear how much they wanted.[2] On the other hand, we also requested them not to come bother us after we paid what they demanded. They wanted more than $600 a month for protection.

Sometimes, impatient gang members do not even wait until the grand opening ceremony to make their move. Should they learn that someone is about to open a new business in their territory or that a commercial organization is in the process of setting up a new business, they will search out the proprietor and ask for protection money.

Once a business is targeted, a group of gang members will enter the place and ask for protection money.[3] Younger members will remain outside the store and watch the streets while older or more experienced members talk to the owner. More than 86 percent of the potential victims in my survey indicated that the gang members who approached them spoke Cantonese. Customarily, the gang members first congratulate the owner, saying *hoi moon tai kat* (good fortune once the door is open), which means best of luck to you on the opening day of your business. Then they go on to identify themselves: "We are from Mott Street; we own this area.[4] If you want to avoid trouble, you have to pay us *po oo fai*. We want $360 as 'lucky money' for the grand opening ceremony and $100 a week for protection."[5] Because most Chinese merchants are well aware of this gang practice, most of them are prepared; they sit down with the extortionists and discuss how much they can pay, if anything.[6] This process is known as *kong so*.

Kong so is probably one of the most significant and complicated aspects of the gang extortion process. It determines the victim-offender relationship for years thereafter, including how much will be paid, how often, and to whom, and what norms and rules are to be observed after payments are made. An agreement between a victim and a gang may include the following "contractual" terms, which are often violated by gang members:

1. The store owner will pay $300 a month protection money to the gang.
2. Payment will be made only to a designated collector or to the gang leader himself. If someone else collects the money, the gang leader has to inform the owner in advance.
3. After payments begin, the gang leader will assume responsibility for ensuring that his followers will not ask the business owner for money on an irregular basis. Nor will his followers be allowed to sell items to the owner during major holidays. Moreover, members of the gang will pay the full price for the goods and services they consume. If they do not, the owner will deduct the amount from the monthly protection payment.[7]
4. A receipt will be offered to the owner for each payment.

The ability of potential victims to negotiate hard and come up with a better deal may depend on their business and personal characteristics. According to qualitative data collected from the follow-up study, business-related factors may include the following:

1. *Business size.* Well-established, big firms often have less bargaining power than smaller businesses. Large businesses in the community are often seen as "fat sheep" by the gangs and as ready for exploitation.
2. *Projected profitability.* Businesses assumed to be very profitable may have less room for negotiation because of their profitability—real or imagined—than businesses expected to generate little, if any, profits.
3. *Type of business.* Certain types of businesses, such as restaurants and retail stores, may not be able to negotiate as flexibly as others, such as, say, medical clinics. They are more vulnerable because they are more likely to involve cash transactions and have heavy customer flow.
4. *Legal status of the business.* There are three types of businesses: legal, semilegal, and illegal. Operators of illegal establishments, such as gambling dens and prostitution houses, have little power to barter since there is no legal recourse for settlement of potential disputes with the gangs. Owners of clinics and car repair shops who conduct legal businesses but do not have licenses to operate (semilegal businesses) may also have little room for negotiation. Their access to legal relief is impeded by their own business practices, but less so than that of operators of illegal enterprises.[8]
5. *Location.* Businesses located at the heart of a gang's turf may find themselves less successful in negotiations than those situated on the outskirts of a gang's turf.

The following business and personal characteristics of the victim may also play an important role in deciding the outcome of a negotiation:

1. *Length of time in the business community.* A business owner who has been active for many years may be more knowledgeable about negotiating than an uninformed newcomer.
2. *Extent of involvement in community affairs.* Members actively involved in community affairs may be able to demand "face" (paying less) from the gangs than those who have never participated in community affairs.
3. *Connection with one or more gang leader.* A person who can say something like

"I know some of your *dai los*" may get a better deal than someone who knows no gang leaders. Those who were former gang members themselves may avoid paying protection money of any kind, except for some lucky money that will be demanded during grand opening day ceremonies.[9]

4. *Background of the chief negotiator for the business owner.* If a powerful community leader or a former gang leader represents a business owner in the negotiation, the chances of the business owner getting a better deal may be significantly enhanced.[10] If the business owner is a newcomer and represents himself or herself in the negotiation, he or she is more vulnerable.

There are also factors that might influence a gang's willingness to negotiate with a business owner. Some of those factors include:

1. *The gang's perceived level of control in the area where the business is located.* This factor may or may not correlate with the location factor already mentioned. It depends mainly on the gang's perception, not on the presence and threat of rival gangs or the business community's attitudes toward gangs.

2. *The financial situation of the gang's vice enterprises.* In certain circumstances, gangs may be more desperate for money than at other times. For example, when a number of gambling dens or prostitution houses are closed down by the police and regular income from the vice industry is choked off, the legitimate business community may become the sole source of income for the gangs, who then toughen their negotiations.

3. *The gang's perception of a business owner's demeanor before and during negotiations.* If the gang assumes that a business owner understands the practice of the extortion well and reacts in compliance with the customs regulating it, the gang may tend to be more lenient in negotiation.[11]

In sum, all of these factors come into play as merchants and gang members negotiate. However, even if the situation favors the merchant, it may not mean that he or she will avoid extortion altogether. Favorable circumstances only help to minimize victimization. A community leader acknowledged that certain businesspeople who have all the right connections still have to come to terms with extortion by the gangs:

> In Chinatown, many so-called people who have face are also extorted. For example, Mr. XXX is considered a big shot in the community. So what! His store has been frequently hassled by a gang. These bad boys only care about collecting money. They don't care if you have face or not. They'll approach you anyway. If you refuse to pay, they just turn your business upside down. In fact, when these people who have face are victimized by gangs, they are less likely than ordinary merchants to reveal it, because they are afraid they will be laughed at. There's a large restaurant in Chinatown owned by a group of big shots. When it was opened, six gangs showed up for lucky money. Each gang asked for $XXX.[12] If they didn't pay, don't even think about doing business in Chinatown.

Most merchants, acting on the presumption that it is difficult, if not impossible, to elude the gangs, try to negotiate with them. A business owner revealed how he pleaded with a group of gang members to reduce his payment: "The store is just opened. I am not sure how the business is going to turn out. Give me a break;

let me pay you $100 now [as lucky money for the opening celebration] and $100 a month in the future."

More often than not, the gang members will accept the business owner's offer and in return, more for symbolic purposes than for anything else, will give the owner a gang member's nickname and a beeper number, and urge him or her to call if he or she has "trouble."

From then on, gang members will collect their protection money monthly. When the collector arrives, the owner or an employee hands over an envelope containing cash. As the practice becomes routine, few words are spoken between the gang member and the owner or his or her employee. In some cases, after handing over the envelope, the owner is offered a receipt, indicating that the protection money for a specific month has been duly paid.

A gang member told us how the criminal act is carried out in a methodical way:

> If there is a new store, I go in with a few guys. I do the talking. "This is my street, and you want your store here. Just give me the money. Three times a month. We'll burn it [the store] if you don't pay." It works. Sometimes they cheat, like saying the business is not good. Then I'll pull out a gun.

From an examination of how gang members approach store owners and of their methods of making demands, it is clear that they view themselves as the "owners" of the area in which the stores are located and that those who do business in their territory must accordingly pay them for the privilege of doing business. A gang member succinctly expressed this mentality: "I normally tell an owner the following when I ask him or her for protection money: 'This is our territory. You open a store here, you got to pay protection money. If you don't want to pay, get the hell out of here.'"

Often, gang members ask owners to pay them an amount that has cultural significance for the Chinese. Most such amounts symbolize prosperity or luck. For example, merchants may be asked to pay $64 a week for protection. The amount is equivalent to eight times eight. In Cantonese, the number eight is pronounced *bat*, which is similar to the pronunciation of prosperity—*faat*. Therefore, 64 signifies double prosperity.

Otherwise, gang members usually demand from business owners an amount that carries meaning within the triad subcultural legends.[13] Gangs may, for example, ask for $360 or $1,080 as lucky money during grand opening ceremonies. The number of oaths a new triad member has to take is 36, and the number of monks who formed the secret society considered to be the predecessor of the triad societies was 108. Authorities theorize that gang members intentionally use these numbers to indicate that they are part of the triad legend. This may instill additional fear in their victims.

A business owner described how he was victimized by gang members for protection money, and the intricacy of negotiating with them, by alluding to other gangs in order to minimize the pressures on him:

> When the store was opened in 1985, they asked for $360 a month. At that time, some restaurants [in the neighborhood] were paying $300 to $500 a month. I

negotiated very hard with them and tried to reduce the amount of payment. They said, "If you don't pay $360 now, the next time will be $720, the next time will be $1,080." They called and warned us. When their *dai lo* came to negotiate, he said, "If you don't pay, and my little brothers come and disrupt your business, I am not going to be responsible." I knew what he meant because when I worked in a store before, more than a dozen little fellas came in during the busiest hour and tried to create a scene. But I was not afraid. That's why I was able to reduce it to $XX a month.[14] They were not happy with the amount, but I told them some stores did not have to pay. Normally, their attitudes were good, but when they wanted to increase the payment they looked very mean. Often, one would come in to collect the money, and the rest [three to four guys] would wait in a car parked outside. It's like they were coming to collect rent, saying "its time to collect money." They liked to say something like "If you rent a house you pay rent. This street is ours, that's why you must pay us."

Paying a gang member protection may frustrate similar attempts by other members of that gang, or of a rival gang. A merchant told how he prevented additional gang harassment by paying protection money:

Once, a group of Fuk Ching came and asked for money. I called the beeper of the gang who we were paying protection money. They talked it over the phone. The Fuk Ching thought I was lying when I told them that I am already paying the X gang. After that incident, the Fuk Ching never showed up again.

Another business owner described how he handled the gang extortion situation:

I asked the *dai lo* to send the same person every time for the money. If somebody else was going to show up, the *dai lo* was supposed to call and let me know. I do not buy items from gang members for an inflated price. If the sellers are Y gang members, I will tell them that I already paid them protection money. If members from another gang come to sell items, I told them I already bought it from the Y gang.

For some businesses, paying protection money may not necessarily result in curtailing additional problems. A restaurant owner was upset when he talked about the futility of paying protection money:

We paid a gang protection money, but after they got paid, they did not give a damn. Twice, they bumped into members of a rival Fuk Ching gang inside my restaurant, and they immediately got into a fight. Their attitude is: "If you have problems, they are yours, not ours. You paid us, we won't bother you." They don't have any morality!

Although some business owners, mostly in Manhattan's Chinatown, indicated that they had been paying protection money for more than 15 years,[15] others, especially those in the loosely controlled sections of Queens and Brooklyn, said they had succeeded in terminating their regular payments when the leaders of the gangs were arrested. A business owner from Queens reported how this happened:

We paid protection money [$100 a week] to the Green Dragons. After the leader of the gang was arrested, we told the gang's little brothers, "Your *dai lo* is in jail now. You can't protect us anymore. Why don't we wait until your *dai lo*'s released and we will resume the payment." They left and haven't come back so far.

Nevertheless, stopping protection payments to a gang that has been confronted by the police in Queens may not mean peace for a business owner, because Chinese gangs based in Manhattan's Chinatown may attempt to invade the territory and fill the vacuum. According to a member of a Manhattan-based gang:

> Because there's few new stores in Chinatown, we go to Queens to fight for new turf. In Queens, there's no clear-cut gang territory. Besides, we have many people in Queens. We were once in a Queens restaurant which was paying protection to the Fuk Ching. I told the owner, "So what! From now on we are going to take care of you. If the Fuk Ching have a problem with this new arrangement, ask them to find me." Since then, I collect money from that restaurant regularly.

Some owners may resist such demands. Under these circumstances, gang members may be forced to carry out their threats. For example, a Born-to-Kill member explained how he and his peers reacted to a business owner who refused to succumb to their demands:

> Once, we damaged a store because the owner refused to let us collect the protection money. We threw chairs, broke the window, beat up the owner and the workers. I was still in the restaurant when the cops who happened to pass by walked in. It was late in the afternoon, between 4:00 to 5:00 P.M. We all got busted.

Most gangs perceive well-established businesses—especially the large restaurants—in the three Chinese communities of New York City to be potential targets for generating a stable and lucrative income. When a major restaurant in Chinatown opens its doors, there is always the potential for gang conflict because more than one gang may attempt to add the restaurant to its list of victims. An owner of a major restaurant in Manhattan's Chinatown explained how a potentially explosive situation developed when he opened up his restaurant:

> My business is very large, and that's why when it was opened, many gangs came for protection money. Every gang wanted $600 monthly payment. I found someone to talk to all the gang leaders. They sat down and *kong so*. My man told them that only one gang will be paid $400 a month. They had to figure out among themselves which gang was entitled to receive the money. After that, they did talk it out, and only one gang showed up for the protection money. I don't know how they settled it.

Lucky Money

Lucky money also is known as *cha cheen* (tea money), *hung bao* (red envelope), or *lei shi* (good for business). Unlike demands for protection money, demands for lucky money are sporadic, spontaneous acts committed irregularly, predominantly by ordinary gang members, probably without the knowledge of their *dai lo*s. Demanding lucky money occurs most often on major holidays, such as the Chinese New Year.

Typically, a group of gang members will approach a business. Two or three older members will enter the business premises while the rest remain outside. When demanding money, gang members will usually cite the following reasons:[16]

One of our brothers is *soi jaw* [literally, "hit by misfortunes" which could mean killed, arrested, or jailed]. We need some money.

A brother was killed. We need money for his funeral.

We need money to *yum cha* [drink tea or eat].

Today is our *dai lo*'s birthday. We need money to buy him a gift.

As they did when they asked for protection money, gang members often spoke Cantonese (89% of the time) when they approached merchants for lucky money. Also, the amount of money extorted often had a special meaning. For instance, some owners were asked for $188, which can be interpreted as "double prosperity all the way."[17] In some cases, gang members demanded $108 or $360. More often than not, however, they asked for about $100 and were offered $50. They usually took whatever was offered and departed.

During the Chinese New Year, many businesses in Chinatown are overwhelmed with gang demands for lucky money. A restaurant owner recounted in an interview that a group of 30 gang members showed up and asked for *hung bao* during the Chinese New Year. He gave each a red envelope containing $5.

Another restaurateur, from East Broadway, described how he was often asked for lucky money by members of the Fuk Ching and other gangs:

> Three to four young Cantonese-speaking Fuk Ching walked in. They own this area. All male. They were ordinary members. Very polite. They did not ask for a certain amount. There's no reason to argue with them, so we paid them more or less, and they accepted whatever amount we gave them. We paid because it signifies luck. My partner knows their *dai lo*, that's why we were not afraid of them, nor worried that they might cause trouble in the store. We see them on the street all the time. This street is theirs. From 1988 to 1990, we were extorted a few times, each time we paid $20 to $30. When we opened the restaurant in 1988, a group of Ghost Shadows showed up and asked for lucky money. We paid them $40. They said it sounded "dead, dead, and dead."[18] So they insisted on getting $50. The Flying Dragons also came. We paid them $30 to $40. Because of the opening ceremony, they all came. But these two gangs never showed up again. Since the establishment of the Fukien American Association here, troubles never stopped.

Another merchant from East Broadway explained his philosophy of paying lucky money. He described his rationale for selecting which individual would be his extortionist: "If a black [African American] came extorting money from us, we of course won't pay. Even with Chinese, we always ask them which gang they belong to. If they are from Mott Street, we won't pay. We will pay only the Fuk Ching who reign on our street."

Should a business owner refuse to pay lucky money, gang members' reactions depend on (1) how desperate they are for money, (2) whether they control the area, (3) what their perception of the profitability of the business is, and (4) how the business owner reacts. Common gang reactions to resistance include cursing the owner and the businesses and engaging in outrageous behavior in the store, but doing nothing further, or warning the owner to be careful and saying something to the effect that "we will be back and you better pay next time." The gang members may appear again and disrupt the business. For example, gang members may stand outside a restaurant or grocery store and tell customers not to patronize the store, saying something such as "the food is poisoned, don't buy it." Also, gang members may create a scene inside the business premises during peak business hours, by such acts as breaking windows, damaging locks, shooting at the store, or even setting the business on fire.

Chin (1990) observed that motivations for gang extortion in the Chinese community may not be strictly financial. He surmised that Chinese gang extortion may be classified into four types. The key objective of the first, and most common, type of extortion is obtaining money. The victimizers and victim may not know each other, and regardless of how the victim reacts to the victimizers' demands, the victim is unlikely to be physically assaulted in this type of extortion.

The second type of extortion is symbolic extortion, which is used as a display of power to indicate control over a territory. Money is not the primary goal; gang members usually demand only free food or other small items, such as cigarettes, or they ask for discounts from business owners. This type of extortion occurs almost on a daily basis, and the victims are usually small store owners or peddlers who do business within a tightly controlled gang territory.

The third type is extortion for revenge. Gang members extort from the victim because the victim previously antagonized the gang, or the gang is hired by an adversary of the victim to extort from the victim as a form of revenge. Because monetary gain is not the motivating factor, victims of this type of extortion are likely to be robbed, beaten up, or killed, even if they do not resist the extortionists. In this case, extortion is used simply as a cover for revenge.

The fourth type is instrumental extortion, which is used to intimidate the victim into backing down in certain business or personal conflicts. In this type of extortion, the victim is also vulnerable to assault and harassment. The extortionate act is, more than anything else, a message sent to the victim by his rival through gang members. Gang members may also rob or extort money from the victim for their own sake. Instrumental extortion is usually the result of conflicts pertaining to business territories or to business or gambling debts.

In short, a gang's propensity for attacking a proprietor or damaging a property may depend more on the underlying motive for the extortion than on the predicted reaction of the victim.

Forced Sales

Gang members often sell relatively inexpensive items at inflated prices on major holidays—for instance, tangerine plants and firecrackers during the Chinese New Year, mooncakes during the Mid-Autumn or Moon Festival, and Christmas cards or whiskey during the Christmas holidays.[19] Data from the business survey suggest that at least 75 percent of these incidents occur during the Chinese New Year. A 34-year-old proprietor described the gang practice:

During the past Chinese New Year, a group of teenagers who appeared to be gang members came to me and said, "Happy New Year. Please take this New Year card and pay us $180. It means that you will prosper in the coming year." You know the first digit denotes "one whole year," and the second digit is pronounced the same as the word "prosperity" in Cantonese. They said that, and they all laughed at me.

Another merchant was asked to buy a tangerine plant and firecrackers:

During the Chinese New Year, several youths showed up with a tangerine plant and asked us to buy it. They asked for $50, but we didn't think the plant worth $50. So we negotiated. They said, "It's once a year, just think of it as helping the 'brothers'." On July 4th, three kids showed up with a box of firecrackers and asked for $200. We said we had already bought some. They left.

Some bakery shops, though they sell mooncakes, which normally are priced at $15 to $20 a box, are compelled to buy mooncakes from gangs. A manager of a bakery store was put in an awkward situation when he was asked to buy an item of which he had too many:

During the Moon [Mid-Autumn] Festival, two young gang members came and said, "Today is the Moon Festival. Please buy this box of mooncakes." I said, "We sell mooncakes too. Why should we need this?" They said, "We have an under-standing with your boss. You've got to buy our mooncakes on the Moon Festival." I asked, "How much is a box?" They said, "Well, $100 a box, no big deal."

Generally a gang will place a large order for mooncakes with the bakeries in Chinatown before the Mid-Autumn Festival and anticipate that it will have little trouble selling the mooncakes during the festival. Sometimes the gang pays for the items; sometimes it does not. The owner of a bakery store told an interviewer how one gang went about its "purchases": "Weeks before the Moon Festival, they [gang members] ordered 250 boxes of mooncakes. When they picked up the cakes, they paid for 200 boxes, but didn't pay for the rest. Of course, I have to offer them the wholesale price, plus a 20 percent discount."

Data from the business survey show that gang members asked business own-ers to pay $50 to $360 for a box of mooncakes, $80 to $120 for a box of fire-crackers, and $50 to $100 for a tangerine plant or a box of oranges. Most mer-chants did not refuse to buy them, but did invariably try to bargain with the sellers.

Business owners gave examples of a few incidents in which they were asked to buy items for exorbitant prices. For instance, a restaurant owner in Queens was forced to buy a paper fan for $360 that was worth no more than $20. A newspaper account reported that a Chinese business owner was asked by a gang to buy a box of mooncakes for $2,000 (*Sing Tao Jih Pao*, 1991d). Sometimes the practice of forced sales is employed by gang members as retribution against a merchant who has refused to pay protection money. A jeweler in my sample told how he was asked to buy a gun for thousands of dollars:

I was asked by a gang to pay protection money, but I refused. They came back a couple of times, but I still said no. Then one day, the leader of the gang showed up with a Uzi machine gun. He said, "I want you to buy this gun for $3,000." I told him I did not have that kind of money right away and asked him to come back later. When he returned the next time, I called the police and he was arrested.

Theft of Goods and Services

The fourth type of extortion involves asking for free goods or services. This is known as *shik pa wong faan* (eating the villain's meal) or *tai pa wong hei* (watching the villain's movie), meaning that the extortionist is a "villain" who cannot be refused. Victims are mostly owners of restaurants, bakeries, barbershops, videotape rental stores, and other retail enterprises such as groceries and optician shops. Restaurants and videotape rental stores are most likely to be targets for this type of extortion because gang members routinely have collective meals and watch videotapes.

Gang members assume that restaurant owners in their territory should provide free meals to show respect. As one restaurateur observed:

> During the Chinese New Year, more than ten gang members came to my restaurant and ate. Later, they said they had no money. You cannot prevent this because you can't ask people at the door whether they are going to pay or not. They said, "We are from Pell Street. This is our New Year dinner party. We didn't bother you over the year. It is your honor that we came here to eat during the New Year." They left after they said that. They didn't even give me a chance to respond.

It is almost impossible for a restaurant owner to prevent this type of gang behavior. A businessman in Queens explained some gang tactics:

> Usually, about 10 people come and occupy a big table. After eating, one person will ask for the check while the others start leaving the restaurant. Then, instead of paying, the guy who asked for the bill will sign his name on the bill and leave. Meanwhile, other people with him will be outside the restaurant already. It's difficult to physically grab any of these people before they leave.

Even if a restaurant is paying protection money, it may still be required to provide gang members with free dinners, albeit in a more orderly manner. Another restaurant owner described the complexity of negotiating with different members of the gang to which he was paying protection money:

> They [gang members] will come to me before they come for dinner. We will negotiate. They will say that these [free meals] will occur two to three times a year, especially when their *dai lo* celebrates his birthday or the gang has something else to commemorate. They want us to pay for their celebrations. We will discuss with them what kind of dishes will be on the table when they come. If they want to order a particularly expensive dish, we will tell them that it will not be served.

Videotape rental stores are sometimes asked to provide special accounts for gangs, free of charge. When gang members walk in and mention the special account to a clerk, they are entitled to check out as many tapes as they like and to keep them for as long as they wish. Some owners said they feel fortunate when the tapes are returned.

It appears that some gangs do this to compel store owners to pay protection money, instead of harassing them constantly for free or discounted goods and services. Some owners stated that when they agreed to pay protection money, they explicitly asked the gang leaders to tell their followers that their business was paying protection money and should be left alone. Even so, paying protection money by no means assured immunity from harassment by young gang members who defy their leaders' orders or were never told to stop requesting free services.

Many gang members enjoy watching Chinese martial arts films, which often are shown in movie theaters in Chinatown and sometimes lead to the eruption of gang violence. A respondent who owned a movie theater in Chinatown told an interviewer how he dealt with gang members who frequented his place:

> My theater is the only theater in Chinatown that insists gang members must buy tickets—at half price, of course—given that they could identify which gang they belong to. I can do that because I hire a non-Asian guard. Even so, they came in a bunch, two to three times a week, and I figure I lost at least $1,200 a month because of this. However, from what I know, other theaters in the community fare worse than me. They are letting the gang kids go in free after 10:00 P.M. It's like the theaters are being taken over by the gangs in the late evening.

Social Organization of Gang Extortion

From the responses of business owners who participated in the business survey, we have seen that gang extortion exhibits certain patterns. However, in order to understand those patterns, we need to know how gang members select their targets; who, if anyone, orchestrates gang extortion activities; whether there is a division of labor among gang members in demanding money from merchants; how the proceeds are distributed; whether extortion is a group venture or an individual activity; and what roles the tongs play in gang extortion. To answer these questions, I needed to collect data from the gang members themselves. I therefore designed a gang study. I shall now turn to the data I collected from the gang study.

Selecting Targets

Do Chinese gangs approach all Chinese-owned businesses in the New York City metropolitan area indiscriminately, or do they victimize only certain businesses owned by Chinese? Data from the gang study suggest that gangs do take into consideration particular factors when they search for targets, findings that appear to match the findings from the business survey.

The first is the location of the business. Some gang members indicated that they mainly choose businesses located at street level, not those that operate on the second or third stories of buildings, as is quite common in New York City: "We extort money from any business that has a storefront. We do not collect money from the stores on the second floor and above."

It is not clear why gang members prefer to exploit businesses on the street level. Possibly, they do so because it is easier to enter and exit these premises. Also, most cash businesses such as restaurants and retail stores are likely to be located on the street level, whereas the second and third floors of buildings are often the locales for professional offices and garment factories.

Another aspect of store location is that most gangs approach only merchants within their turf. There may be two reasons for this. The first is that in comparison to potential victims outside their turf, business owners within their territory may be less likely to resist their demands. A subject stressed that his gang exploited only businesses within its turf because it was easier: "We target only Chinese take-out restaurants within our area because thy won't give us hassle."

The second reason is that by selecting merchants in its turf a gang may avoid unnecessary skirmishes with other gangs. And if members of a gang go outside their territory on criminal explorations, they may not be supported by their gang leaders should conflicts arise between them and members of other gangs. A street-level *dai lo* made this clear when he said: "If you go to another gang's territory to extort, you are on your own." This rule does get broken, however. Some subjects in this study disclosed that they have entered a rival gang's turf to extort money. It is not clear whether they acted on their own or with the sanction of their *dai lo*. It appears that some *dai lo*s are very strict about the policy of victimizing only merchants within their territory while others adopt a freewheeling attitude.

Another factor that affects target choices concerns the ethnicity of the store owner. Most respondents emphasized that they approach only Chinese merchants with whom they can communicate. A few subjects indicated that their targets sometimes included not only Chinese but also Korean and Japanese merchants. This was the exception, however. Only one said he and his associates exploited non-Asian businesspeople, but only when they were desperate for money. In this respect, the data from the gang on the selection of targets matches the data from the business owners.

A third factor in selecting merchants to extort from is the type of business. Many gang members said that their favorite targets are businesses with high cash flow, such as restaurants and retail stores.

As mentioned earlier, gang members are always on the alert for newly opened businesses. There are two reasons for this: one, gangs are confident that new businesses will always be willing to pay them lucky money; and two, by being the first gang to approach a business for protection money, especially if the business is located on neutral turf, the gang hopes to gain an edge on other competing gangs for establishing regular protection money payments.

Some gangs rely on their members and on female associates for information on potential victims. One subject said that employers who hire gang members and rich people who often visit Chinese-owned nightclubs and massage parlors may end up being victimized by gangs: "Some of us used to work as waiters or delivery boys, so we know which restaurants have a lot of cash. Also, the girl I am living with is working in a nightclub. She will tell me what is a good target."

Most respondents suggested that the size of a business is not a factor in their decisions. In selecting victims, two gang members had this to say:

> We approach any Chinese business, doesn't matter whether small or large. We only approach Chinese because we can talk to them. These businesses have to be within our territory.

> We collect money only from Chinese and Korean stores. Anything like restaurants, grocery stores, whorehouses. Size makes no difference.

From the interviews with gang members, it is apparent that Chinese gangs prefer to victimize mainly Chinese-owned businesses located on the street level. Consequently, restaurants and retail stores are favorite targets of gangs. Some gang members may go into a rival gang's territory to extort money, but the practice is likely to be discouraged by gang leaders.

Assigning Responsibility

According to research conducted by Skolnick et al. (1988), Fagan (1989), Padilla (1992), and Taylor (1990), a division of labor exists among gangs that are organized for drug selling. Therefore, we might want to ask whether there is a similar division of labor among Chinese gangs in carrying out extortion activities. That is, who makes the decisions about which stores to approach and how much money to demand? Do some gang members specialize in extortion? And do different gang members play different roles in the extortion process?

My data suggest that for Chinese gangs, extortion is a relatively highly organized activity. First, only gang leaders select the businesses to be exploited. Ordinary members confront only those merchants selected by their leaders. The following account suggests that gang leaders are normally in control of extortion activity: "We do what our *dai lo* asks us to do. Most of the time it is well planned."

Under most circumstances, only a *dai lo* will decide which store to approach and how much money to demand. However, it is very unlikely that he will become personally involved in the extortion, unless his subordinates have trouble collecting the money. Three subjects explained the role of *dai los* in the extortion racket as follows:

> Our *dai lo* will only set the principle for our extortion business. We do the actual work of collecting money from the store. A *dai lo* will be involved only if there is trouble collecting.

> We often go in with at least three members. Our *dai lo* is rarely directly involved.

> If there is a new restaurant, *sai lo* [little brother or ordinary gang member] will go collect money first. If unsuccessful, the *dai lo* will go.

There are, however, certain businesses that only *dai los* handle and with which they do not trust their subordinates: these are mainly "major" businesses, and gang members are usually kept in the dark about such extortion activities. Ordinary members do not know how and with whom arrangements are made, how much money their *dai los* receive, or why gang members are asked by their *dai los* to stay away from these establishments.

On rare occasions, a *dai lo*, most likely a street-level leader, may be the first from a gang to approach a merchant. An ordinary member described his gang's practice:

Most of the time, the *dai lo* tells the owner, "I am in charge of this area, you should help our operating cost." We won't say it directly. We give them a price, sometimes they negotiate. We take $700 to $1,000 a month from large restaurants, and $100 a week from take-out restaurants. It depends on the area where the business is located. We normally send only two to three guys because we do not want to scare the customers.

When a group of gang members (usually four or five) shows up in a store to demand money from the owner, each person is assigned a specific role. One person will do the talking, some will keep an eye on the customers, making sure no one calls the police. Another member will watch the street. If the group arrives in a car, one stays behind the wheel. One subject explained how his gang carries out such an assignment from the *dai lo*. It is done with careful preparation and division of labor:

> I always go into a store with three brothers. One does the talking, which I do most of the time. One makes sure no one uses the phone in the store. Another makes sure nobody leaves the scene. One stays outside in the street. I got arrested last time because I was with two new members, and the owner was able to leave the scene to find the police. We stayed in the store too long, and I didn't know we were taped by the restaurant's video camera.

Distributing the Income

After gang members collect money from store owners, there is the question of what they do with it. Are the criminal proceeds turned over to factional *dai lo*s (gang leaders who are in charge of a particular faction within a gang) or to the highest leader? If so, how do the leaders distribute the proceeds? Do the *ah kung*s (tong members who are in charge of the gangs) receive a portion of the money?[20] Prior to this study, little was known about the allocation of extortion money among Chinese gangs. Law enforcement authorities speculated that gang leaders often mishandled the funds and thus precipitated intragang conflicts.

My respondents suggested that different gangs have different ways of handling extortion-related income. Some gangs turn all the money over to a *dai lo*, and he disburses it among the members. Other gang members turn the money over to a *dai lo*, and the money is kept by him. In turn, these gang members receive a regular salary from the *dai lo*.

Another subject indicated that he turned over only a portion of the proceeds from extortion to the *dai lo*: "We give half of it to the leader. We share the rest among the group. We used some of it for rent."

Four street-level *dai lo*s (the lowest ranking clique leaders, who report to the faction *dai lo*s) explained how the proceeds from extortion are actually distributed:

> I "own" a store.[21] I collect the money and share some with my followers. Sometimes, I go with other members. I then get some of the money.[22] *Dai lo* gets the most.

> I keep 70 percent; the factional *dai lo* takes 30 percent. Among the 70 percent, I personally keep 20 percent; the rest goes to the little brothers.

I give 30 percent to my *dai lo*; I keep 40 percent. The rest is given to the little brothers to split.

I give 50 percent to my *dai lo*. The 50 percent I have, I keep 20 to 30 percent for myself, and the rest will be given to my followers.

In sum, Chinese gangs handle the money from extortion in four different ways:

1. Gang members will hand all the money from extortion over to their *dai lo* (usually to a faction *dai lo* in a tong-affiliated gang or a *dai dai lo*, primary leader, in a nonaffiliated gang), and he will keep all of it. The *dai lo* will offer his followers regular allowances on a weekly basis and pay for their food and other expenses.[23]
2. All the money collected from business owners will go to the *dai lo* first, and then he will split it in any way he sees fit.
3. Street-level *dai lo*s or associate leaders will turn in a certain percentage of the money to the faction *dai lo*, keep a certain portion for themselves, and distribute the remainder among ordinary gang members.
4. Members of the clique that is directly involved in the extortion will keep all the money and split it among themselves. Those who do not participate in the act personally will not get anything. The *dai lo* usually will not receive any money from the extortion.

Generally, a faction *dai lo* receives from 30 to 60 percent of the extortion money, and a street-level *dai lo* keeps 15 to 40 percent of such money. Ordinary members may not gain much from extortion because either they receive only relatively low regular allowances or they have to share their small percentage of the income with the entire group. In this respect, my findings are similar to Padilla's (1992) finding that young ordinary members of drug gangs often receive very little from their gangs' lucrative drug trade.

Group versus Individual Extortion

Gang researchers have found that criminal activities committed by gang members are not always sanctioned by their gang as a group. In other words, some members "freelance" in certain crimes, and their activities have nothing or very little to do with their gang as a whole. Thus, we need to ask the question whether among Chinese gangs most extortion is committed on an individual basis or on a collective level.

Most of my subjects in the gang study indicated that extortion is a group venture and the money gained from extortion is group money. Members are usually not allowed to participate in extortion without the knowledge of the gang. If they do, they risk punishment. When asked whether extortion is a group project, gang members made the following remarks:

Extortion is a gang business.

Extortion money is group money; it doesn't matter who collected it. There is no freelance. Money goes to the gang.

The money is for the whole gang. We do it together.

It's a group thing.

There is no freelance. If someone *log kaak* [cheats] he will be beaten.

However, one subject indicated that shaking down Chinese merchants is carried out both on a group and an individual level in his gang. Another respondent said that "extortion is basically a group undertaking, but a few attempts are freelance." Still another subject indicated that, for his gang, exploiting store owners is "mostly freelance."

Gang Extortion and Tongs

Although there is evidence that certain tongs play an important role in facilitating gang member involvement in providing services for the flourishing vice businesses in the community, little information is available on the function, if any, of these same tongs in extortion activity. My subjects, being mostly ordinary gang members, knew very little about the role and connection of the tongs with gang extortion activity. Only one subject from a tong-affiliated gang claimed with certainty that "the uncle collects a certain percentage of the protection money," and another subject revealed that the *ah kungs*, along with the *dai dai lo*s, take care of extortion of the major businesses in Chinatown personally.

Nevertheless, some interviewees in the business survey were convinced that the tongs, or at least some tong members, play an important role in promoting extortion in the community. When asked whether he ever thought of approaching the tong in his area for help against harassing gang members, a store owner replied:

> I won't ask for help from the association because the association itself is a troublemaker. For me, they [tong members] and the ones who came to ask for money from me [gang members] are the same people.[24] There's no sense in asking them [tong members] for help.

Even if the *ah kungs* are not actively involved in gang extortion, they may be in a position to prevent it. They may be able to intervene with the *dai dai lo*s to ensure that street-level leaders and ordinary gang members are cautioned not to bother a particular store. One merchant explained how he avoided the gangs by joining a tong: "After joining the X association, nothing happened anymore. If there is trouble, I will go the X association's president or senior members and ask them for help."

Another merchant, an influential figure in the community himself, remembered how he was able to avoid gang extortion by asking for help from a tong leader but could not avoid the reach of the tong:

> After I opened a business in Chinatown, I came across a tong leader in the street of Chinatown. He said he already told the kids not to bother me. Then he asked me to go to his tong and chat with the president. When you are invited like this, can you turn down the invitation? If they ask you to go to their association and have a talk you gotta go. But once you got there, there's nothing to discuss but to donate *heung yau cheen* (incense oil money). I paid them a few hundred dollars. It was a different form of extortion!

Yet another community leader indicated that the tongs are positioned to influence gang extortion activities. He mentioned that he often sought help from the On Leong and the Hip Sing associations when members of his organization were subjected to extortion by gangs:

> If a member of our association was extorted and asked us to intervene, we approach the On Leong and Hip Sing and find someone who is influential enough to mediate. Some extortions occurred because our members may have stepped on a business rival's toes or may have owed gambling debts to the gambling houses. We will let our members handle these cases themselves. Otherwise, if the money is not a lot, we ask our members to pay, just to gratify those bad kids. If the money is a lot, we talk to the ultimate leader and ask to pay a little less. The bottom line is we look at it case by case. If there is gross injustice, we'll intervene, but our policy is not to interfere as much as possible.

Gang Member Perceptions of Extortion

My gang member subjects expressed the view that collecting money from Chinese merchants is relatively easy and has little stigma attached to it. According to one subject, the relationship between the extortionists and their victims is much more cordial, even compassionate, than an uninformed outsider could imagine:

> We know all the owners; we call them by their first names. They treat us like nephews. If we ask for $20, they'll give us $40. After we eat in their restaurants, we would like to pay the bills, but they insist on treating us. So we tip 75 percent of what we eat. The waiters like us. Sometimes the merchants only have half the money [we asked for], so we'll have to try to live with it. It's never their [the merchants'] fault. We will never broke their stores. We don't want to scare them. This is one of the worst things to do.

A member of the Born-to-Kill also stated that extortion is a rather effortless endeavor: "We just go in; the money is there. For new stores, the *dai lo* would talk to the owner, tell him that we are members of the Born-to-Kill, and set the price. The *dai lo* decides the date to collect. He never has any problem."

Summary

In New York City's Chinese communities, there are at least four forms of extortion that are committed by gang members against Chinese businesses: (1) demands for regular payment of protection money, (2) intimidations for lucky money on an irregular basis, (3) the forced selling of items at inflated prices, and (4) the theft of goods and services. None of these extortion practices is unique to New York City's Chinese community. These activities appear to be prevalent in Hong Kong and Taiwan (Zhang, 1984; Chi, 1985). No research has been done to show whether Chinese store owners in San Francisco, Los Angeles, Chicago, Boston, Vancouver, and Toronto are subjected to the same patterns of extortion.

This study suggests that gang members spend a substantial amount of time sizing up victims, convincing them to pay, working with them to develop mutually acceptable payment schedules, collecting money, and distributing the proceeds. The study also found that street-level leaders and faction *dai los* are the major beneficiaries of gang extortion. It is not clear to what extent, if any, the top leaders and the *ah kungs* derive financial gain from extortion rackets. However, the top leaders and the *ah kungs* apparently condone the exploitation of business owners in the community. They may intervene only if it is personally profitable and beneficial to them.

The activities of organized crime in Chinatown have created a climate of suspicion and fear. Organized crime and extortion seem deeply rooted in the community's social fabric. They drain away the community's resources and create a chaotic and pernicious social milieu in which victimizers and victims frequently negotiate the criterion for "normal" extortion.

5

Victim Reactions to Gang Extortion

Chinese businesspeople are often characterized by journalists as powerless victims frightened into silence by ruthless Chinatown gangs (Howe and Pak, 1972; Penn, 1980; Kerber and Gentile, 1982; Louttit, 1982). According to media accounts, many Chinese merchants are so often exploited by gangs that the merchants see themselves as hapless victims, and the majority not only comply with gang demands but also seem disinclined to report such demands to the police. Even those who do reach out to the police are assumed to be reluctant to testify in court out of fear of gang vengeance. Since most business owners remain silent about the crimes committed against them, it is assumed that in Chinese communities gang extortion is not only pervasive but also grudgingly tolerated.

Police claim rather defensively that Chinese immigrants are unwilling to report crimes to authorities (U.S. Senate, 1992). The police believe that a substantial number of Chinese are robbed in the subways by non-Chinese, but few complaints about these incidents reach the police. Law enforcement officials theorize that Chinese are targeted by robbers because the Chinese ethnic group has a reputation for being generally compliant and unlikely to contact authorities.

A paucity of empirical data on why business owners in Chinese communities seem tolerant of gang intimidation and crimes, how many merchants resist, and what their reasons are for doing so is available. Data about reporting rates of gang extortion, the reasons for nonreporting, Chinese merchants' perceptions of the criminal justice system, and common tactics business owners employ to reduce the risk of being victimized are also scarce.

In this chapter, I will examine the victims' justifications for either complying with gang demands or resisting them, the prevalence of reporting crime to law enforcement authorities, the reasons for reporting and nonreporting, the victims' perceptions of the criminal justice system, and their patterns of adaptation to gang victimization.

Justifications for Yielding to Gang Demands

Most subjects of the business survey (327 out of the 416 who were approached by gang members, or 79%) submitted to demands by gang members for money or goods and services. Many reasons were offered for acceding to gang demands. One rationale may be described as sociocultural: some businesspeople construe extortion demands not as criminal per se but as consistent with Chinese customs and social traditions. As long as gang members assert themselves during Chinese holidays and behave deferentially, so that the cultural norms of the holiday are not violated, many merchants seem willing to comply with their demands. When asked why they paid the gangs, the merchants justified their compliance in general ways. In the words of several:

> When they asked for money, they didn't physically attack me. Besides, they were very polite. This [asking for money by gang members] is expected in Chinatown. Nothing unusual.

> It was Chinese New Year, and it is a tradition to give lucky money during the New Year. For Chinese, it is quite natural and normal. If they came another time, then it is something else.

> It's [gang extortion] part of doing business—period.

When gang members come to sell items on the Chinese New Year, it is culturally almost impossible for merchants to refuse. For Chinese business owners, "harmony" is a prerequisite for prosperity. That is, without harmony there can be no prosperity. It is customary not to refuse a request from a "well-wisher" during the Chinese New Year holiday, even if that person is a gang member; to do so would disrupt harmony at the beginning of a year, and this might bring bad luck throughout the entire year. Moreover, Chinese merchants believe that everybody is entitled to make a little extra money during the New Year.[1] Given these beliefs, gang members who appear with tangerines[2] and say "Happy New Year, we wish you prosperity" compel owners to give them $50 to $100 in cash. Owners feel they cannot refuse to accept somebody's "goodwill."

Business owners also rationalize giving money to gangs as "reciprocal face giving behavior." Chinese cultural expectations require that people know how to "give face" to others—especially to those who deserve it or are in a position to demand it—to show respect. Not giving face to a person, especially in response to an overt request, is a serious humiliation to someone who is expecting such a gesture. When face is given, the recipient is obliged to reciprocate. Gang members normally demand to be given face. Some business owners may take the initiative and offer gang members a discount without having to be asked. In this manner, the business owners express their understanding of *jo yan* (how to behave like a human being). In return, gang members are supposed to be more "reasonable" than they otherwise would be in dealing with the business owners. A substantial number of business owners who paid protection money to gangs mentioned "reciprocal face giving" as the major reason for their compliance. A restaurateur explained how he viewed the offering of discounts to the gangs as "giving face":

> The kids from this block come to our restaurant and eat. They normally come in a group. It's not that they didn't pay. It's our rules to give them face by giving them a 20% discount. It's a good thing for all of us because it's "mutual face giving." We have some kinds of mutual understanding: they should not come more than once a month.

The concept of face has a double function in victimization: it relates both to submission to gang extortion and to reluctance to disclose to others that one is in fact being persecuted by gangs. For many Chinese merchants, especially those considered by the community as influential figures, revealing to others details about victimization is equivalent to "throwing away one's face," or worse, having "no face." A community leader explained why Chinese extortion victims are unwilling to talk about their victimization: "The Chinese want people to 'mind their own business,' and they like to have face. That's why they don't want other people to know that they are extorted."

Other merchants were willing to pay extortionists, however reluctantly, because they saw payment as a practical way to deal with the problem. Many businesspeople realize that the police cannot protect them or their businesses 24 hours a day and believe that if they refuse to pay, a gang might damage their property or disrupt their business. They soberly calculate the costs and benefits of not paying and conclude that in the long run, it might be cheaper to pay. The following reasons were often mentioned by merchants who perceived their compliance with gang demands as nothing less than a prudent decision:

> I paid because I am afraid of their retaliation. I own a small business. I cannot afford to pay for any damage to the store.

> I was afraid they would come and sit in the restaurant if I refused to pay. If that happened, customers would be afraid to come into my restaurant.

> I can't fight directly with the gang. Otherwise [if I don't pay], I can't do business because we are easy targets.

> If you decide to fight the gangs and refuse to pay, they will break your windows and damage the locks. If you claim for compensation from your insurance company, they will increase your insurance fee. This way, you pay more. It's [resistance] not better than paying the gangs.

There are other advantages to paying the gangs. Paying up enables businesspeople to concentrate on their businesses instead of on the gangs. As mentioned earlier, commercial rents in Chinatown are relatively high, and business competition is fierce; consequently, most store owners are deeply involved in the daily operations of their businesses and work long hours to make sure they survive. As a result, there is little time to be concerned with issues and activities that are not business related and that are, in terms of dollar costs, rather petty. Chinatown store owners seem determined to invest all their energy into their businesses and are willing to pay a price for peace of mind.

Another reason Chinese business owners submit to gang demands rests on superstition and folklore. Many Chinese people heed the maxim of "converting big problems into small problems, and small problems into no problems." According to this cultural maxim, no one should magnify problems. Others believe that disaster in life is inevitable for everybody, but that money can be spent to prevent or delay it. Many business owners see the gangs as potentially disastrous to them and their businesses, so they are prepared to spend a small amount of money to send the gangs away. The following views, expressed by some merchants, exemplify traditional feelings about the relationship between money and disaster: "Losing some money helps avoid misfortune," "Spend some money to avoid bigger trouble."

The opening ceremony of a business is symbolically important to Chinese store owners because they believe that the first day of business dictates the future. Everything must go smoothly at the opening celebration to ensure a good future. If something goes wrong, it implies bad luck. Consequently, Chinese merchants are careful in picking the day for the occasion; some even consult a fortune-teller to choose the right day. For this reason, Chinese merchants are most vulnerable during the opening ceremony of their business. If gang members appear and congratulate the owners, the owners are unlikely to refuse a demand for money. They regard payment as a way to generate luck; the money paid is known as *lei shi*, money that is "good for business."

Resistance and Avoidance

Overall, the Chinese business owners in this study offered relatively little resistance to gangs. Only 86 (or 21%) of the 416 proprietors who had been approached by gangs said they did not comply with the gangs' demands. In comparison, according to the National Crime Victimization Survey (NCVS) data, victims usually take some self-protective measures in slightly more than one-half (51%) of all personal victimizations (Hindelang et al., 1978). Chinese business owners were least likely to refuse gang demands for free goods or services (9%), followed by forced sales (20%), asking for lucky money (33%), and protection (46%). The respondents may have been most reluctant to succumb to gang demands for protection money because in the case of protection, unlike other types of extortion, once the victim agrees to pay, he or she may have to pay regularly for quite some time.

Merchants reported many reasons for refusing the gangs. Some willingly gave gang members money during major Chinese holidays but persistently refused to do so if gang members harassed them at other times. A 43-year-old proprietor from Hong Kong expressed his feelings about being asked for money during the Christmas holiday:

> When these gang members came during the Chinese New Year, I always paid them *lei shi*. This is our custom, that's fine. However, when they showed up for money during Christmas, I told them, "This is not Chinese holiday, come back on Chinese New Year." Also, when these kids came to sell firecrackers and moon-cakes on Chinese festivals, I normally bought them. Once, they came to sell turkey on Thanksgiving. I said, "This is not our holiday, I am not celebrating it. You have to wait until the Chinese New Year." They left without a word.

Other business owners developed other resistance tactics because they believed that once they yielded, systematic attempts to exploit them would become the norm. A 45-year-old Taiwanese store owner in Flushing, Queens, explained why he was determined to fight against the gangs:

> A group of gang members came for extortion money. They showed up three times, but I refused. I even called the police. At one time, a couple of police

officers were inside my store, but the gang members still came in and said, "You've got to pay us. You should know that there are three guns pointing at you from the outside." They dared to say that because they knew the police didn't understand Cantonese. I didn't want to pay because I know that there is no end to this once you start paying. The third time they were here, the police arrested them.

Most store owners who refused to pay were more subtle in rejecting gang threats. Many business owners simply indicated that the owner was not in the store and asked the gang members to come back later.[3] If gang members came to sell items, the business owner might tell them that they had already bought the items and would show them the tangerines, firecrackers, or mooncakes that were placed in the store for that purpose.

Some store owners offered gang members food and drink instead of money. A 58-year-old woman who owned a small store in Manhattan's Chinatown explained that she always tried to cajole gang members with smooth talk and soft drinks when they came for money:

> I can't speak English, and I don't have the time to seek help from the police. On the other hand, I can't afford to pay them whenever they come and say, "Auntie, one of our brothers just got out of jail, we need money to eat." What am I supposed to do? What I did was, I always asked them to sit down and take a rest, said nice things like "Big Brother, have a bottle of bean milk." They drank the milk, hung around for a while, and left. I saw this as a way to send away the *wan shan* [god of misfortune].[4] They also came to sell a tangerine plant during Chinese New Year. I pointed at the entrance to the basement and said, "Big Brother, we already got the plant right there." They left. You can't be outright blunt in dealing with these youngsters, you know.

Some merchants spurned the gangs because they were irritated by their crude behavior. These merchants regarded themselves as law-abiding, hard-working business owners who had nothing to be afraid of, and they viewed gang members as a bunch of parasitic street thugs who prey only on those who do not dare to stand up to them. A 45-year-old woman from Hong Kong explained how she refused to pay protection money to a group of teenagers:

> Members of the XX gang showed up and asked for $300 a month for protection. I replied, "I can't pay you this kind of money. Business competition is fierce here, I am barely surviving." They threatened to disrupt my business and hurt me. I said, "Look, I am not going to pay no matter what. You guys are so young, why don't you go to school or find a job?" Two of them appeared to be upset, but the rest of them didn't say a word. They left me alone.

Some merchants were able to resist extortion attempts because they themselves were active or former members of a gang or tong. One store owner in his early 30s, who, during in our interview with him, acted as if he were part of the gang subculture, claimed that he was not at all intimidated by gang members:

> A group of Ghost Shadows came and wanted extortion money from me. I said, "No money, get lost right away." They left the store immediately. They should have figured out who I was before they approached me for money. I am amazed

that they had the guts to come before they even knew anything about me. These Shadows are all garbage.

When a 63-year-old tong member who owned a store in Manhattan's Chinatown was approached for protection money, he was quite bold in dealing with the gang:

A clique of gang members asked me for protection money. I said "no" to them, and they threatened me. "We'll burn your store and kill you," they said. I told them, "Do what you have to do; I'm waiting for you, anytime!" These guys thought that everybody in Chinatown was afraid of them. The more you pay them, the more you are afraid of them, the more they harass you. I've been in Chinatown for so many years, I've experienced every circumstance you can imagine; I'm not afraid of them. In fact, if they act arrogantly, I'll call the police and arrest them. If they are polite and humble, I may let them survive.

Not all store owners who resisted the gangs were as fortunate as the merchants quoted above. Some were attacked or even killed. A manager of a well-established business initially defied a gang, but later found out that it was a titanic task to keep on fighting, and eventually caved in:

When they came and asked for $500 a month for protection, I refused. I said, "I know a lot of people in Chinatown." They replied, "It doesn't matter. You still have to pay." I asked them to let me think about it, and they left. I called 911 right away, and the police didn't even bother to show up. What's the point in calling the police? When they came back the next day, I said I needed more time. In the next few days, they robbed a customer in the toilet room, asked a customer who was sitting in the dining area to "borrow" his wallet and took all the cash, stood in front of the store in the evening—about 20 of them—and stared at the employees who were leaving after work. Finally, when one gang member threw a jumbo firecracker behind the counter and burnt the leg of an employee, I got so perturbed that I chased them with a knife. However, after that, I decided to pay them exactly what they asked for.

More often than not, resistant owners must endure a traumatic process of negotiating with the extortionists, by seeking help from underworld figures or the police, while worrying about personal safety for themselves, their families, employees, and customers. A restaurateur explained in detail how complicated and risky it was to confront a group of gang members. His account characterizes the plight of many businesspeople:

I arrived in the United States about 15 years ago. Upon my arrival, I started a business in Manhattan's Chinatown. During that time, I established a good relationship with tong members and elders. A few years ago, I opened a Chinese restaurant in Flushing, Queens, with a few business partners. My partners maintained a close relationship with members of the Chinese underworld, and my restaurant catered to people who stay out late in the evenings, so many criminal elements congregated in my restaurant. My partners offered discounts to those who were associated with the criminal world, sometimes as high as 50 percent or more. During that time span, everything went very well, except that the restaurant had to offer heavy discounts to some customers.

Later, I became the sole owner of the restaurant. I decided that it was time to get rid of the discounts. I made up my mind that I was not going to offer more than a 10 percent reduction.

One day, a group of people showed up at my restaurant and asked me to pay them for laying off an employee who worked for me at another restaurant I owned. I sold that restaurant. The group told me that the employee is a good friend of theirs, and she suffered financial loss because of my decision to sell the restaurant. When I refused to pay, they threatened me.

I decided that I should talk to the leader of the gang. I did talk to some leaders in Manhattan's Chinatown, but the issue could not be settled because the group who demanded money from me were members of a Queens-based gang, formed by predominantly young people from Taiwan who have no relationship with Cantonese gangs and tongs in Manhattan's Chinatown.

I did not report the extortion to the police. I tried to solve the problem by myself. I armed myself with a revolver, and I was ready to fight them myself, and with the help from a couple of good friends.

One day, a couple of young kids showed up and tried to rob the restaurant. Both sides opened fire, but nobody was hurt. The police later arrested the kids, but could not press charges because the police officer who first arrived at the scene forgot to register the gang members' guns which they seized. As a result, the district attorney who was in charge of the case asked me to fabricate something so that he could press for other more serious charges against the kids. I refused to do so because I was more concerned with the arrest and indictment of the gang leaders than the kids. I was convinced that the leaders gave the kids orders to rob my business or at least sanctioned the robbery. However, the police simply ignored my request for arresting the leaders. I was disappointed. I have little interest in the kids, and I did not want to provide wrong information simply to make a criminal case. The whole episode ended as a result of my reluctance to press charges against the kids. After the incident, the gang did not show up again, and I sold the restaurant a few months later.

I went through a very stressful period. I was angered, afraid, and emotionally drained during the standoff with the gang, which lasted for a few months.

Another business owner explained how a gang tried to extort money from him and how he reacted to the situation. From his description of the incident, it is apparent that gang members can be rather tactful, but at the same time, by resisting them one could put one's life in jeopardy:

I owned a nightclub in Flushing, Queens. Most Chinese nightclubs are located in midtown Manhattan, with only a few in Flushing, Queens. These clubs are normally open until four o'clock in the morning and are frequented by mainly businessmen, gamblers, and gang members. The clubs hire third-rate entertainers from Hong Kong and Taiwan to perform in the establishments, along with a small band. The places also hire young girls to work as bar girls, accompanying the customers while they drink, and allowing customers to check out the girls after business hours. Many shoot-outs have occurred in these Chinese nightclubs over the past several years.

I opened the nightclub with three partners. Many young kids, including members of the Taiwan Brotherhood gang, came to my nightclub. Several kids will come in and have a fight amongst themselves or throw bottles and cups on the floor. They would get into a conflict with the armed Caucasian guards and would stay long after the business was closed. I did not pay attention to any of these kids and tried to concentrate on running my business.

One day, a number of young people approached me and asked for protection money. I told the kids that I would like to talk to their leader. Finally, through a middleman, I met the leader of the gang in a restaurant in Queens. I told the leader that I knew his "big brother," who was then living in Taiwan, and I showed him the name card of his big brother. The leader immediately retreated, saying that it was all a mistake. I treated him to a nice dinner and assumed that things were all settled once and for all. However, the next day, the leader, along with his followers, came to my nightclub and created a scene by throwing glasses on the floor. There was an argument between the guard and the troublemakers, but I did not call the police.

One day, I was again approached by a lieutenant of the gang, asking me to explain at an upcoming meeting with his leader why he had been contacted by the police. He suspected that I was responsible for it. I did show up for the meeting, and the gang members kidnapped me and took me to a nightclub in midtown Manhattan where the gang hung out. At the nightclub, I was threatened with a gun by one of the young gang members. The leader of the gang showed up later, pretending that he had no knowledge of his followers' actions and asked me to forgive his negligence. I saw the whole episode as a conspiracy by the gang to coerce me into paying protection money to them.

Later on, as I expected, word was sent to me and my business partners that it would be easier to just pay the gang. I discussed the issue with my partners, and most of them tentatively agreed that the gang should be paid. However, when I approached the gang to discuss a payment, the leader changed his mind. Instead of protection money, the leader demanded to be a partner of the nightclub, the so-called dry partnership.[5]

I decided that this was not going to work, allowing the leader to become a partner without any investment on his part. I reported the case to the police, asking for police protection. With the attention from the police and pressure from one of the Chinatown adult organizations (a partner of mine is very close to the leader of the Tsung Tsin Association), the gang retreated. A few months later, we sold the business.

Some nightclubs in New York City are owned by people who are ex-gang members. Their experiences in gangs tended to make them underestimate the magnitude of the threat from the extortionists, and violence often erupted as a result of the nightclub owners' refusal to take the gangs' threat seriously.

Table 5.1 shows the association between the personal and business attributes of my respondents and their likelihood of resistance to gang extortion in general. The base rate for resistance was 21 percent (86 out of the 416 who were approached). The bivarate table indicates that none of the personal characteristics under consideration were critical in determining the likelihood of resistance to the gangs. The subjects' age or number of years in the United States, which are not shown in table 5.1, did not have any significant effect on their resistance rate.

However, business type was correlated with resistance. Factories were not only the least likely to be approached but also the most likely to challenge the gangs. Since factories normally carry little cash and their operation does not rely on good public image, they are in a position to resist gang demands. Restaurants

Table 5.1. Association between Subjects' Personal and Business Characteristics and Resistance to Extortion[a] (N = 416)

Personal	N Approached	% Resisted	Business	N Approached	% Resisted
Sex			Type of business**		
Male	327	20	Restaurant	177	12
Female	89	25	Retail food store	97	27
Country of origin			Retail nonfood store	70	29
Hong Kong	230	18	Service	55	22
Taiwan	68	24	Factory	17	35
China	60	20	Neighborhood		
Other	58	28	Manhattan's Chinatown	240	19
Education			Queen's Chinatown	76	28
No schooling	6	0	Brooklyn's Chinatown	32	19
6th grade or less	44	9	Manhattan non-Chinatown	27	22
7th to 9th grade	49	27	Queens non-Chinatown	12	8
10th to 12 grade	142	18	Brooklyn non-Chinatown	29	24
College	154	24	Sole owner of business?		
Graduate school	16	25	Yes	181	24
English proficiency			No	225	17
Poor	109	20	Estimated profitability		
Average	142	22	Good	189	18
Fluent	163	20	Average	144	25
Affiliation with community organization?			Poor	82	20
Yes	95	24	Manhattan's Chinatown (N = 240)		
No	319	20	Vietnamese zone (Born-to-Kill)	21	33
			Italian zone (Ghost Shadows)	55	27
			On Leong zone (Ghost Shadows)	58	10
			Hip Sing zone (Flying Dragons)	21	5
			Tung On and Tsung Tsin zone (Tung On)	9	0
			Fujianese zone (Fuk Ching)	61	20
			Other core zone (No dominant gang)	10	20
			Outskirts (No dominant gang)	5	20

a. Number of missing observations: Education = 5; English proficiency = 2; Estimated profitability = 2; Affiliation with community organizations? = 1; Affiliation with community organizations? = 2. Percentage have been adjusted accordingly. Percentage of the subjects who have experienced attempted victimization but successfully resisted was 21%

** p ≤ .01

were not only the most likely to be targeted but also the least likely to resist the gangs. Restaurateurs may be reluctant to antagonize the gangs because their businesses could easily be disrupted by malicious gang members. Street location was also associated with resistance. Although these data are not shown in table 5.1, store owners on Pell, East Broadway, Bowery, Division, and Bayard were less likely to resist than merchants on Center, Eldridge, and Canal.

Although businesses in Queens were more likely to oppose gang demands, their rate of resistance was not significantly higher, statistically speaking, than that of businesses in other boroughs. Likewise, there is some variability in the resistance rate for businesses located in the various Chinatown zones, but the differences are not statistically significant. Store owners within the Tung On territory were not only more likely to be approached than those in other zones (see table 3.7) but also least likely to defy the gangs. No other business characteristic was affiliated with resistance to gang demands.

It appears that there is a significant association between the level of vulnerability to attempted extortion and the level of resistance to gang demands. Businesses more likely to be approached were those whose owners admitted yielding to gang demands. Certain areas of Manhattan's Chinatown, reported to be most vulnerable to attempted extortion, were also areas where resistance to gangs was weakest.[6]

In examining the association between a merchant's personal and business characteristics and the likelihood of his or her resistance to specific gang demands (these data are not shown in table 5.1), I found that variables associated with resistance were not the same for all forms of extortion. In comparison with business owners in the Chinatowns of Manhattan and Queens, merchants in Brooklyn's Chinatown were significantly more likely to resist attempts for protection money. When gang members asked for lucky money, younger business owners were more likely to resist than older merchants. And, those who spoke English fluently were less likely to comply with gang demands for lucky money. People who owned the building in which their business was located were also more likely to resist paying lucky money. Retail food stores and garment factories were more likely to resist buying items from the gangs than were other businesses such as restaurants and wholesale supply firms. Finally, merchants who had lived in the United States longer were more likely to resist extortion than those who had arrived more recently.

Overall, restaurants were the least likely to resist gang extortion, and factories were the most likely to; the more highly educated businesspeople were more likely to resist than were the less well educated. The use or absence of threats by gang members was not a factor in store owner resistance.

Reporting Crime to the Police

Law enforcement authorities have attributed the persistence of gang extortion to two factors: the victims' willingness to submit to gang demands, and their reluctance to seek help from police (Kinkead, 1992; U.S. Senate, 1992). They have expressed frustration not only because of low report rates but also because of the reluctance of Chinese victims to testify in court when arrests are made. As a result, the law enforcement authorities have viewed the situation of Chinatown residents in general, and Chinese merchants in particular, as one of living in a "subculture of fear" (R. Wu, 1977; *World Journal*, 1994b).

Little is known about how much gang extortion goes unnoticed by law enforcement authorities. Nor are there data about why Chinese victims in general seem unwilling to contact the police. The police often cite fear, the language barrier, and a lack of trust as major factors in victim underreporting.

Table 5.2 shows the reporting rate and reasons for not reporting by type of victimization. It also includes the 1990 NCVS reporting rates for purposes of comparison. The data show that the reporting rate for forced sales was only 4 percent. The reporting rate for respondents who were shaken down for protection money (24%) was higher than the reporting rate for any other type of attempted extortion. In comparison, the overall reporting rate among victims of gang extortion (20%) was substantially lower than the reporting rate for all personal crimes (38%) (these rates are not shown in table 5.2) and the reporting rate for personal robbery (50%) disclosed in the 1990 NCVS report (Bureau of Justice Statistics, 1992).[7] Because the NCVS data do not include the reporting rate for extortion, it is not known whether Chinese victims are less likely than members of other ethnic groups to report extortion.

Why are Chinese business owners relatively reluctant to contact the police when victimized? The police have speculated that many are immigrants who were exploited by law enforcement authorities in their country of origin. As a result, they tend to distrust the police in the United States (U.S. Senate, 1992). Other observers believe that the language barrier is the main reason that Chinese victims avoid the police (President's Commission on Organized Crime, 1984). Table 5.2 illustrates the reasons for not reporting illegal gang behavior given by respondents in this study and compares them with the reasons cited by respondents in the NCVS study.

The major reason the Chinese victims in this study were unwilling to report extortion was that they did not consider the crime important enough. Many business people were annoyed by gang practices of asking for money or free goods, but they did not view the gangs' acts as a serious threat because little money was lost or because they were not harmed or threatened by the offenders.[8] However, that a crime was not important enough to report was rarely mentioned in the NCVS data (Bureau of Justice Statistics, 1992). In the words of one of the respondents in my study: "I paid them a small amount of money, and they didn't hurt me. Besides, they asked for it in such a polite manner. This is expected in Chinatown, nothing extraordinary."

The second most frequently mentioned reason the respondents in this study gave for not reporting extortion was that they assumed it was useless to approach the police because there was no proof of the crime, the loss was not covered by insurance, or they were convinced the police could not recover the extorted money or goods. This was also a common reason cited in the 1990 NCVS study by victims not reporting personal robbery to the police.

Table 5.2. Reasons for Not Reporting Extortion to Police, by Type of Victimization[a]

	Protection (N = 130)	Lucky Money (N = 246)	Forced Sales (N = 308)	Theft of Goods or Services (N = 103)	NCVS Personal Robbery (N = 1,149,710)[b]
Total nonreporting rate	76%	82%	96%	84%	50%
Object recovered/ offender unsuccessful	13%	13%	5%	0%	19%
Lack of proof/ insurance would not cover/unable to recover property	16	22	18	22	14
I can handle it myself	0	2	4	12	12
Police ineffective, inefficient, or biased	9	7	1	6	11
Private or personal matter	3	0	0	0	9
Police would not want to be bothered	4	8	3	1	8
Fear of reprisal	21	6	6	19	7
Too inconvenient or time-consuming	5	7	2	2	7
Reported to another official	0	0	0	0	7
Will report if happens often	2	2	0	2	2
Not aware crime occurred until later	0	0	0	0	1
Crime not important enough	23	28	29	34	1
It's a way to generate luck	2	4	1	0	0
This is expected in Chinatown	4	1	1	1	0
We need the items anyway	0	0	3	0	0
See it as gift giving	0	0	9	0	0
See it as ordinary sale	0	0	9	0	0
Other reasons	2	1	7	3	3

a. Percentage who cited this reason for not reporting crime to police. Respondents could provide more than one reason.

b. 1990 NCVS report (Bureau of Justice Statistics, 1992). N = number of victims.

Fear of gang reprisal was the third major reason cited by my respondents for not reporting victimization by gangs. Respondents were concerned that if they contacted the police, gang members might return and harm them, damage their property, or disrupt their business.[9] In the NCVS survey, fear of reprisal ranked seventh.

Others did not report extortion to the police because they did not pay the gang or because they did not view the attempted extortion as a crime and thus saw no reason to contact the police. Also, many respondents thought extortion was not worth reporting because they believed the police did not consider gang extortion as serious as violent and drug-related crimes. Some respondents stated that contacting authorities did not necessarily result in police action. Even when the police arrived, they sometimes advised the business owners to comply with gang demands or told them that the police could do nothing about the matter because there was no proof of a crime. In most instances, the police filed a report and told the proprietors to call them when the gang members approached them again.

Table 5.3 shows the reasons given by Chinese victims of gang extortion, robbery, and burglary and NCVS victims of personal robbery for reporting those crimes to the police. Chinese victims of gang extortion contacted law enforcement

Table 5.3. Reasons for Reporting Victimization to Police, by Type of Victimization (Percentage Distribution)[a]

	Overall Gang Extortion ($N = 416$)	Robbery ($N = 53$)	Burglary ($N = 162$)	NCVS Personal Robbery ($N = 1,149,710$)[b]
Total reporting rate	20%	72%	24%	50%
To recover property	0%	0%	0%	18%
To catch or find offender	10	4	8	14
To prevent further crimes by offender against victim	24	0	0	10
To punish offender	1	0	0	10
To prevent crime by offender against anyone else	1	2	0	9
To stop or prevent this incident	20	0	0	8
Duty to notify police	4	0	2	7
To improve police surveillance	17	30	25	3
Needed help because of injury	0	0	0	1
To collect insurance	0	4	8	1
Good relationship with police	6	0	0	0
Being threatened	4	0	0	0
Because it was a crime	4	54	39	13
To have a police record	0	4	13	0
Some other reason	10	0	6	6
Not available	0	0	0	1

a. Percentage who cited this reason for reporting crime to police. Respondents could provide more than one reason.

b. 1990 NCVS report (Bureau of Justice Statistics, 1992). N = number of victims.

Table 5.4. Personal and Business Characteristics by Victims' Reporting Behavior[a]

	Protection (N = 130)	Lucky Money (N = 246)	Theft of Goods or Services (N = 103)	At Least One of the 4 Types (N = 416)
Total reporting rate	24%	18%	16%	20%
Sex				
Male	22	19	14	20
Female	35	14	25	23
Country of birth				
Hong Kong	19	15	17	14
Taiwan	47	24	9	30
China	27	25	22	21
Other	20	12	7	16
Education		*		
No schooling	none[b]	20	0	17
6th grade or less	13	6	13	16
7th to 9th grade	24	0	0	10
10th to 12th grade	22	21	27	21
College	28	24	10	23
Graduate school	50	18	33	31
English proficiency				*
Poor	18	8	10	12
Average	28	18	17	23
Fluent	25	23	19	23
Type of Business				*
Restaurant	25	22	18	25
Retail food store	23	11	6	14
Retail nonfood store	17	25	21	21
Service	33	6	8	15
Factory	33	23	none	18
Neighborhood				
Manhattan's Chinatown	24	13	15	16
Queens' Chinatown	23	24	15	28
Brooklyn's Chinatown	19	14	25	16
Manhattan non-Chinatown	33	33	none	26
Queens non-Chinatown	33	25	none	25
Brooklyn non-Chinatown	27	28	20	35
Any franchise?		*		
Yes	23	29	20	25
No	25	15	14	19
Were you threatened?	*	**		***
Yes	36	34	20	41
No	17	14	13	14

a. Data on forced sales are not presented because only 13 of 308 subjects (4%) reported the crime to the police.

b. None = No base N.

*$p < .05$; **$p < .01$; ***$p < .001$

authorities mainly because they wanted to prevent the offenders from committing further crimes against them, to stop or prevent the particular incident, or to improve police surveillance. Unlike NCVS subjects, Chinese victims were motivated neither by recovery of property nor by the conviction that extortion is a crime for which the authorities need to be notified. Yet, when asked why they notified the police when their businesses were robbed or burglarized, most respondents in my study replied that these were serious crimes which must be reported. The data presented in table 5.3 illustrate that Chinese business owners and NCVS subjects appear to have significantly different reasons for reporting victimization to law enforcement authorities.

The relationship between merchants' personal and business characteristics and reporting behavior are presented in table 5.4. One of the best predictors for reporting crime is the offender's use of intimidation or threats when demanding money. The data suggest that if victims are threatened, regardless of the type of threat or the form of extortion, they are more likely to contact the authorities. This suggests that when threats are made by offenders, victims may consider the crime more serious and therefore be more likely to call the police. However, gang threat was not one of the major reasons cited by the respondents for their decisions to report gang extortion to the police (see table 5.3). The data also show that Chinese merchants who spoke fluent English reported extortion at a higher rate than those who spoke little English. Other personal characteristics such as sex, age, education, country of origin, length of stay in the United States, and affiliation with community associations were not important factors associated with reporting behavior (with the exception of an association between education and reporting of demands for lucky money).

Among business characteristics, business type and neighborhood were associated with reporting behavior in general. That is, restaurateurs were most likely to contact the police while owners of retail food stores were least likely to. Also, respondents who operated businesses in Manhattan and Brooklyn outside the Chinese communities in those boroughs were more likely to report extortion than were store owners within the Chinese communities, although the difference in reporting rates was not statistically significant. Merchants in Manhattan and Brooklyn's Chinatowns were less likely to contact authorities than were merchants in Queens' Chinatown. Owners of large businesses (those with more than one branch) were more likely to report being approached by gang members than were owners of small businesses.[10]

In sum, the data suggest that incident-specific correlates, such as threats or the seriousness of the crime, play a major role in predicting reporting behavior, followed by environment-specific correlates, such as type of business or neighborhood. Victim-specific correlates were the weakest in predicting reporting behavior among the victims in this study. My findings support the hypothesis proposed by researchers such as Hindelang and Gottfredson (1976), Garofalo (1979), and Skogan (1984) that reporting behavior is basically incident-specific. That is, victims are most likely to report a crime to police if they consider the crime to be serious.

Reducing Risks

Although Chinese merchants are rarely assaulted while being subjected to extortion for small amounts of money, some officials believe that the existence of Chinese gangs and the publicity about their violence have had a profound impact on the lifestyle of many Chinese entrepreneurs. It is reported in the local media that many store owners are reluctant to identify themselves as owners out of fear, and many carry guns or make friends with crime figures for protection. According to these accounts, fear of crime, whether from gangs or other offenders, compels merchants to take extraordinary security measures in conducting their business and has altered the relationships between business owners, their patrons, and the public at large.

To assess the accuracy of these claims, I asked respondents whether they changed their lifestyle, altered their business practices, or increased their business security measures because of gang harassment. Twenty-two percent of the respondents stated that they had changed their lifestyle. The adjustments mentioned most often included dressing in ordinary clothes, not wearing jewelry, carrying little money, and driving inexpensive automobiles. In short, the common strategy was to maintain a low profile and to avoid being noticed as a prosperous business owner. The following example demonstrates the extraordinary effort one business owner took to avoid being noticed. A young woman who owns a retail store in Manhattan's Chinatown tried not to drive her brand new Mercedes Benz around the community. On one occasion, when she had to drive, she encountered gang members to whom she was paying protection money. She was so frightened by the prospect of the gang members seeing her driving an expensive car that she hid her head under the steering wheel until they passed.

Twenty-nine percent of the respondents said they altered their business practices to avoid being victimized by gangs: they closed their businesses earlier than usual, hired only acquaintances or friends, kept only a small amount of cash in the store, or did business only with regular customers.

Almost six respondents in 10 revealed that they increased business security measures in order to prevent crime. Many business owners installed alarm systems, video cameras, or iron gates on their business premises. In order to discourage gang members with beepers from hanging around, some stores removed public phones. To avoid the possibility of gang members' robbing customers in rest rooms, the owners locked the rest rooms or remodeled them so they could not hold more than one occupant at a time.

Other measures adopted by the business owners included (1) only hiring workers who spoke fluent English, so that when gang members came, the workers communicated with them only in English, thus deterring them; (2) employing managers who know how to cope with gang members; (3) departing from the business premises in a group at closing time; (4) carrying guns; and (5) hiring non-Chinese employees, under the assumption that gangs would not bother non-Chinese.

In sum, many Chinese merchants changed their lifestyle and business practices or increased security measures because of the gang problem. Many respondents were reluctant to discuss what they did because they did not want outsiders to know what risk management tactics they used. After all, some of the adjustments in behavior might not be viewed as socially desirable. For example, some merchants initiated contacts with tongs for protection. Under such circumstances, the merchants might be obligated to donate a certain amount of money to the tongs as a membership fee. The tongs issue a receipt to the donor, and the receipt is posted at the business entrance as a deterrent to gangs. Tong membership or a receipt from a tong, however, is by no means a certain guarantee of thwarting gang demands. Some business owners who joined tongs or offered them money were still subjected to extortion by gangs.

The data show no appreciable difference between victims of extortion and nonvictims in adjustment of lifestyle in response to the gang problem in the Chinese community. Respondents in Brooklyn's Chinatown, however, were more likely to alter their lifestyle than were respondents in other areas, and business owners in the core area of Manhattan's Chinatown were less likely to adjust their lifestyle in the face of gang threats. Respondents in the Chinatowns of Queens and Brooklyn were more vigilant and more cautious than respondents in Manhattan's Chinatown. Business owners outside the three Chinese communities were more likely to do something to protect themselves from the gangs than were those within the Chinese communities.

Perception of the Criminal Justice System

Other than Song's study (1992), there has been no research on how Asian communities in America view the criminal justice system. In order to understand why Chinese business owners are more likely to change their lifestyle and business practices than to seek help from the police to protect themselves from gangs, we need to examine their impressions of the criminal justice system.

According to Song (1992), perceived police prejudice against Asians is one of the major concerns of Chinese in southern California in combating crime in their communities. The Chinese media in New York City have reported extensively on several incidents of police insensitivity to and brutality against Chinese victims and Chinese offenders. In a few kidnapping incidents, relatives of victims have even blamed the police for the death of their loved ones because they claim the authorities were more concerned with the arrests of the offenders than with the rescue of the victims (*Sing Tao Jih Pao*, 1993f). The media have also reported that because of these incidents, the relatives of kidnapping victims have given up the idea of seeking help from police and pay kidnappers immediately to save the victims' lives.

Community leaders also see police ineffectiveness as a major reason for the escalation of gang violence in the Chinese community. When major gang-related violent incidents occur, community leaders will often accuse the police of ineptness. A prominent community leader who took part in this survey expressed his frustration with the police as follows: "Personally, I am very disappointed with the development of the gang problem in Chinatown. I am almost ready to give up. The police are mainly concerned with heroin trafficking. They ignore the gangs."

When asked how he viewed the relationship between the police and the Chinese, another community leader concluded that the relationship was relatively weak, mainly because of police insensitivity to the culture and lifestyle of Chinese people:

> It's not that the Chinese do not want to cooperate with the police. It's the police who do not want to cooperate with the Chinese. The police are slow. If they investigate a crime, they want to start from the very basic. Most Chinese have to work, but the police like to ask a lot of questions. They want the victims and witnesses to go to the precinct, but many of them cannot afford to miss a day of work. Besides, there is a communication problem between the police and the victims. Also, the police do not treat the victims sincerely. They are not polite to Chinatown residents. Moreover, the police could not solve the crime in the community. Sometimes we talk very loud. The police then think we are berating them. They see us as a group of people without much cultivation. They look down on us.

One business owner even concluded that employees from the city health department were worse than gang members and expressed his disenchantment with public institutions in general: "In fact, people in the food industry dislike the health department the most. They often come to bother us and issue tickets—it's like legitimate extortion. They don't understand the way we operate our businesses. For them, everything is a violation."

My interviewers asked the victims what occurred after they reported crimes to police. Most said that nothing significant happened, that the police arrived on the scene after the perpetrators were long gone, filed a report, and asked them to call if and when the perpetrators showed up again. One subject claimed that the police laughed after they learned that the incident was one of Chinese against Chinese. Some were told by the authorities that gang extortions were small matters and that they should not be so concerned. However, a few respondents indicated that contacts with the police resulted in the arrests of the perpetrators. One subject said that after the gang members were arrested, they were back in his store within half an hour taunting him, "Here we come again. So what!" For some subjects, though, contacts with the justice system led to more police officers patrolling their areas.

Table 5.5 shows the victims' evaluation of police performance and their forecasts for their future reporting behavior. From 43 to 55 percent of the respondents said the police satisfactorily explained to them what action they would take. From 42 to 61 percent of the respondents said they found the police helpful. The data, therefore, do not support the assumption that the police are callous and generally treat Chinese crime victims disrespectfully. The majority of the respondents indicated that the police were polite to them.

Nevertheless, those who were subjected to demands for protection and lucky money were more discouraged by their encounters with the police than encouraged by them. Table 5.5 shows that 33 percent of the protection victims and 22

Table 5.5. Victim Assessments of Police Effectiveness, Politeness, and Future Reporting Behavior by Type of Victimization[a]

	Protection (N = 31)	Lucky Money (N = 43)	Robbery (N = 38)	Burglary (N = 137)
Did the police satisfactorily explain what action they would take?				
Yes	43%	55%	53%	45%
Did you find the police helpful?				
Yes	42	61	47	45
Did you find the police polite?				
Yes	87	93	95	93
Are you more or less likely to contact the police in the future?				
More	7	14	32	13
Same	60	64	62	81
Less	33	22	5	6

a. N = number of victims who approached the police.

percent of lucky money victims felt that they would be less likely to contact the police if and when they were victimized again. However, the robbery and burglary victims in my sample appear to have had a different experience with the police than protection and lucky money victims. Victims of robbery and burglary said that they would be more likely to contact the police in the future, even though their assessments of police effectiveness and politeness were almost the same as those of protection and lucky money victims. This is probably because they view robbery and burglary as serious crimes.

According to data that are not included in table 5.5, most respondents (61%) thought the police were effective in dealing with crime in their neighborhoods, while some (13%) were not sure whether the authorities were competent. Only 26 percent did not think the police were capable of fighting crime in their community.

When asked whether they thought the police were prejudiced against Asians, almost half of the respondents (47%) responded affirmatively, and 29% said they thought the police were probably biased. Only one-third of the subjects (34%) were convinced that the authorities do not discriminate against Asians. Thus, the data suggest that as many as two out of three Chinese merchants question police impartiality in dealing with Asian victims.[11]

The interviewers of this study also asked the respondents their perception of the whole criminal justice system. Most thought that the system is too lenient with criminals and said that suspects are often released on bail, those who can afford expensive defense lawyers often get away with crime, and punishment, if any, is often minimal and has little or no deterrent effect. On the other hand, the respondents noted that the system seems too harsh on crime victims. Victims are required to spend a substantial amount of time cooperating with a justice system that is overwhelming and inefficient. Also, there are too few foot-patrol officers, not to mention police officers who speak their language and understand their culture. Several respondents said they thought the system "sucks" because "it treats the criminals better than the victims."

Most respondents said they would like to see an increase in the number of foot-patrol and plainclothes officers working in their neighborhoods—preferably Chinese police officers. Almost all the respondents expressed the desire to have more Chinese officers working in their neighborhoods. They would also like police captains who understand Chinese culture and the Chinese community to be in command of the Fifth and Seventh Precincts, the two precincts that cover the core areas of Manhattan's Chinatown. Moreover, they suggested that precinct chiefs should not be rotated as often as they are now.

The majority of the respondents proposed that the criminal justice system get tough with lawbreakers. In general, they said suspects should not be set free on bail, murderers should be sentenced to death, chronic offenders should be locked up for prolonged periods of time, juveniles who commit serious crimes should be treated as adults, the procedure for reporting crimes should be simplified, the courts should be more efficient, and tougher gun control laws should be adopted. If Chinese offenders are convicted for serious crimes, such as murder or heroin trafficking, they should be deported. Many respondents indicated that they would like authorities to target gang leaders rather than ordinary gang members because the leaders are the main instigators and benefactors of gang activities. They also said that gang leaders should be held responsible for their followers' activities, even though the leaders may not be directly involved in those activities.

Some subjects suggested that a special task force should be created to deal specifically with gang extortion in the Chinese communities. They said that another agency should be established to educate Chinese businesspeople on how the criminal justice system works, to instruct victims on how to report crimes, and to restore the Chinese business community's faith in the criminal justice system.

In brief, most subjects considered the criminal justice system to be too easy on the perpetrators and to provide little or no protection for the victims of crime. They proposed that the American criminal justice system could learn something from the Chinese system—a system that, in the words of one of the respondents, sets out to "execute the wrongdoers and protect the innocents."

Summary

The data suggest that most Chinese business owners comply with gang extortion demands because such practices are considered consistent with Chinese customs and not worth resisting. Businesspeople are generally willing to pay the gangs some money to avoid further, more significant problems. The idea of refusing gang demands is not appealing to the victims because their businesses could be disrupted or their properties damaged.

A small number of business owners did refuse to be victimized by the gangs. Some eluded the gangs with relative ease, but most expended considerable time and energy ridding themselves of the gangs. These resistant business owners rarely sought help from the police in confronting the gangs.

When Chinese business owners chose not to report crimes, the reasons most often cited were that the crime was not important enough or that contacting the police would be useless, followed by fear of reprisal from the gangs. The most significant predictor of crime reporting behavior was the seriousness of the extortion, as manifested by the gangs' use of threat in the process of extortion.

Many business owners in Chinese communities are forced to hide their ownership identities and their economic success for fear of gang extortion. They are also coerced into changing their business practices and increasing security precautions. Fear of extortion among business owners has created a business milieu in which only relatives and close acquaintances are to be trusted and strangers are viewed with suspicion. In other words, only *guan xi* (a personal relationship) can help members of the Chinese community establish a business or employer-employee relationship.

The majority of the Chinese merchants would welcome a tougher criminal justice system. They would like to see harsher punishment for offenders, the reinstitution of the death penalty in New York State, and the deportation of chronic Chinese criminals. Most merchants desperately want a dramatic increase in the number of Chinese police officers in their neighborhoods.

After careful examination of the quantitative and qualitative data collected for this study, I find that gang extortion in the Chinese communities of New York City is both institutionalized and normalized. Institutionalization occurs when certain behavioral patterns are integrated into the social routines and customs and are expected by individuals, groups, and organizations in a specific community. That is, gang extortion in the Chinese community has become so common and so pervasive that residents, business owners, community leaders, law enforcement authorities, and various community associations have come to take it for granted. Many Chinese businesspeople stated that they have become so accustomed to being approached by gang members that they now view such approaches as part of doing business in their communities. Some owners revealed that when discussing the gang issue with their business partners before the grand opening ceremony for their business, they and their partners decided to put aside a certain amount of money as a gang offering.

The tongs and other community associations are fully aware of the gang extortion problem; yet, leaders of these organizations say that the problem has existed for a long time and there is little they can do about it. In fact, many community associations have benefited indirectly from the threat of gang extortion because some owners either "donate" money to these associations or maintain a good relationship with their officers, believing that this will provide protection.[12] In other words, the vulnerability of Chinese businesspeople to gang victimization in some ways contributes to the status of certain community associations and their leaders.

Gang victimization of business owners is not only institutionalized but also normalized. That is, certain local norms shape the behavior of gang members; they tend to follow these norms ritualistically when they approach merchants for money. The norms concern the amount of money to be requested, the demeanor to be displayed by gang members, and the timing and frequency of extortion attempts. As long as gang members adhere to these norms, their activities fit the pattern of acceptable behavior not only from the victims' standpoint, but also from the standpoint of the law enforcement community and certain powerful community leaders. The latter are in a position to punish gang members whose extortion activities are not "normal" or that may go too far and violate expectations of tolerable behavior.

So far, there is no theory about why gang extortion is prevalent in Chinese communities and why victims react to it the way they do. The development of such a theory would require comparison of the social environment and victim-offender relationship for gang extortion with those for other interpersonal crimes such as domestic violence and prison victimization. All three types of victimization occur within a closed society in which victims and offenders interact on a daily basis.

Members of the larger society, in general, and law enforcement authorities, in particular, often find it extremely difficult, if not impossible, to intervene in these types of victimization, mainly because both the victims and the offenders do not want to disclose the incidents to outsiders. In addition, both victims and offenders may share the same social, cultural, and economic characteristics. Consequently, in these types of crime, victims may reluctantly continue to be victimized, rationalize and justify their victimization, and seek help only if they are convinced that their lives may be in jeopardy should they resist the perpetrators of the crime.

6

Gang Characteristics

Few empirical studies on Chinese gangs exist. Consequently, we know little about the social background of Chinese gang members, the social processes of and reasons for their joining and leaving Chinatown gangs, the structure of the gangs, the levels of gang cohesion, and the nature of the relationship between the gangs and community organizations. This chapter sheds some light on the characteristics and social dynamics of Chinese gang members and their organizations.

Attributes of Gang Members

Newspaper accounts and government reports on Chinese gangs usually focus on gang activities and ignore the social structure of gangs and the background of the people involved in gang activities. In only one study, conducted in San Francisco by the Institute of Scientific Analysis (Toy, 1992a, 1992b; Joe, 1993, 1994), were a substantial number of Chinese gang members interviewed for the purpose of examining their age, country of origin, education, family background, and other vital demographic and socioeconomic characteristics.

Sex

My study indicates that gang membership is restricted to males, which reconfirms the findings of Toy (1992a) and Joe (1994) on Chinese gangs in San Francisco. According to my male subjects, females are not considered for gang membership. They possess little knowledge of and have no interest in male criminal activities. Nevertheless, many young Korean and Chinese females do hang out with members of Chinese gangs in New York City. Asked about her role in extortion activity, a female subject replied: "I do not get involved. If I am with them while they are collecting money from a store, I stay outside the store."

Some subjects, both male and female, indicated that women are asked to leave when men begin to discuss gang business. They also stated that females are discouraged and dissuaded from learning about gang activities and structure.

Most young women become associated with Chinese gangs through male gang members with whom they attend school. Females with problems at school or at home may find affiliation with gangs appealing because the gangs provide money, food, and a place to stay for females who are seeking sanctuary from school or from home. Some young women find hanging out with gang members fun; others become affiliated with gang members because they like the protection gangs provide. Gang affiliation makes the young women perceive themselves as desirable or important, and the females who hang out with gang members typically boast about their affiliation with the gangs.

Although fun, excitement, and power are associated with hanging around with gang members, the respondents recognized that doing so could also be dangerous because the women could be sexually exploited. According to a female subject, only those who are steady girlfriends of gang leaders are immune from rape by gang members. Another female respondent indicated that once, while visiting a nightclub, she was drugged by male gang members with whom she hung out. She believes that if she had not left the premises before losing control, she would have been raped. Still another female subject revealed that she always took her drink with her when she went to the rest room so it could not be spiked while she was away. Also, women gang associates were susceptible to rape if they violated certain gang rules or dated members of a rival gang. A male gang member attested to this by saying that women who ignored gang rules would be "served," meaning they would be raped by one or more gang members.

Little is known about whether female affiliates of Chinese gangs are forced to work in prostitution houses. None of the eight female subjects interviewed was being coerced into working as a prostitute. However, one subject indicated that gang leaders would assign females who were considered promiscuous to work in Chinatown massage parlors owned by the gang.

A female subject summed up her ambivalent feelings about being affiliated with gang members: "They [gang members] could be fun, and they could be dangerous. When you are with them, you get someone to back you up. People help each other out. However, you really get sick of it too."

Another female subject attempted to leave a gang by seeking help from her parents. She went to stay in Hong Kong temporarily, but later rejoined the gang because, as she put it, she missed them:

> Girls can't go out with members from other groups. Also, boys are not supposed to tell girls anything about the gang. These things bother me. However, girls want to be popular. If you hear Canal Boys [Born-to-Kill], the top gang, girls like to be known to be with them. If I was offered to choose again, I wouldn't want to be in it. I don't want to spend the rest of my life like this. I want to meet more friends, but they won't trust me if I get to know others. They keep doing the same routine. It's like a waste of time. I want to go to college. A lot of kids I know, they are dropping out [of the gang]. I want to have a future. Last year, I really hated them. I asked my parents to send me to Hong Kong. I was with them for four years. However, after staying away from them for a while, I really missed them. I eventually came back and hung out with them again.

Females are not considered gang members, but they nevertheless play an important role in a gang's daily activities. Some women are asked to carry guns for males because females are less likely to be searched when stopped by police.

Also, females often work as the "eyes and ears" of the gangs because they are not ordinarily criminally suspect, and they may hang out with more than one gang.[1] For example, as one female subject observed: "Girls can be really important because we can do things without being detected. That is, we are less noticeable. For example, we often go check out places [for rival gang members or police officers] for our boys."

Also, the girlfriends of gang leaders become the "elder sisters" of ordinary gang members, and they are obliged to look after the male gang members, especially when the leaders are on the run or imprisoned.

Age

Many law enforcement authorities claim that Chinese gang members are usually older than African American or Hispanic gang members (Bresler, 1981; Posner, 1988). A police officer who worked in Manhattan's Chinatown indicated that labeling Chinese gangs as youth gangs is not appropriate because most gang members are in their late 20s and early 30s (Chin, 1986). He insisted that gangs in Chinatown should be viewed as adult gangs.

My study does not support this observation. The average age of the 62 gang members who participated in my study was approximately 19 years. The majority (82%) were 20 years old or younger, and about one in three were 18 years old (see table 6.1). Only three subjects were in their late 20s or older. Most of the Chinese gang members who participated in this study were teenagers rather than adults; however, I did not interview any high-level gang leaders, and it is probable that the leaders may be older than their followers. Joe (1994) also found that most Chinese gang members in San Francisco were teenagers. My research suggests that Chinese gang members are not normally older than members of other ethnic gangs (Los Angeles County District Attorney, 1992; Conly et al., 1993).

Country of Origin and Ethnicity

The media often describe Chinese gangs as immigrant gangs, which implies that it is mainly foreign-born Chinese who join the gangs (Rice, 1977). For example, the 25 Ghost Shadows members convicted for racketeering activities in 1985 were all born abroad (Polsky, 1985). The majority of the gang members in my study were immigrants. However, more than one-third of them were born in America (see table 6.1). Joe (1994) also found that there are a substantial number of American-born Chinese in San Francisco's Chinese gangs. It is possible that, while mainly young immigrants joined Chinese gangs in the 1960s and 1970s, more and more American-born Chinese were lured into them in the 1980s and 1990s. Thus, theories on Chinese gangs formation would be flawed if they ignored the possibility that a growing number of American-born Chinese are joining gangs.

Among foreign-born subjects, most were born in either Hong Kong or China. The rest came from Vietnam, Taiwan, Korea, or Cambodia. Subjects born in Korea were all Koreans, whereas subjects from Vietnam and Cambodia included

Chinese, Vietnamese, and Cambodians. The average number of years the foreign-born subjects had been in America was 9.3, which indicates that most were not recent immigrants. This was also the case for members of San Francisco's Chinese gangs—their average length of stay in America, according to Joe (1994), was 10.8 years.

In terms of ethnicity, most subjects (68%) identified themselves as Cantonese or Toisanese (see table 6.1). This finding is not unusual because most immigrants

Table 6.1. Personal Characteristics of Chinese Gang Subjects ($N = 62$)

	N	%
Age		
16 and younger	7	11
17	8	13
18	19	31
19	8	13
20	9	14
21 and older	11	18
Place of birth		
United States	22	35
Hong Kong	15	24
Taiwan	3	5
China	9	15
Vietnam	5	8
Other	8	13
Ethnicity		
Cantonese/Toisanese	42	68
Taiwanese	4	6
Korean	3	5
Vietnamese	3	5
Vietnamese Chinese	3	5
Other	7	11
Education		
6th grade or less	1	2
7th to 9th grade	7	11
10th to 12th grade	40	64
College	14	23
Attending school or employed?		
Yes	49	79
No	13	21
Ever arrested?		
Yes	32	52
No	30	48
Ever imprisoned?		
Yes	9	15
No	53	85

from Hong Kong declare themselves as Cantonese and the Cantonese are the most dominant Chinese group in the United States (Zhou, 1992).

Over the past ten years, throughout the United States, there has been a noticeable increase in gang involvement among adolescents from Vietnam, Laos, Cambodia, Taiwan, the Philippines, China, and Korea (Butterfield, 1985; Badey, 1988; Vigil and Yun, 1990). In southern California, young immigrants from Vietnam, Laos, and Cambodia have been very active in gang activities (Butterfield, 1985). Two relatively new gangs in New York City, the Green Dragons and the Fuk Ching, were founded in the 1980s by Fujianese youths from China (Dannen, 1992). While ethnic differences within Chinese gangs appear to be fading, Chinese gangs are interested in recruiting mainly Asian youths. The more powerful gangs, such as the Flying Dragons and the Fuk Ching, now have factions consisting of mainly Korean or Fujianese teenagers, and the Born-to-Kill gang is made up predominantly of Vietnamese or Vietnamese-Chinese (English, 1995). Of the 62 male subjects in my study, only one was white. Table 1.1 (in chapter 1) shows which ethnic groups play dominant roles in Chinese gangs in New York City.

Education and Employment

Among the 62 subjects in my study, 38 (61%) were either full- or part-time college or high-school students (data not shown in table 6.1). Only a few stated that they spoke English poorly (10%) or read and wrote English inadequately (8% and 7%, respectively) (data not shown). In light of these findings, the contention by some observers that most Chinese adolescents enter gangs because of language barriers should be re-examined. Most (87%) had a 10th grade or higher educational level (see table 6.1). Among the 14 subjects who indicated that they had some college education, only two were not attending college at the time the interviews were conducted.

Contact with the Criminal Justice System

About half the subjects stated they had been arrested at least once (see table 6.1), mostly for minor crimes, and most were released without being imprisoned. During the interviews, several subjects jokingly referred to their arrests as being "invited to the precinct to sip tea." Only nine subjects (15%) were ever incarcerated. Their prison terms ranged from one to three years. Only a few of those arrested had been put on probation.

Family Background

The study found no evidence to support the hypothesis proposed by Posner (1988) that many Chinese gang members are living in America without their parents. Only three subjects indicated that either one or both parents were absent.

Only one subject stated that his parents were born in the United States. The average length of stay in the United States for the subjects' fathers was 14.7 years, and for the subjects' mothers, 14.4 years (see table 6.2). According to Joe (1994),

Table 6.2. Subjects' Family Characteristics
$(N = 62)$[a]

	N	%
Mother's occupation[b]		
Garment factory worker	35	61
Homemaker/unemployed	8	14
Store owner	3	5
Street vendor	2	3
Cashier	2	3
Other	8	14
Father's occupation[c]		
Restaurant worker	19	35
Garment factory worker	8	15
Unemployed	6	11
Driver	3	6
Retired or deceased	3	6
Other	15	27
Mother's education		
No formal education	5	13
Elementary school	6	15
Junior high school	8	20
Senior high school	18	45
College	3	7
Father's education		
No formal education	3	8
Elementary school	5	13
Junior high school	7	19
Senior high school	13	34
College	10	26
Living with parents?		
Yes	45	73
No	17	27

a. Number of missing observations: Mother's occupation = 4; Father's occupation = 8; Mother's education = 22; Father's education = 24. Percentages have been adjusted to account for this.

b. Average number of years in the United States: 14.4.

c. Average number of years in the United States: 14.7.

the average length of stay in the United States for the parents of San Francisco's Chinese gang members was also about 14 years.

Like the members of other ethnic gangs, most Chinese gang members in my study were from working-class families. Only one subject's father and three subjects' mothers were professionals. Most subjects' parents either worked in restaurants or in garment factories. Three subjects stated that their mothers had attended college, and 10 subjects reported that their fathers had attended college.

Most of the subjects lived with their parents (73%). Only seven subjects lived in "gang houses." I found no evidence to support the contention that young

Chinese gang members are under the constant authority and control of gang leaders or tong elders. The majority of them still live with their parents and are under the guidance (to the extent that adolescents ever are) of their parents.

Most subjects (65%) stated that they either occasionally or rarely saw their parents. Sung (1977) found that most immigrant parents work long hours in restaurants and garment factories and have little time for their children. More than half of the subjects (54%) indicated that they got along with their parents. And most (76%) said that their parents did not understand them. It is apparent that most subjects did not have a satisfactory relationship with their parents. However, it is not clear whether their dissatisfaction led them to join gangs or if their involvement in gang activities generated unhappy parent-child relationships.

Profiles

Profiles of two deceased gang leaders are provided here to bring the human element to the discussion of the characteristics of Chinese gang members. These brief case histories are constructed from newspaper and magazine articles.

MICHAEL CHEN

Before he was killed in 1982, Michael Chen was a leader of the Flying Dragons. Chen, a Cantonese, was born in China in 1950. When he was 13 years old, he immigrated to New York City from Hong Kong with his mother and a sister. There they joined his father, who had left China when his mother was pregnant with Chen. After his arrival, Chen worked as a delivery boy for a Chinese restaurant in upper Manhattan while attending Seward Park High School, near Chinatown. After his graduation from high school, Chen attended college briefly. Chen's father earned his living as a taxi driver.

In 1976, Chen was arrested in Queens for homicide, but the charges were dismissed. The following year, he was indicted in the slayings of two members of the rival Ghost Shadows during a brazen shoot-out in the crowded Pagoda Theater on East Broadway in Manhattan's Chinatown. However, he was later acquitted. Chen, who was known as "The Scientist" because of his "cool" and patient ways, rose to become the leader of the Flying Dragons in the late 1970s. He owned three expensive sports cars and dressed only in designer clothes. He was considered to be extremely good to his parents and especially affectionate toward his grandmother. Chen had a reputation for being polite and never seemed outrageous or rude. He did not drink, smoke, or gamble, and was generous toward others (Breslin, 1983). He did, however, have a weakness for women.

On March 13, 1983, Chen's body was found on the ground floor of the Hip Sing Credit Union, which was located across the street from the Hip Sing Association on Pell Street (Weiss, 1983). He was apparently murdered with a handgun. According to various sources, Chen received a telephone call in the early morning. He left his apartment, which was above the Hip Sing Credit Union, and showed up at a coffee shop adjacent to the credit union. Neighbors heard the gun shots, but no one bothered to call the police. No suspect was arrested, and the case has never been solved. The police theorize that the killing was carried out by people whom Chen knew well because he would not have gotten out of bed at that time to meet strangers. The fact that the credit union where Chen's body was found was operated by the Hip Sing Association, an organization affiliated with the Flying Dragons, also led law enforcement authorities to speculate that the murder was at least sanctioned by the Hip Sing.

Chen thought of himself as a businessman and had invested in a nightclub in Flushing, Queens, and a meat market and paper supply house in Manhattan. Before his demise, he allegedly told his friends he was contemplating completely dissociating himself from the gangland of Chinatown and transforming himself into a respectable businessman.

ANDY LIANG

Andy Liang was a member of the Fuk Ching gang and later a leader of the Tung On gang. Liang's family immigrated to the United States in 1982 from Guangdong, China. Liang was born in 1963. He attended school briefly after his arrival in America, but quit when he had trouble following the academic demands and joined the Fuk Ching gang. Liang's family, which consisted of his parents and a younger sister, lived in an apartment on Eldridge Street, in Manhattan's Chinatown. His parents worked long hours in garment factories to make ends meet.

Liang was in a car with two other Fuk Ching members in September 1985 when three men opened fire on them. One of the other Fuk Ching gang members in the car was killed. Liang's criminal record included a conviction for assault in 1985 in Brooklyn, for which he was put on probation, and a conviction for robbery in 1986 in midtown Manhattan, for which he was put on probation for five years. In 1986, Liang's 12-year-old sister was strangled to death by a deranged neighbor. In April 1987, Liang was shot three times on East Broadway by members of the Flying Dragons. He recovered from this attack only to be shot and killed on Division Street in June 1988 by a prominent Chinatown businessman. When the police arrived at the scene, they found Liang had been shot 19 times. The businessman was later acquitted on the grounds that he had been acting in self-defense (Fraser, 1991). Before his death, Liang had been living in a Tung On gang apartment located at the headquarters of the Tsung Tsin Association. The gang was providing protection to a gambling establishment within the building.

Entering and Leaving Gangs

Although the reasons for and social processes of recruitment and induction into African American and Hispanic gangs have been extensively studied by social scientists, little empirical work has been done on the movement of Asian youths into gangs. Chin (1990) hypothesizes that Chinese youths participate in delinquent behavior because they are unable to cope with problems they face in school, their families, and the community. Their transformation from delinquents to gang members is propelled by their association with adult crime groups and the internalization of the norms and values of the triad subculture. According to Toy (1992a), young Asians in San Francisco join gangs mainly because they need protection or because they grow up into the gangs. Song et al. (1992) theorizes that Chinese youths are involved in gang activities because of identity crises and negative reactions from law enforcement authorities. Many official reports and popular books on Chinese gangs charge that young people in Chinatown join gangs mainly because they are lured by the opportunity to make money (U.S. Department of Justice, 1985, 1988; Posner, 1988).

In this study, most respondents gave more than one reason for becoming gang members. The top five reasons, in order of importance, were money, protection, fun, brotherhood, and power/status (see table 6.3).

Half of the 62 subjects mentioned making money as one of the primary reasons for joining a gang. They were impressed by the amount of money gang leaders appeared to have and were excited by their generosity with money. The would-be gang members knew that by becoming a gang member they would be able to make at least some money by watching the streets or protecting gambling houses. Moreover, they were aware of the gangs' pervasive involvement in extor-

Table 6.3. Reasons for Joining
and Leaving Gangs[a]

Reasons for Joining (N = 62)	
Money	31
Protection	23
Fun	18
Brotherhood	15
Power/status	10
Girls/sex	9
Excitement	8
School problems	5
Family problems	4
Free food/materials	3
Drugs	2
Other	4
Reasons for Leaving (N = 32)	
Urged by family members	5
Saw that members got into trouble	5
Got arrested	4
Saw that members got killed	4
Went back to school	4
Gang life not glorious	3
Risky	3
Maturity	2
Can't make money	2
Police harassment	2
Other	1

a. Number of respondents who said these were reasons for joining or leaving gangs. Respondents could provide more than one reason.

tion and related crimes involving businesses in the community. One subject asserted that gang activity was "all about making money." Studies of other ethnic gangs also suggest that financial incentives are one of the most important factors in the decision to enter a gang (Taylor, 1990; Jankowski, 1991; Padilla, 1992).

The second most often cited reason for entering a gang was self-protection. Many subjects joined gangs because they were frequently attacked by school-mates, who may or may not have been gang members. The subjects found that hanging out with members of a Chinese gang was the most effective way to deter such attacks. One subject explained that he joined a Chinese gang because it offered him much-needed protection:

> I was attacked by black or Hispanic schoolmates several times. The teachers never listened to my side of the story. They stole my sports jacket, and they insulted me with racial slurs. My friends always came to help. I needed their friendship for self-protection. So I joined them.

Fun and brotherhood were also mentioned as major reasons that gangs were appealing to the subjects. One respondent said he joined a gang simply because he was asked to "play": "My friends knew some [Flying] Dragons. My friends asked me whether I would like to *po* [hang out] together and play, and do some dark society thing. I said, 'OK.'"[2]

Power/status was another reason many Chinese subjects gave for joining gangs. The respondents realized that being a gang member signified power and status, and this translated into the power to approach Chinese businesspeople for money and favors. Being a gang member also involved being feared by ordinary Chinatown residents, and gang members had the opportunity to be affiliated with some of the most powerful figures in the community.

Sex, women, excitement, school problems, and family problems were also mentioned by subjects as reasons for involvement in gangs. Only two subjects mentioned drug use as a reason for joining a gang. According to Fagan's study (1989), African Americans and Hispanics join gangs for the following reasons: material incentives, recreation, a place of refuge and camouflage, physical protec-tion, rebellion, and commitment to community. It appears that Chinese youths join gangs for reasons that are not dissimilar to those of youths from other ethnic groups.

Recruitment and Membership

It is not known how Chinese gangs recruit new members. Almost all the respon-dents in this study stated that they joined gangs voluntarily. Only one felt that he was somehow pressed to join. Over the past 25 years, there have been reports in local newspapers that adolescents were forced to join gangs in Chinatown (*World Journal*, 1980a). According to these reports, those who refused the invitation were severely beaten by gang recruiters. I found no evidence to substantiate these reports. One subject revealed that the intensity of his gang's recruitment de-pended on how many members were arrested: "If some brothers are arrested, we recruit more often, like every two months. Otherwise, once every six months."

Although the initiation ceremonies of triad societies are well documented (Morgan, 1960; Booth, 1991), little is known about how adolescents are inducted into Chinese gangs in the United States. Chin (1990) found that the Flying Dragons' initiation ceremony is similar to that of the triad societies. For example, new members have to take oaths, drink wine mixed with the blood of other new recruits, and pay tribute to *Guan Gong*.[3] A member of the Flying Dragons described the initiation ceremony:

> At the initiation ceremony, I had to take oaths, bow to the gods, and drink wine mixed with blood. Two *dai lo* and two uncles [tong members who play the role of middlemen between the tong and the gang] were present at the ceremony. After the ritual, one of the uncles gave me a *hung bao* with cash inside and congratulated me: "Now you are part of the family."

Another gang member also indicated that he was asked to take oaths when he joined: "I had to take the gang oaths. The ceremony was performed inside a restaurant."

However, not all Chinese gangs conduct an initiation ceremony. It seems that the non-tong-affiliated gangs are less likely to carry out initiation ceremonies than are gangs that are affiliated with tongs.[4] According to a subject who was a member of the non-tong-affiliated White Tigers gang: "I became a member by accepting their invitation. We went to a restaurant and celebrated. There was no initiation ceremony. We just drank together until we got drunk."

Another subject, a member of the non-tong-affiliated Born-to-Kill, confirmed the former's claim: "For Vietnamese, there was no ceremony. They introduced us to other members. We do not have a formal initiation ceremony."

Most subjects were extremely proud of their membership in a Chinese gang, at least initially. When asked how he felt after joining the Flying Dragons, a subject replied excitedly: "I felt very good, very powerful, very resourceful."

Dissociating: Reasons and Processes

My study suggests that membership in a Chinese gang does not last for life. Members did drop out of the gangs and did not experience retaliation from their peers for their actions. The reasons for leaving most often mentioned by those subjects who stated that they had left the gangs ($N = 32$, or about half of the sample) included being urged to leave by family members, seeing other members get into trouble, being arrested, seeing members of the same gang being killed, and deciding to go back to school (See table 6.3). Of the 32 former gang members in the sample, at the time of the interviews, 14 had left the gang less than a year ago, 8 had dropped out of the gang for one to two years, and the rest had dissociated from the gang for about three years. The average length of gang membership for the former gang members was about two years; and for the active gang members, it was about three years.

Some left the gangs because their family members were deeply concerned and anxious about their involvement in gang activities. In some cases, parents, siblings, or girlfriends urged the subjects to leave. In other cases, family members sent the subjects away, either abroad or out-of-state, so they could avoid gang peers. One subject indicated that he finally left his gang when his mother threatened to kill herself if he continued his gang association.

Some decided to leave their gangs because they had seen too many fellow gang members get into trouble with the law. One left because his *dai lo* was sent to jail. One street-level leader said he quit because his followers were constantly being arrested for getting into fights and he simply did not want to be bothered by these incidents anymore.

Some dropped out of the gangs after being arrested by police. For some of the respondents, being arrested amounted to what Garfinkel (1956) called a "degradation ceremony." Certain youths came to realize the risk of being incarcerated and decided that being a gang member was not worth it, especially when they found out that their *dai lo* might not bail them out if they were arrested. One member put it this way:

> Because my friends got into trouble with the law, we were running into a cage. It was like a cycle. You bailed out someone with money collected from protection rackets, you got caught, you had to pay more. A friend of mine was caught and needed $3,500 for bail. *Dai lo* said he didn't have the money. Then I told myself, "Forget about it. What's the point in being a member of the gang."

Others left their gangs after they witnessed close friends being killed. Under such circumstances, they either felt guilty for their friends' deaths or feared they might be murdered too. One subject gave the following account of his decision to leave his gang:

> A friend of mine was dancing with a girl from another gang. A guy pulled the girl away from my friend. We assumed he was a Tung On. We approached him and asked, "Who the hell are you?" He said, "If you want to know, we'll go outside." That's when we got outside. They had three guys. They had people outside carrying weapons. This guy shot at my friend. My friend was dying in my arms. We all left the scene before the police arrived. I still feel guilty for leaving my friend there to die. He might have survived if I had stayed there with him. I still have nightmares about the incident and see him in these dreams. I saw many other friends get killed. It's not worth it. Because they died for stupid reasons, like over a girl. After my close friend was killed, I was pretty determined to leave.

Still others left because they eventually came to realize that being a gang member was not as glorious as they thought before joining. They became disillusioned when they found that gang leaders were not really concerned for their well-being and that close friends may kill one another over money or women. They said there was no "righteousness" among gang peers and, after a while, extorting money from merchants could be not very glamorous. According to a subject:

> I felt like I had the potential to do something else. I felt that the life of a gangster was not glorious anymore. It is a way of life that is filthy and corrupt. Also, there were so many intergang fights. The gangs only know how to victimize their own people. It is really disgusting.

Another subject decided to leave because he realized that his gang activity was becoming more and more serious.

At the beginning, it was a lot of fun. However, later I found that this was a dead end. I committed some minor crimes, such as extortion and protecting gambling places, after I joined the gang. Later on, I began to get involved in serious crimes, such as assault and home-invasion robbery. It got more and more risky.

Leaving the gangs was not that difficult for most subjects. Most dropped out simply by not showing up at the gangs' hangouts. Their gang peers may have called them at home or at their beeper numbers, but if they ignored the calls, they were left alone after a while.

Some talked to their *dai lo*s about their decision to leave. They often said they wanted to go back to school or were tired of being a gang member. Interestingly, more often than not, their *dai lo*s were supportive and urged them to study hard. One said: "I talked to my *dai lo* that I was fed up with it. College is good for me. My *dai lo* said, 'Be a good kid.' It was fine with him."

However, a few were threatened when their *dai lo* or gang peers found out they planned to leave the gang. One subject was able to leave only because his elder brother was himself a senior member of the gang and was able to get him out: "I was just an ordinary member. I left Chinatown for about four months. My elder brother talked to someone. My brother was also a gang member. He said it wasn't an easy task. We were threatened."

Some were subjected to extortion by their gangs, and some were even assaulted. One subject said: "I had to pay thousands of dollars to my gang before they let me leave. I saved that money for many years from gang activities, so I didn't mind paying them."

On the basis of what former gang members had to say about their experiences in dissociating themselves from their gangs, it appears that the level of difficulty a gang member had in extricating himself depended on the rank he held in the gang, how much he knew about the gang, and whether he intended to join another gang, as well as what particular gang he belonged to, what his leader was like, and what reasons he cited for leaving. If the subject was an ordinary gang member who knew very little about his gang's involvement in more serious crime, he would be able to leave relatively easily. If, on the other hand, the subject was a senior gang member and had an intimate knowledge of gang activities and membership, he might not be allowed to leave his gang readily (Ng and Tharp, 1983).

Structural Characteristics

There are avid debates among gang researchers on how street gangs are organized, and many questions about this issue have been raised. How well organized and cohesive are gangs? Is their structure horizontal or vertical? Are there different ranks within a gang? How much control do gang leaders have on ordinary members? What are the rules and norms of the gang subculture, and how committed are gang members to these rules and norms? Are street gangs affiliated with adult crime groups? What is the relationship between gangs and the community? Can gangs be classified according to the uniqueness of their structure and activity?

Some researchers have proposed that some gangs are well-organized, hierarchical criminal organizations (Whyte, 1943; Cloward and Ohlin, 1960; Spergel, 1964; Taylor, 1990; Jankowski, 1991). According to these researchers, there is a division of labor among gang members, and leaders are in complete control of all gang activities. There are norms and rules for members to follow, and violators are severely punished. In sum, gangs are organized as paramilitary units rather than as collections of self-serving individuals. Taylor described what he called "corporate gangs" as follows:

> These well-organized groups have very strong leaders or managers. The main focus of their organization is participation in illegal money-making ventures. Membership is based on the worth of the individual to the organization. Promotion inside the infrastructure is based on merit, not personality. Discipline is comparable to that of the military, and goals resemble those of Fortune 500 corporations. Different divisions handle sales, marketing, distribution, enforcement, and so on. Each member understands his or her role and works as a team member. Criminal actions are motivated by profit. (1990: 7)

Other researchers have challenged the notion that gangs are well-organized entities (Yablonsky, 1970; Hagedorn, 1988; Moore, 1991). For them, most gangs are loosely organized, and gang leaders know very little about their followers' daily activities and exercise little control over them. The leadership structure either does not exist or it changes rapidly. Members come and go, gang activities are rarely planned, and most gangs lack any deliberate, rational organizational purpose. According to Hagedorn:

> Milwaukee's gangs come in a variety of forms and shapes, but none that looks like a pyramid. They are all age-graded, with the gang beginning as a group of friends and youth roughly the same age. As the group ages, a new age-graded grouping forms from neighbors, acquaintances, and relatives. (1988: 87–88)

According to law enforcement authorities, Chinese gangs are better organized than other ethnic gangs because they are closely associated with adult crime groups and are more involved in profit-generating criminal activities, such as extortion, the smuggling of aliens, gambling, and prostitution, which require the gangs to function as units with their own specific tasks (U.S. Department of Justice, 1988; U.S. Senate, 1992). Steady income from these illegal activities also enables Chinese gang leaders to enjoy control of their members, to restrain members from involvement in reckless violence, and to stabilize the hierarchical structure of the gangs. In brief, people in the law enforcement community generally agree that all Chinese gangs are "organized gangs" similar to Cloward and Ohlin's (1960) "criminal gangs," Spergel's (1964) "racket gangs," and Taylor's (1990) "corporate gangs."

Although there are official law enforcement assumptions about Chinese gang structure, there are no empirical data on the size, infrastructure, norms, and values of Chinese gangs. In the following sections, I will try to shed some light on the structure of Chinese gangs, by analyzing the information from my interviews with former and active gang members.

Size

The New York City Police Department's Asian Gang Intelligence Unit, which operates out of the Fifth Precinct, in Manhattan's Chinatown, can only guess at the size of the major gangs in their area. And Intelligence Division detectives who cover the entire city believe that a gang's size is not stable but that it is fluid and is built around a hard core of 20 to 30 members.

I asked the subjects in my study about gang size. Most were either reluctant to answer the question or not sure how many members actually belonged to their gang. Other studies have also found that gang members generally do not know how many people belong to their gangs at a given time (Yablonsky, 1970). Those in my study who volunteered an estimation were not consistent in their assessments of gang size. Nevertheless, I think it is worthwhile to present what they said about the size of their gangs.

A member of the Ghost Shadows said there were 70 to 80 active members in his gang, including those who were active in Queens. A subject who belonged to the Born-to-Kill (BTK) thought that there were some 150 core and 70 peripheral members in his gang. Another BTK member estimated that there were 300 members. A member of the Flying Dragons said his gang had about 200 members. A youth belonging to the Taiwan Brotherhood revealed that there were 12 to 15 core members and 40 to 50 peripheral members in his group. A member of the White Tigers said his gang had 10 core members and 20 to 30 peripheral members.[5]

After examining the data from the questionnaires and taking into consideration the information collected from informal talks with the subjects, we can safely say that there are hard-core and peripheral members in all the Chinese gangs in New York City. The smaller gangs such as the White Tigers, Green Dragons, Taiwan Brotherhood, and Golden Star appear to have a maximum of 20 core members and 50 peripheral members. Major gangs such as the Ghost Shadows, Flying Dragons, Tung On, Fuk Ching, and Born-to-Kill may have fewer than 100 core members and an unknown number of peripheral members. The number of members in a particular gang might change dramatically, especially when a gang is indicted by federal prosecutors as a racketeering enterprise or has been glamorized in the media after committing a reckless violent crime and attracts thrill seekers.

Faction and Clique

How cohesive are Chinese gangs? Are Chinese gangs monolithic organizations or coalitions of age-graded groups? These are important questions that need to be answered before we can fully understand the structure of Chinese gangs and the function that violence plays in them.

A unique aspect of Chinese gang structure is the prevalence of various factions within it—this is especially true of gangs based in Manhattan's Chinatown. For example, the Flying Dragons have six factions—three in Manhattan and three in Queens. Each of the three groups in Manhattan occupies a street—namely, Pell, the Bowery, and Grand. The Pell Street group consists of mainly American-born Chinese, and the other two groups are made up of predominantly Cantonese youths. The three Flying Dragons factions in Queens are the Chinese Flying Dragons, the Korean Flying Dragons, and the Grand Street faction in Flushing. Like the Flying Dragons, the Ghost Shadows have three groups in Manhattan's Chinatown—namely, the Mott, Bayard, and Mulberry factions. Each reigns in those particular streets in the Chinese community. The same is true for the Born-to-Kill, the Tung On, and the Fuk Ching. This study did not find factions among gangs based in Queens and Brooklyn.

According to my respondents, rivalry among factions is common. This is confirmed by the media in their many reports on incidents of intragang violence.[6] The Pell and the Grand factions (Manhattan) of the Flying Dragons are often in conflict with each other. In 1991, a member of the Grand faction was shot and killed by a member of the Pell faction. According to a member of the Grand faction, he was not allowed to appear in Pell Street. If he had to go there, he was obliged to inform the Pell group through his *dai lo* so that his coming and going would not be a surprise. Likewise, factional killings are not unusual among the Ghost Shadows. In 1991, there was a shooting between two factions of the Ghost Shadows, and an innocent bystander was killed by a stray bullet (Steinberg, 1991). In 1985, an outburst of violent activities among two rival groups of the Tung On shocked the Chinese community (Ibert, 1985). My data strongly suggest that there is little cooperation among the various factions of a Chinese gang and that these factions or subgroups can be considered gangs in and of themselves.

In New York City's Chinese gangs, each faction may consist of two or more cliques. Like other ethnic gangs (Los Angeles County District Attorney, 1992), Chinese gangs depend on cliques as their basic building blocks. However, Chinese gang cliques are not formed according to age, as Hagedorn (1988) found was the case with Milwaukee's non-Asian gangs, but rather are headed by clique leaders who have executive authority at the street level. The relationship between a clique leader and his followers is probably the strongest relationship within the hierarchy of a Chinese gang, regardless of whether or not the gang has factions. Cliques that belong to a faction may compete with one another for the attention of the faction leader, but their relationship appears to be much more cordial than the relationship between factions.[7]

My data suggest that non-tong-affiliated gangs appear to be more cohesive than tong-affiliated gangs. This may be because non-tong-affiliated gangs are smaller and lack competing factions. Because there are more direct interactions among members of non-tong-affiliated gangs, there are fewer intragang conflicts than there are in tong-affiliated gangs. Also because smaller amounts of money are at stake, there tends to be less friction. In tong-affiliated gangs, cooperation among factions is almost nonexistent; however, as has been noted, cliques within a faction seem to be able to coexist rather peacefully.

Affiliation with Adult Organizations

According to local and federal authorities, certain Chinese gangs in San Francisco and New York City are closely associated with adult organizations known as tongs.

Those Chinese gangs function as "street muscle" for the tongs, performing such tasks as guarding gambling clubs and massage parlors sanctioned by the adult group, collecting debts for gambling clubs, protecting the territory of the adult organization from outsiders, and occasionally working as couriers for heroin trafficking groups (U.S. Department of Justice, 1985, 1988; U.S. Senate, 1992). According to the authorities, those Chinese gangs are tightly controlled by tongs, there is an alliance between those gangs and the tongs, and the tong-affiliated gangs are better organized and tend to be more involved in income-generating criminal activities than non-tong-affiliated gangs (Bresler, 1981; Posner, 1988, Kinkead, 1992).

Other observers, mainly researchers in California and Canada, have claimed that gangs are only loosely affiliated with tongs and that tongs exert little or no control over gangs. Moreover, there has been no evidence to date to sustain the conclusion that gangs and tongs are affiliated on an organizational level: only certain tong members are associated with gang leaders (Dubro, 1992; Toy, 1992b; Joe, 1994). Based on data collected from 70 gang members in San Francisco, Toy concluded that:

> Contrary to popular belief, tongs do not have direct control of gangs nor are the arrangements permanent. Tong members often use certain respectable gang leaders as liaisons between the tong and the gangs in order to carry out specific criminal activities. More often than not, the average gang member is not aware of the particulars of this connection. Tongs have had little to do with the actual recruitment of gang members; they only play a part in financing the gang. In doing so, they enable selected gangs to become recognized and powerful. (1992b: 656)

Joe also reached the conclusion that the relationship between gangs and tongs in the Bay Area was "nonexistent":[8]

> The majority of members in the eight groups [studied] knew little or nothing about the tongs as well as triads. Although the SSs [Suey Sings] and the WCs [Wah Chings] have been "associated" with two Bay Area tongs in the past, their current connections are nonexistent or tenuous at best. Most teenage and adult members in these two institutionalized groups were not aware of the tongs although a few of them mentioned that these were the elders in Chinatown. (1994: 404)

Toy's and Joe's findings, however, may not be applicable to the situation on the East Coast. At the 1991 U.S. Senate hearings on Asian organized crime, in response to Senator William Roth's questions, a member of the Ghost Shadows described the tong-gang relationship in New York City as follows:

> Mr. Chu: The present relationship, the Ghost Shadows protect the territory and interests of the On Leong Association. They have the backing of the On Leong Association to operate in these territories. Ghost Shadows, like in my incident, when they are fugitives from the law, it is the On Leong Association that takes care of them, sends them to different cities to avoid capture or prosecution. They

also send the Ghost Shadows out to the different chapters to carry out any means of enforcement that they have to do.

Senator Roth: Could the Ghost Shadows survive as a separate organization without the On Leong Tong?

Mr. Chu: Financially, they can survive without the On Leong Association. They are now more dependent on the moneys they make from the drug dealings and extortions. To operate in that certain territory, they have to have the approval and the backing of the On Leong Association. If they fell into the bad graces of the On Leong, the On Leong would replace them with another street gang. (U.S. Senate, 1992: 34–36)

My data appear to be more in accord with the Ghost Shadows member's testimony than with the research findings and conclusions of Toy and Joe. I found that, with the exception of the Born-to-Kill, the major Manhattan-based Chinese gangs are affiliated with certain adult organizations. Certain tong members who are known as *ah kung* (grandfather) or *shuk foo* (uncle) serve as mentors for the gang members and play the role of liaison between tongs and gangs. During the interviews, gang members often talked about those mentors with respect and fear. When asked how he viewed the *ah kung* of his gang, a subject exclaimed, "*Ah kung* is very ferocious, very powerful, very capable."

I found that most tong-affiliated gangs have more than one principal or primary leader. For example, the Flying Dragons have two or more *dai dai lo* (big big brothers), who are very close to certain officers or members of the Hip Sing Association. These *dai dai lo*s control the various factions of the gang. Each faction has a *dai lo* (big brother) and one or more street-level *dai lo* (clique leader) who are known as *yee lo* (second brother) or *saam lo* (third brother). Each street-level *dai lo* is in charge of several *ma jai*s (little horses) or *leng jai*s (little kids).[9]

The *dai dai lo*s take orders from one or more *ah kung* or *shuk foo*. The *dai dai lo*s then convey orders to the *dai lo*s, who in turn relay them to the *yee lo*s or *saam lo*s, and the latter provide instructions and orders to the *ma jai*s or *leng jai*s. Most instructions from the *ah kung*s to the gangs have to do with collecting gambling debts and protecting gambling dens and prostitution houses in the tong's territory. I did not find the *ah kung*s or *shuk foo*s to be actively involved in commanding gang members to commit violent crimes or participate in international crimes such as heroin trafficking or the smuggling of aliens. According to the subjects in my study, the only connection between tongs and gangs appears to be around gambling debt collection. Two subjects made the following comments about the tong-gang connection:

We rarely take orders from the affiliated-tong, unless someone owes gambling debts to the tong or certain gambling places. We go collect the money for them.

We hang out at the adult organization's building and play mahjong in their gambling places. The uncle will tell the *dai lo* what to do.

The *ma jai*s [ordinary gang members] seem to have little knowledge of their faction *dai lo*s, nor of the *dai dai lo*s, *ah kung*s, or *shuk foo*s. They take orders only from their immediate leader, who is the street-level *dai lo*. They are in-

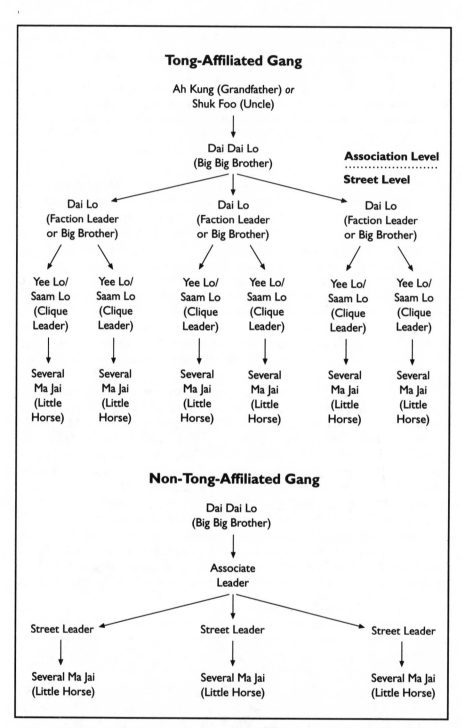

Figure 6.1 Typical Organizational Structure of Tong-Affiliated and Non-Tong-Affiliated Gangs

structed by gang leaders not to ask questions about the leadership structure. Likewise, the street-level *dai los* are only familiar with their immediate leaders— the faction *dai los*—and rarely have the opportunity to deal directly with the *dai dai los* or *ah kungs*. Thus, there is evidence that tong-affiliated Chinese gangs are hierarchical. Ordinary gang members may meet those above their immediate leaders only during their initiation ceremony. Figure 6.1 shows how factions and cliques are related to the key leaders and to the adult organizations.

In sum, most Chinese gangs and the tongs are linked through certain tong members and gang leaders. The limited number of tong members who serve as *ah kungs* may or may not be officers of the tongs. My data do not support the assumption that there is a full-fledged organizational-level alliance between tongs and gangs. If a tong needs help from its affiliated gang, the message will be conveyed to the *dai dai lo* by the *ah kung*. The *dai dai los* will then make a decision about which faction might be best suited for carrying out the *ah kungs* orders.

Some *dai dai los* are also officers of the affiliated tong. Before his arrest for heroin trafficking, a *dai dai lo* of the Flying Dragons was elected national manager of the Hip Sing Association, an important position within the organization. When the gang leader was robbed of $40,000 in cash and shot by unknown assailants at an attorney's office in Chinatown, the Hip Sing Association posted a $10,000 reward for information that might lead to solving the case.[10] Likewise, the highest leaders of the Ghost Shadows and the Tung On gangs have, at times, served as officers of their affiliated adult organizations. Some ordinary gang members also join the affiliated tongs, but it is not clear why some do and others do not.

On occasion, the relationship between tongs and gangs is established not only through formal appointments but also by means of family ties. For example, in the late 1980s and early 1990s, leadership of the On Leong Merchant Association and the Ghost Shadows gang was believed to be controlled by three brothers. J. Caleb Boggs III, staff counsel to the Senate's Permanent Subcommittee on Investigations testified:

> The president of the On Leong Association is Wing Wah Chan. Wah was previously New York Chapter President until his brother, Wing Yueng Chan, resigned as national president in April, 1989. A third brother, Wing Lok Chan, aka "Lok Jai," is the main leader of the affiliated Ghost Shadows gang. (U.S. Senate, 1992: 67)

Likewise, the younger brother of the president of the Tung On Association was alleged to be a former leader of the Tung On gang (Meskil, 1989). Table 1.1 (in chapter 1) shows the affiliation between gangs and tongs in Manhattan's Chinatown.

Territory

Every Chinese gang in New York City maneuvers in its own territory. When subjects were asked whether their gangs had a territory, all but one answered negatively. Manhattan's Chinatown is divided into several gang turfs, and each gang normally control two or three blocks (see figure 1.1 in chapter 1). The gang territories in Queens and Brooklyn are more spread out, with the Green Dragons in control of Jackson Heights and Elmhurst, the White Tigers and the Taiwan Brotherhood in control of Flushing, and the Golden Star in control of Brooklyn.

Tong-affiliated gangs usually claim those streets belonging to the adult organization with which they are associated. For example, the Ghost Shadows' major territory is Mott and Bayard Streets, and it is no coincidence that the adult organization affiliated with the Ghost Shadows, the On Leong Association, also reigns in these two streets. Likewise, the Hip Sing Association is located on Pell Street, and the Flying Dragons, the gang affiliated with the Hip Sing, has a strong hold on Pell Street. Since most Chinatown gangs have more than one faction, each faction normally occupies one block.

Division of Labor

According to my survey of Chinese gang members, some gangs, especially those not affiliated with a tong, have no distinctive division of labor. Members are considered by the *dai lo* and among themselves as equals. In the non-tong-affiliated gangs, members are collectively involved in extortion, fighting, and other activities. In the tong-affiliated gangs, however, there is some division of labor, and certain members are assigned by the *dai lo* to be street watchers, debt collectors, protection money collectors, or enforcers. Members of tong-affiliated gangs do not have the ready access to their *dai lo*s that members of non-tong-affiliated gangs do, possibly because tong-affiliated gangs are in general much larger.

Gang Lifespan

Table 6.4, which is based on media accounts and gang intelligence reports, shows when Chinese gangs were established and their lifespans. Of the 15 gangs listed, only five have dissolved. The Continentals, the first and only gang of American-born Chinese, disappeared from Chinatown quickly because it could not compete with gangs of predominantly foreign-born Chinese, such as the Ghost Shadows and the Flying Dragons. The Continentals' inability to integrate with a tong also diminished its status within the community. The Ching Yee became obsolete after two members were brutally murdered by a rival gang. The White Eagles collapsed because the gang was expelled from Mott Street by the On Leong Association and replaced by the Ghost Shadows. After several of its leaders were ambushed on Mott Street by the Ghost Shadows, the Black Eagles gang also faded from Chinatown. The Kam Lun gang lasted less than a year because of the downfall of the affiliated Kam Lun Association, which was ruthlessly attacked by a rival group. The Ghost Shadows and the Flying Dragons, two gangs that control the core areas of Chinatown, have existed for more than a quarter of a century. They are deeply entrenched in the community because of their affiliation with two of the most powerful community associations. As long as the tongs remain in control of Chinatown and the gangs are able to maintain good relationships with the tongs, it is unlikely they will be removed from the community.

Table 6.4. Lifespan of New York City's Chinese Gangs:
1960–present

Name	Period	Lifespan (in years)
Continentals	1961–1964	3
Ching Yee	1964–1970	6
White Eagles	1964–1980	16
Black Eagles	1967–1980	13
Ghost Shadows	1966–present	30
Flying Dragons	1967–present	29
Tung On	1974–present	22
White Tigers	1980–present	16
Hung Ching	1980–present	16
Golden Star	1980–present	16
Kam Lun	1982–1983	1
Born–to–Kill	1983–present	13
Fuk Ching	1983–present	13
Green Dragons	1986–present	10
Taiwan Brotherhood	1989–present	7

Norms and Rules

According to subcultural theorists, a gang represents a subcultural group with its own norms and values (A. Cohen, 1955; W. Miller, 1958; Wolfgang and Ferracuti, 1982). Research has shown that certain gang norms are similar to the norms prevalent in the gang's underclass community. Chin (1990) proposed that a specific system of norms and values is closely followed by Chinese gang members. He concluded that the norms and values of the Chinese secret societies, triads, tongs, and gangs are compatible with and shared by members of a Chinese criminal subculture historically and popularly known as *jiang hu*, or the "dark society."[11] In order to understand the behavioral patterns of gang members, their coping mechanisms, and the sources of gang conflicts and tensions, it is important to examine some of the norms and values that characterize and define the gangs.

Some of the norms and rules most often mentioned by my subjects were:

- Do not go to another gang's or another faction's territory without good reason or the permission of your *dai lo*.
- Do not look for trouble, especially by engaging in street fighting or reckless shootings.
- Do not betray your gang—do not leak information about your gang to outsiders, especially when you are arrested and interrogated by police.
- Do not threaten store owners when they refuse to pay protection or extortion money— you should know how to collect the money without threats or the use of force.
- Do not hang out with members of rival gangs.
- Do not use drugs.
- Do not become involved in heroin dealing.
- Listen to the *dai lo* and follow his instructions carefully.
- If you see members of another gang on your turf, beat them up.
- Respect the *ah kungs*.

- Do not kill anyone who belongs to the same gang.
- Do not flirt with another member's girlfriend.
- Do not ask too many questions about gang business.

A member who violates these norms and rules might be punished by his peers or *dai lo*, either lightly or severely. He could be physically assaulted or killed. One subject had the following to say about punishment for violators: "If you break the rules, you get beat up. I saw a lot [of this sort of punishment]. Like if you did something wrong, you have to light up a cigarette and have to burn your arm or palm. The *dai lo* may get his follower killed if the latter joins a rival gang."

When asked why and how certain members are promoted and become leaders, my subjects cited the following qualities or conditions that are considered by primary gang leaders and tong members as essential for leadership. Leaders must:

- Be able to recruit many followers.
- Be good at dealing with business owners—that is, be capable of collecting money from merchants in the territory regularly without using threats and violence.
- Possess a stable source of income (either legitimate or illegitimate) and be generous with money.
- Be willing and capable of negotiating with rival gang leaders when there are inter-gang or intragang conflicts.
- Have good relationships with elders of the affiliated tong.
- Be trusted by the primary leader.
- Have guts and be aggressive.
- Know how to make money.
- Be low-key.
- Be good at interpersonal relationships in general.

When someone is promoted and becomes a leader, that does not mean the position is permanent. On some occasions, a *dai lo* might be either forced to leave the gang or killed. One subject provided a chilling account of promotion and demotion within his gang:

> If a *dai lo* got killed or jailed, someone will be promoted. In this situation, everybody has an equal chance of being promoted. However, even after one is promoted as a leader, he may be disliked by *shuk foo*. If that's the case, *shuk foo* could put him [the *dai lo*] up at the altar [meaning, have him killed]. *Shuk foo* is a very ferocious person. He makes the decision.

Nevertheless, according to the data collected from the gang study and my years of observation of the development of Chinatown gangs in New York City, gang leadership is relatively stable. Several well-known *dai dai los* have been able to remain in power for many years. Very rarely has a *dai dai lo* or a faction *dai lo* been disposed of by the affiliated tong or by their followers.

Summary

In examining the data collected from Chinese gang members in New York City, I found few differences between members of Chinese gangs and members of other ethnic gangs. Members of Chinatown gangs, like members of gangs in the black and Hispanic communities, are predominantly underclass adolescents who enter the gangs for material gain, protection, power, and excitement. Also, the average length of membership of Chinese gang members appears to be similar to that of members of other ethnic gangs. There is no evidence to suggest that once a Chinese youth enters a gang, he will be unable to dissociate himself from the gang or be forced to remain in the gang for a prolonged period of time.

The connection between street gangs and adult organizations is a structural aspect of Chinese gangs that is different from that of other ethnic gangs. Although some researchers have found black and Hispanic gangs to have been affiliated with adult groups at one time or another (Moore, 1978; Vigil, 1988), the relationships appeared to be less permanent and pervasive than such relationships in the Chinese community. However, the gang-tong linkage does not seem to tighten gang cohesion, and in this respect there is little difference between Chinese gangs and other ethnic gangs.

My findings do not support the assertion made by some observers that a well-organized, monolithic, hierarchical criminal cartel, sometimes referred to as the "Chinese Mafia," exists in the United States and in many other nations. Secret societies, triads, tongs, and gangs are alleged to be the building blocks of this organization. My findings also do not support the notion that a chain of command exists among these various crime groups or that they coordinate with one another routinely in international crimes such as heroin trafficking, money laundering, and the smuggling of aliens. Instead, my data suggest that in most cases gangs are not controlled by tongs. Rather, the gangs work for tongs and adult crime groups on an ad hoc basis. Furthermore, gang cohesion is strained by the lack of cooperation among the various factions of a specific gang.

An important aspect of Chinese gang structure is the existence of a small number of tong members who serve as mentors for tong-affiliated gangs. According to my subjects, these mentors, who are called *ah kung* or *shuk foo*, appear to play an important role as criminal middlemen in connecting the tongs and the gangs, and in providing gang leaders and ordinary gang members with guidance in developing and nurturing criminal careers within the Chinese community. The law-enforcement community appears to know very little about these tong members, and as a result, most of them remain immune to prosecution. Most officers of the tongs are not *ah kungs*, and some of the *ah kungs* may not even be listed as tong officers. Ordinary gang members do not have access to the *ah kungs*, which makes the task of identifying and prosecuting the *ah kungs* all the more difficult.[12]

After examining some of the structural characteristics of Chinese gangs, we may ask what constitutes the most appropriate label for Chinese gangs. Are Chinatown gangs similar to Cloward and Ohlin's "criminal gangs" and Taylor's "corporate gangs"? Or are they comparable to Cloward and Ohlin's "violent gangs" and Taylor's "territorial gangs"? In order to answer these questions, we need to take into account the following: (1) not all Chinese gangs in the United States are alike, and there appear to be dissimilarities between Chinese gangs on the west coast and those operating on the east coast of the United States; and (2) even on the east coast, there are two major types of Chinese gangs—those that are affiliated with tongs and those that are independent. Before we can decide which types of classification are most appropriate for Chinese gangs, we must examine the criminal patterns of Chinese gangs. Consequently, I will first examine gang aggression in chapter 7 and than explore the patterns of Chinese gang criminality, other than extortion and violence, in chapter 8.

7

Gang Violence

Chinese gangs have a reputation for violence (Daly, 1983; Dannen, 1992). Since the mid–1970s, violence has often erupted in the Chinese communities in North America. In 1977, for instance, five people were killed and eleven were wounded when three assailants opened fire on customers inside a Chinese restaurant in San Francisco's Chinatown (Ludlow, 1987). In 1982, masked gunmen shot dead three young Chinese and seriously wounded seven others in a bar in New York City's Chinatown (Blumenthal, 1982). Similar incidents have occurred in Seattle (Emery, 1990), Boston (Butterfield, 1991), Vancouver (Gould, 1988; Dubro, 1992), and Toronto (Kessel and Hum, 1991; Lavigne, 1991; Moloney, 1991). Most of these incidents were reported to be related to Chinese gangs, and in some, innocent bystanders were wounded or killed.[1] Law enforcement authorities believe that the emergence of Vietnamese and Fujianese gangs, drastic shifts in political alliances among Chinese community organizations, rapid but destabilizing economic expansion in Chinese communities, and the involvement of Chinese gangs in heroin trafficking and in the smuggling of aliens have created an escalation in gang violence over the past few years (U.S. Senate, 1992).

Although there have been anecdotal reports in the media and de facto charges made in official indictments, there has been no reliable information on the frequency and seriousness of aggression involving Chinese gangs.[2] The patterns and causes of such aggression have yet to be empirically and systematically examined.

Lack of research has limited the development of theoretical explanations for gang violence in the Chinatowns of North America, although two hypothetical interpretations of Chinese gang violence emerged in the late 1970s. In the first, according to Thompson (1976), Chinese gang violence is a cover-up for racketeering activities such as gambling and prostitution. Violence among Chinese gangs is therefore thought to be condoned or encouraged by adult criminal groups in order to divert police attention from rampant organized crime activities in the community.

The second perspective, in many ways similar to the first in its orientation, was proposed by Takagi and Platt (1978). They hypothesize that violence in American Chinatowns is not instigated by members of street gangs. Instead, adult organizations, which control organized crime and the community's political economy, plot violent activities in the Chinese community. Takagi and Platt conclude:

> We have tried to carefully distinguish two different kinds of crime in Chinatown: "organized" rackets and violence associated with those who control the political structure and legitimate business; and ordinary "street" crime. The violence so much in the news today has more to do with the former than the latter. . . . There is no evidence to support the argument that violence is related to youth gangs. Organized violence appears to be related to the business of protection rackets and political intimidation of progressive organizations rather than to an "irrational" youth "subculture." (1978: 22)

In this chapter, I will examine the participation rate of gang members in gang violence in New York City's Chinatown; the frequency, typology, and causes of such violence; and the restraining mechanisms on such violence. Specifically, I will estimate the general level of aggressive behavior among members of Chinese gangs and explain how and why Chinese gang members direct their aggression toward members of rival gangs, members of their own gangs, and nongang victims. The mechanisms used to check gang aggression in the Chinese community will also be discussed. Finally, prior explanations of Chinese gang violence will be evaluated in light of the findings. Instrumental violent crime such as robbery and kidnapping will be discussed separately in the following chapter, which focuses on profit-generating gang activities other than extortion.

Media Reports

Between 1968 and 1992, at least 340 incidents of Chinese gang-related violence were reported in the newspapers of New York City.[3] An analysis of the media accounts suggests that during that time, there was a steady rise in the amount of Chinese gang-related violent activity. However, it is not certain whether the media reports reflect an actual increase in gang-related violence or simply a propensity among journalists to report gang violence in Chinatown more often.

Most Chinese gang-related violence reported in the media includes either assaults on (30%) or murders of (44%) gang members. Only 42 incidents of violence (13%) were reported to be robbery related, and only 10 (3%) were reported to be extortion related.

According to media accounts, 51 percent of the incidents occurred in the streets. However, unlike other ethnic gangs (Sanders, 1994), Chinese gangs were rarely involved in drive-by shootings. Violent confrontations among gang members often erupted in the streets when two groups came into contact with each other either accidentally or intentionally. Other high-risk places for gang aggression included recreational centers such as billiard halls or movie theaters (17%), public places such as parking lots (11%), restaurants (8%), home of the victims (7%), and business premises (6%).

Almost half (49%) of the violent incidents covered by the media took place in core areas of Manhattan's Chinatown, 20 percent in Queens, and 10 percent in Brooklyn. If the violent episodes that occurred on the outskirts of Manhattan's

Chinatown (8%) and in other parts of Manhattan (7%) are included, then about 64 percent of all incidents of violence happened in Manhattan. The media data show that a gun was used in 86 percent of the violent incidents and a knife was involved in at least 6 percent of them.

More than half (53%) of the incidents of violence involved only one victim. Most (82%) involved Chinese offenders and Chinese victims. In only 14 incidents (5%) were non-Asian victims involved, and none of the non-Asian victims was reported to be a gang member. About 42 percent of the incidents resulted in the death of one or more victims. Victims were killed execution-style in 54 of the incidents (17%).

In brief, an examination of media accounts of Chinese gang violence suggests that most incidents of violence occurred in the streets of Manhattan's Chinatown. In most circumstances, a gun was used. However, only half of the incidents led to the death of one or more victims. And most incidents of violence involved only Chinese gang members. Whether the media accounts present an accurate portrayal of gang violence remains to be seen.

Participation and Frequency

Respondents in my survey of gang members reported that they were fairly active in violent activities such as simple assault, shooting, and robbery. Almost all (96%) admitted they had assaulted someone in 1991, the year prior to the interviews.[4] Eighty-two percent revealed that they had committed at least one robbery, and 52 percent acknowledged that they had used a gun against someone in 1991 (see table 7.1).[5] My respondents appeared to have a higher participation rate in simple assault (beating), aggravated assault (shooting), and robbery than did the gang members in other ethnic communities studied by Fagan (1989). These findings are consistent with the findings of the Los Angeles County District Attorney (1992) that members of Asian gangs are relatively active in violent crimes.

Table 7.1 shows that most respondents were regularly (i.e., three or more times per year) involved in simple assault (93%) and robbery (70%). About one out of two subjects (67%) said that they were frequently (i.e., 12 or more times per year) involved in simple assaults and 54 percent in robberies, while only 5 percent said that they frequently opened fire on others. Again, in comparing these figures with Fagan's (1989) study, it seems that Chinese gang members are more regularly and frequently involved in assaults and robberies than are members of other ethnic gangs, though members of other ethnic gangs may be more frequent participants in shootings or in chronic aggravated assault.

According to the data presented in table 7.1, participation in assault was second only to theft of goods and services, which was the most frequent reported criminal activity.[6] Frequent involvement in simple assaults was less likely than frequent involvement in providing protection to illegal businesses, theft of goods or services, and alcohol use. However, the respondents were more likely to engage in violent crimes than to participate in other drug and nondrug crimes traditionally considered typical gang activities. Also, participation rates and frequency

Table 7.1. Frequency and Participation Rates in Criminal Activities
        (*N* = 62)

Self-Reported Criminal Activities	At Least Once	Regular: Three or more Times	Frequent: Twelve or more Times
Individual violent acts, prior year			
Simple assault	96%	93%	67%
Robbery	82	70	54
Shooting	52	33	5
Victimization of businesses			
Theft of goods or services	97	93	87
Protection	90	88	78
Asking for lucky money	86	82	61
Forced sales	68	53	22
Drug use[a]			
Alcohol	94	91	73
Marijuana	52	37	21
Crack	10	3	0
Cocaine	10	3	2
Heroin	8	2	0

a. Reported involvement in a drug sale was 17%.

of involvement in two types of violent crime—robbery and shooting—were considerably higher than frequency of hard drug use. Thus, we may conclude that violent activities such as assault, robbery, and shooting were frequent activities among Chinese gang members we interviewed.

The gang members we interviewed also indicated that their peers' were involved in such activities. When asked about how many members of their gangs were involved in a list of crimes, most (71%) responded that fighting was the activity that most gang members were regularly involved in (see table 7.2). Sixty-

Table 7.2. Frequency and Participation Rates in Criminal Activities
        by Other Gang Members (*N* = 62)

Reports of Others[a]	At Least a Few	Several	Most
Fighting	100%	97%	71%
Extortion[b]	100	95	68
Guarding gambling houses	97	83	62
Gambling	96	81	52
Drug use	81	54	12
Drug sales	72	47	8

a. The question presented was, How many members of your gang were actively involved in the following activities in the past year?

b. The word extortion here denotes all four kinds of gang victimization of business owners mentioned above.

eight percent of the respondents indicated that most members of their gang were involved in extortion, and 62 percent believed that most members of their gang were providing protection to illegal gambling establishments. Thus, fighting appears to be the most prevalent activity among Chinese gangs, surpassing extortion and guarding gambling establishments, the two activities suspected by law enforcement authorities of being the main activities of Chinese gangs (U.S. Senate, 1992).

Table 7.1 also suggests that gang members are relatively inactive in hard drug use, although they do consume alcohol. Only about one in two gang subjects used marijuana at least once in 1991, and only one in five reported frequent marijuana use. Only 8 to 10 percent of the respondents reported having used crack, cocaine, or heroin at least once in 1991. About 2 to 3 percent of them admitted to regular use of hard drugs, but none admitted to frequent use of crack or heroin. In comparison, more than 70 percent of the Los Angeles gang members are reported to use drugs, usually about once a week (Los Angeles County District Attorney, 1992). Other researchers (Fagan et al., 1986; Hagedorn, 1988) also reported extensive drug use by Hispanic and African-American gang members. The Chinese gang members in my sample appeared to be more interested in gambling than in drug use. Over half the respondents reported that most of their fellow gang members were active in gambling (table 7.2). Since guarding gambling establishments is a major function of Chinese gangs, many gang members may have learned to gamble while protecting gambling establishments.

Although law enforcement authorities and the media have attributed the dramatic increase in Southeast Asian heroin in the United States to Chinese gang involvement (Kerr, 1987a; Bryant, 1990; U.S. Senate, 1992), only 17 percent of my subjects reported that they had ever participated in a drug sale. According to one report, about half of the Los Angeles gang population sells drugs in any given year (Los Angeles County District Attorney, 1992). This issue will be discussed in detail in the following chapter.

Typology and Causes

Gang violence is a term used to refer to violent activities involving gang members. Gang violence may be classified into three types, depending on the gang affiliation of the victim: intergang violence, intragang violence, and violence directed at nongang victims. In the first, the aggressor and the victim belong to different or rival gangs. In the second, both the aggressor and the victim belong to the same gang. Interfactional and intrafactional disputes may also be included in this category. In the third type of gang violence, the victims are usually not affiliated with any gang.

Intergang Violence

Most respondents (92%) indicated that they had been involved in at least one confrontation with a different gang. The most frequently cited reason for inter-

Table 7.3. Causes of Gang Violence ($N = 62$)

Reason	Intergang Conflicts	Intragang Conflicts
Staring/provocative attitude	35[a]	5[a]
Turf warfare	28	1
Girls	6	13
Revenge	3	2
Money	3	15
Misunderstandings	1	6
Pride	1	1
No reason	1	0
Insubordination/disciplinary problems	0	4
Power struggle	0	7
Verbal argument	0	4
Drunkenness	0	1
Jealousy	0	1
Drugs	0	1

a. N = Number of respondents who said these were reasons for conflict. Respondents could provide more than one reason.

group clashes was "staring" (or "looking down") (see table 7.3). These incidents were spontaneous responses to being stared at or being asked "Where are you from?" or "Who is your *dai lo*?" Gang members interpreted this sort of behavior as disrespectful and challenging. A person who stares at another is considered arrogant and aggressive. Asking a gang member the identity of his leader is also construed as a serious challenge; it conveys an intention to belittle or degrade the reputation or power of a gang. These incidents were most likely to take place in recreational centers and restaurants located in neutral areas. Two respondents described separate violent incidents sparked by staring, both of which ended tragically:

> We went to a party and saw that people there were very arrogant. There were a lot of different gangs, and they were staring at one another. I asked my friends whether we needed more men [for support]. They said no, so we began to dance. One guy was perhaps jealous because of whom I was dancing with. He asked me, "Where are you from? Where is your *dai lo*?" I pointed at my *dai lo*. He said, "I want you to leave. . . ." I hit the guy. Everybody jumped in and shots were fired. My friend had a gun. I only had a knife. He fired shots. . . . When we went back a few days later, we were arrested. A friend of mine killed one guy and wounded two.

> We fought with members of a gang in Queens. It happened in a pool hall. My brothers started the conflict. I didn't know why. I wasn't there. I think it was because members of the Queens gang were staring at us. That's why we got into an argument. I got a call from my gang. I went there, but everybody was gone. One of my brothers was killed.

More often than not, staring at members of a rival gang only resulted in fistfights. A respondent described a typical violent incident caused by staring:

I was involved in a fight with the Ghost Shadows. We were staring at one another. They asked, "Who are you staring at?" and pulled out a gun. They threw the first punch. We thought they had only two guys, but after the fight started, three or more of them were involved. We punched them back. After the fight, we were lying on the floor. They told us they were the Ghost Shadows and left.

The display of aggressive attitudes by gang members also triggers conflict. In some cases, trivial matters can set off an incident. Some respondents reported that they attacked other gang members simply because they disapproved of the other gang members' appearance: "We beat up a group of Fujianese at a night club because we didn't like the way they looked. They looked disgusting."

Turf is the second most often cited reason for intergang aggression. As was discussed earlier, all the active gangs in Manhattan's Chinatown have their own turf, which normally includes the commercial areas surrounding the headquarters of the adult organization with which the gang is affiliated. The invasion of a gang's turf not only signifies a threat to its status and authority but also may, if successful, deprive that gang of real income. Moreover, the act is a challenge to the power and authority of the adult organization located in the area. Consequently, protecting turf is important not only for saving face and for financial reasons, but also in order to fulfill a major responsibility delegated to the gang by the affiliated adult organization.[7] Many observers and gang members themselves have indicated that it would be difficult for the gangs to exert control over their turf without the full support of the adult associations (U.S. Senate, 1992). In order to maintain the support of the adult organizations, Chinese gangs will do whatever it takes to protect their turf in Chinatown.

Violence is often sparked by turf wars that occur when one gang wishes to acquire part or all of the territory of another gang, or when two different gangs confront each other over the same piece of unclaimed or disputed territory. Because most core areas in Manhattan's Chinatown have been occupied for decades by well-established gangs and adult organizations, planned turf-related intergang hostilities are more likely to occur in newly developed commercial blocks in virgin territory that has not been claimed by any gang or adult association. Turf wars in certain areas of the Chinese communities of Queens and Brooklyn are common because these areas are not well defined in terms of turf territorial prerogatives and because the tongs do not control these areas. Without the backup of a stable and visible adult organization, a gang's claim to an area is susceptible to challenge and may lead to invasions by other gangs.

A subject from a gang located in Manhattan described how his gang intruded into a rival gang's turf in Flushing, Queens:

We fought with a gang in Queens because our *dai lo* wanted to take over Flushing. We went to Flushing and called their [the rival gang's] *dai lo* and told him to leave Flushing or we would mess him up. Later, five to six members of that gang showed up in a restaurant in Flushing to collect protection money. We tried to talk to them first, but they wouldn't listen. We had 30 guys. They tried to pull out their guns, but we overpowered them before they could reach for their guns. It happened outside a restaurant. They were no match for us. They underestimated us. We just beat the crap out of them. Our *dai lo* told them, "Go home, and tell your *dai lo* this [turf] is ours." However, it [occupying the turf] didn't last too long because Flushing is too far away from Manhattan's Chinatown. It takes half an hour to get there. If someone [a "brother"] is in trouble, it's hard to send help.

In other turf-related incidents, the invading party may have had no intention of taking over a territory and may only have wanted to extort money from business owners in that territory. Such acts were considered serious challenges by gang members.[8] A gang member described how his gang handled such a threat: "We shot at a bunch of XX gang members. They came over to our turf and tried to collect protection money from our store owners."

Some intergang violence was triggered by accidental trespassing into a rival gang's turf. In these instances, in which territorial violations were unintentional and innocent, the gang that controlled the area could not discern the intruders' intentions, so the normal reaction was to treat the event as if it were a deliberate show of disrespect for the gang's turf. A subject revealed how risky it could be for a Chinese gang member to wander into a rival gang's area:

A Chinese gang member walked into our turf and was wandering around. We beat him till he could not get up from the floor. Fifteen of us were beating him. My "brother" said he had seen the guy with the XX gang. If we see a suspicious guy in our turf armed with a gun, we will kill him right away.

Because gang turfs in Manhattan's Chinatown are close to one another or contiguous, it is often necessary for a gang member to walk through a rival gang's territory to reach his own. Violence has often erupted at the edges where gang boundaries meet. This phenomenon has also been observed with African American and Hispanic gangs in Los Angeles (Los Angeles County District Attorney, 1992) and San Diego (Sanders, 1994). Most turf-related intergang violence in Manhattan's Chinese community though, appears to be spontaneous reactions to accidental encroachment rather than planned invasions.

The issue of money is linked closely with the turf issue. This becomes apparent in the struggles over territory. Because income expands when gangs receive protection money from more stores or restaurants, the primary goal of turf expansion is economic. A large turf, especially one situated on busy streets, is very lucrative. As one respondent maintained, turf is equivalent to money for Chinese gangs: "The reason for intergang fights was mainly to expand the gang's turf and to make more money. A larger turf means more income. It's all about money."[9]

Other violent episodes between gangs occur simply because gang members show up at recreational establishments frequented by their rivals:

We were hanging out in a pool hall in our turf. Some Green Dragons walked in. They stared at us. One of my friends was playing video games by himself. One of them came around and questioned my friend. Since that was our turf, we had things like guns and sticks there. We swung at them with pool sticks, hit them until we beat them up. We also shot a guy in the leg. We warned him that if he returned, it [the shooting] was going to be in the head.

Women, revenge, and money were also mentioned as underlying causes for hostilities between members of rival gangs. The fact that some women associate with members of different gangs creates animosity and jealousy among gang members. A respondent explained how a joyful occasion turned into an explosive confrontation because of arguments concerning women:

> Once, a friend of mine just graduated from college, and we decided to have a celebration. A couple of girls were invited to the restaurant, and they brought some Green Dragons with them because one of the girls' boyfriends was a Green Dragon. After we bumped into them, we chased after them. We threw rocks and garbage cans at their cars. Later that night, the two gangs decided to meet. We were prepared to fight, but we talked it out.

Another reason for intergang conflict is revenge. When a gang member has been assaulted or killed by another gang, revenge is sought, and this generates a recurring cycle of violent incidents. Three subjects described the vicious cycle of gang retaliations:

> Once, two to three kids were in "our" pool hall. We knew they didn't belong there. We took them down to the bathroom and mugged them. They said they were members of the XX gang and left. They came back twenty minutes later and shot at the pool hall's window. More than one gun was fired. One of my friends was shot, another guy in the pool hall died. We went after them, but you could rarely find them when you are angry at them. Later, we found a couple of them and robbed them. I wanted to do it by myself, so I told my friends to step back. I wanted them to have a fair chance. I beat them up until they were lying on the floor.

> On one occasion, we fought with the Green Dragons because they came over to "our" pool hall. We didn't like that. We fought, but we were caught unguarded. We used pool sticks and tried to get a gun. The owner of the place helped us. The Green Dragons left but came back again and beat up our *sai lo*. We went to their turf and shot them. We always have to watch over our shoulder. It's back and forth.

> Members of a rival gang came to Canal Street and beat up one of us. The next day, we went back and shot at them.

Drug sales are one of the major reasons for intergang violence among black and Hispanic gangs (Sanders, 1994); however, none of my respondents mentioned drugs as the cause of conflicts among rival gangs. Since Chinese heroin importers are believed to be rarely involved in street sales and only a small number of the gang members in my survey admitted to having been lured into drug dealing, it seems unlikely that Chinese gang members fight for control of street-level drug markets.

The data also show that warfare between Chinese and non-Asian gangs is almost nonexistent. Chinese gang members may fight with members of the Vietnamese Born-to-Kill gang, but not with members of black or Hispanic gangs. Studies of other ethnic gangs confirm that intergang hostilities are basically intraethnic rather than interethnic (Hagedorn, 1988; Jankowski, 1991; Los Angeles County District Attorney, 1992; Sanders, 1994).

Moore (1978), Horowitz (1983), Vigil (1988), and Sanders (1994) point out that machismo, honor, and respect are subcultural values related to aggression among Hispanic gangs. In this study, I find that these values or psychological dimensions of behavior also appear relevant to Chinese gang violence. Although only one subject mentioned pride as a reason for gang aggression, staring and provocative attitudes displayed by rivals—the major etiological factors for gang aggression mentioned by my respondents—could be equated with an affront to a gang's sense of pride and honor. In sum, my findings support the conclusion reached by Reiss and Roth on gang violence, that "gang conflict often occurs when a gang believes that its status or reputation, its turf, or its resources are threatened by another gang" (1993: 142).

Intragang Violence

Intragang violence is defined as violent behavior against members of the same gang. Intragang assaults among Chinese gangs appear to be not as frequent as clashes between members of different gangs. A substantially smaller number of subjects (28%) indicated that they had participated in intragang conflicts. Intragang aggression is less common among Chinese gangs than among other ethnic gangs (Reiss and Roth, 1993; Sanders, 1994). Unlike aggression between rival gangs, however, according to my survey, fights between members of the same gang are mainly over money, women, and power (see table 7.3). Violence among members of the same gang is often spontaneous, and weapons are rarely used.

Money was the most often cited reason for intragang disputes, perhaps because gambling is reportedly widespread among gang members (Kinkead, 1992). Disputes over gambling debts often led to physical confrontations. One respondent described how he got involved in an altercation with a member of his gang: "We fought over money. Last month, we were gambling, and a guy owed me money. We yelled and pushed, but it didn't go too far."

In addition to gambling debts, disputes over the distribution of profits from illegal businesses are also a major cause of intragang tensions. As was mentioned in chapter 4, there are rules about how extorted money should be distributed within a gang. After collecting money from victims, gang members often turn it over to their faction leader, who then distributes it among his followers. If ordinary members and street-level leaders are not satisfied with the way their faction leader handles money, intragang violence may ensue. During the late 1970s and early 1980s, disputes of this kind resulted in several vicious attacks among members of the Ghost Shadows and forced the gang to split into two factions (U.S. District Court, 1985a, 1985b). One of my subjects explained how he became involved in an intragang struggle because of money:

> Once, a guy in our gang said something bad about our group. He expected us to guard the streets. I said, "If you want me to take over [the streets], I'll keep the money [collected from the stores]." I told him he had no rights [to ask for a share of the extortion money]. I told my brothers [ten of them] to jump this guy. It was a fistfight; no weapons were used.

Women were the second most frequently mentioned reason for intragang violence. As was discussed in chapter 6, women are an essential part of Chinese gangs, although they are not allowed to be members. Many Asian females associate with Chinese gangs, and they are often seen in public places in the company of gang members. But qualitative data from the gang subjects reveal little about specifically why and how women associates provoke conflicts within gangs because the subjects rarely elaborated on this issue.

All the gangs in Chinatown have, at one time or another, experienced major internal clashes (Daly, 1983; Meskil, 1989; Chin, 1990). As was mentioned earlier, many Chinese gangs are divided into rival factions, each of which is headed by its own leader. Although the primary leader may try to maintain peaceful coexistence among the different factions under his control, members of the different factions may nonetheless fight among themselves without his knowledge. In fact, some factional clashes within gangs are as brutal as some of the more bloody episodes of warfare between rival gangs (Chin, 1990). A subject explained why members of his faction would fight with members from another faction of the same gang: "The Y faction fights with the Z faction. They don't care that they all belong to the same gang. For our gang, each faction has its own territory, and members are not supposed to go to other factions' territory. You cannot walk on the wrong street."

Thus, the very notion of a street gang among the Chinese appears similar to other ethnic gangs. Although Chinese gangs appear to be relatively well-integrated units, with clear lines of power and authority, they may be more accurately described as loose confederations of smaller cliques precariously held together by a shared interest in a turf that is affiliated with a tong. This description is much like the African American and Hispanic gangs examined by Short and Strodtbeck (1965), Klein (1971), Fagan (1989), and Sanders (1994).

Misunderstandings, bad attitudes, and verbal altercations were also mentioned by respondents as causes of intragang conflicts. Ironically, members of different factions of a gang may attack one another simply because they do not know they belong to the same gang. As was mentioned earlier, some gangs have three or more factions, and there is little communication among ordinary members of these factions. It is not unusual for gang members not to recognize members of other factions. A subject explained how this can happen: "We were walking, they started coming at us. We exchanged words. We hit them. After we fought, the older guy [an "uncle" from the tong] was called and he came over, and then we found out that we belonged to the same gang."

Intragang violence, especially assaults within a particular faction, is also used for disciplinary purposes. Since a gang is an illegal organization, its means for disciplining its members are limited. The disciplinary action usually employed for breaking gang rules or for failing to fulfill gang-related duties is some type of physical punishment. The ultimate punishment may be execution. Two subjects explained why some were attacked by their peers:

> It [the attack] sometimes happens when the followers didn't collect money from the stores, or they mugged people on the streets, or they didn't listen to the *dai lo*, or they complained too much. In these cases, we will punch them a few times.
>
> Small stuff. It's like he's supposed to go up to mug a guy and he didn't do it. He

had to do it because he was the guy with the knife. He was scared, and he backed down. We had four more guys to help him, and the other guys did the mugging. We lost face, so later we beat him up.

Among some black and Puerto Rican gangs, drug use and drug dealing have been found to be responsible for the escalation of violence (Taylor, 1990; Padilla, 1992). The media and some law enforcement authorities have made allegations that Chinese gangs are increasingly involved in heroin trafficking, which, in their view, is also the major reason for violence among Chinese gangs. However, I do not find support for that contention. Drug use and drug dealing were not rampant among the gang subjects we interviewed or the gang members they knew. I also did not find support for the hypothesis that the heroin trade is a catalyst for Chinese gang violence. Klein et al. (1991) maintain that, although crack dealing was alleged to be the cause of the recent escalation in gang violence among black and Hispanic gangs, an examination of official data in Los Angeles did not support such an allegation. A report prepared by the Los Angeles County District Attorney also concluded that: "Contrary to popular belief, most gang homicides are not random shootings nor are they disputes over drugs or some other crime. Gang homicides are the products of old-fashioned fights over turf, status, and revenge" (1992: xx).

Generally, although gang members admitted to participating in violence with members of other gangs and with members of their own gang my study found that for the most part: (1) violence among gang members is freelance and erupts rather spontaneously over personal matters; and (2) gang leaders strive to control and contain violence for purely pragmatic purposes. The issue of obtaining control over violence or holding violence in check is discussed later in this chapter.

Violence against Nongang Victims

In comparison with intergang and intragang aggression, violence against non-gang victims by Chinese gang members is relatively rare. Of the 340 gang-related violent incidents reported in the New York newspapers between 1968 and 1992, only 10 incidents (3%) were reported to have involved extortion-related violence against business owners. Data from the business survey also suggest that victims of extortion were unlikely to be attacked by gangs. Out of 603 subjects, only 2 reported being physically assaulted for resisting the gangs.

As was mentioned earlier, many gang respondents admitted that they were relatively active in committing robberies. Gang members not only mug people in the streets of Chinatown but also rob stores, gambling clubs, massage parlors, and residences. While victims of muggings are unlikely to be injured, victims of other types of robbery may be assaulted or killed by heavily armed gang members. Although the media have reported several robbery cases in which the victims were brutally murdered, there is no statistical information available that would permit us to make a determination of the extent of physical assaults in commercial and home-invasion robberies committed by members of Chinese gangs.[10]

One of the alleged major activities of Chinese gangs is debt collection for gambling dens and alien-smuggling rings (Chin, 1990). Gang members may use violence to coerce debtors who are behind in their payments, or they may assault illegal aliens who default on their payments to smuggling rings in the United States. Recently, several illegal aliens were kidnapped and tortured by Chinese gang members because they failed to repay their smuggling debts (Kifner, 1991; Lorch, 1991; Strom, 1991).[11]

Gang members may also employ violence to silence those who dare to testify against them in court. A Chinese merchant was shot and killed by gang members after he agreed to testify in a robbery charge against the Born-to-Kill gang (Steinberg, 1992; English, 1995). Likewise, a young Chinese female and her boyfriend were abducted and executed by members of the Green Dragons gang after the young woman testified against the gang in a double-murder case (U.S. District Court, Eastern District of New York, 1991; Dannen, 1992). Two prominent Chinatown leaders were also believed to have been viciously attacked for their cooperation with law enforcement authorities (Hetchman, 1977; Gold, 1991). However, the likelihood of Chinatown residents being assaulted for testifying is rare because few are willing to testify against Chinese gangs (*Sing Tao Jih Pao*, 1992a).

Kong So: *A Restraining Mechanism*

Jankowski found that violence among Hispanic and African American gangs "is not unrestrained" (1991: 139). Likewise, it appears that gang violence in the Chinese community is held in check. According to qualitative data from the gang study, factional leaders, perhaps under pressure from top leaders or tong members, instruct street-level or clique leaders to control ordinary members and prevent them from becoming involved in spontaneous violence. One of the most challenging jobs for a street-level leader is to prevent his followers from engaging in deadly confrontations with rival gang members. In instances of disputes or violent confrontations between gangs or within a gang, street-level leaders try to resolve problems through peaceful negotiation, a process known among Chinese gangs as *kong so*.

Many gang members (69%) indicated that when intergang conflicts occurred, faction or street-level leaders from the parties involved selected a place (normally a restaurant located in neutral territory) to sit down and talk, or negotiate. As in formal negotiations between nations, the representatives from each gang are expected to be of equal status. A street leader explained how negotiations are carried out among Chinese gangs:

> [When there is an intergang dispute], I will have to do the negotiation. If they [the rival gang] feel like I am not qualified, they will ask me to send my *dai lo*. Sometimes, when they see that I look young, they will say that I am not qualified. I will then call my *dai lo*, and he will try to regain face for me. If the negotiator from the rival gang is of the same rank as myself, we will sit down and talk.

It appears that whenever intergang conflicts erupt among Chinese gangs, *kong so* is the norm rather than the exception. It is certainly expected to give the parties involved an opportunity to cool down and figure out a nonviolent way to save everyone's face. Money may be relayed to the party that was being insulted or physically harmed. Or else, the party judged to be guilty may treat the "victims" to a lavish dinner, a popular method of settling disputes, known as *bai tai zi* (literally, setting a table). *Bai tai zi* is also a common practice among gang members in Hong Kong and Taiwan for redressing grievances and soothing ill feelings (Zhang, 1984; Chi, 1985).

However, it is not known how often negotiations among Chinese gangs prove to be successful in resolving conflicts. In some cases, fatal shootouts have occurred when negotiations broke down (James, 1991). A street leader we interviewed speculated about how he would react should a negotiation prove unsuccessful: "I will talk to them [the rival gang] first. If the negotiation breaks down, I'll tell them to wait there. I'll then tell my kids to do the attack. I won't show any anger [during the negotiation]."

Another gang member described what led him to participate in a negotiation with a rival gang and what happened when talk failed to settle the conflict:

> A couple of days ago, the XX gang thought that one of our brothers wanted trouble. They speculated that our brother was trying to threaten them. Our brother denied, but they wanted him to apologize. Our brother refused. We went to a restaurant at Lafayette Street to meet with them. At the meeting, our brother refused to apologize. They asked if we wanted to start anything. We walked out and waited. When they came out, we beat them up.

Not only can intergang clashes be resolved through *kong so*, intragang confrontations may also be quelled through the same mechanism. Gang members (84%) said that their *dai los* would intervene when a serious conflict among members developed. If the situation warranted, the *ah kung* (the tong member who acts as the middleman between the tong and the gang) would also step between the warring parties. One gang member explained how it works:

> If the conflict among us is serious, the *ah kung* will have to come out and resolve it. If not, the *dai los* will sit down and talk. If members of other gangs know that we are fighting among ourselves, they will laugh at us. Sometimes we will fight among ourselves, but not openly. We will shake hands and apologize, though we still fight behind the backs of the *dai los*.

The capacity for violence appears to be one of the key defining characteristics of street gang culture. Its employment, however, is shaped and determined by a cluster of constraints related to profit-generating goals. Violence between and among gangs is regulated through an agent or *ah kung* who attempts to channel aggressive behavior in ways that effectively maintain gang coherence. Gang coherence in turn supports the gang's involvement in extortion activities and in the provision of protection services to organized vice industries in the community.

Kong so is a regulatory mechanism designed to achieve several ends; it may mute violence or define its parameters so that the gangs retain their viability and do not self-destruct. Gang leaders have a vested interest in containing and controlling the violent behavior of the members of their gangs. By elaborating the thresholds of permissible and impermissible violence, gang leaders consolidate their authority and manipulate an asset to their own advantage. Violence is a key criminal resource which needs to be utilized and exploited efficiently if it is to be effective. Many gang leaders recognize that this resource should not be wasted.

The identification of *kong so* illuminates many aspects of Chinese gang organization. For instance, we may think of gang structure as both a consequence and an initiator of action. Street gang structure does not simply develop spontaneously or haphazardly. Rather, roles played by gang members are shaped by the criminal activity of the gangs. Moreover, since most of the gangs' criminal activities depend on the needs of the affiliated adult organizations, the power structure of the gangs reflects the needs of the tongs to communicate and effectively use the potential violence of the gangs for their purposes. Also, gang structure works as a control or constraint on the types of criminal activities gangs are likely to engage in. The development of gangs in turfs and the assignment of roles—criminal work roles—within the turf constricts their capacity for freelance crime and may even temper and tame their violence.

Leadership plays a pivotal role in the organization and discharging of collective violence. In order to harness a gang's energies for its projects—whether for turf defense, protection of adult criminal organization enterprises, or credible threats against extortion victims—gang leaders need to create and maintain assymetrical information flows in which *dai lo*s possess greater knowledge and better networks of influence with faction leaders and others than do the members of the cliques.

Summary

Members of Chinese gangs appear to be quite active in committing violent crimes. Most of the gang members in my survey reported regular or frequent engagement in assault, shooting, and robbery. Gang violence in the Chinese community may be categorized into intergang violence, intragang violence, and aggression against nongang victims. Intergang violence appears to be the most common sort of violence, and violence against nongang victims is the rarest. The subjects indicated that provocations and turf warfare were the major reasons for intergang hostilities, and that disputes over money and women were important causes for intragang conflicts. Almost all gang-related violent incidents in Chinatown are intraethnic confrontations.

In studies of African American and Hispanic gangs, involvement in drug use and drug distribution has been found to be a major contributing factor to the escalation of gang assaults and murders (Taylor, 1990; Padilla, 1992). My study suggests that Chinese gang members are, by comparison, less involved in drug use and drug selling. Only one subject reported drug selling as a reason for intragang violence. Thus, the use and distribution of drugs do not appear to be a vital factor in causing violence among the Chinese gang members we interviewed. This finding supports the conclusions of Fagan (1989), Jankowski (1991), Klein et al. (1991), and the Los Angeles County District Attorney (1992) that the use and selling of drugs is not necessarily related to the incidence of violence among street gangs.

Moore (1990) and Jankowski (1991) have stressed the importance of differentiating between gang violence and individual violence in examining the nature of gang aggression. According to both Moore and Jankowski, most violent acts committed by gang members are not specifically motivated by group objectives. I also find that the aggressive behaviors of Chinese gang members are often not sanctioned or known by their leaders. Only a few violent incidents, mainly planned turf warfare, can be defined as collectively based violence, undertaken by the gang as a whole. In most incidents, gang leaders play an important role in the suppression of violence among young gang members because they wish to prevent escalation of minor conflicts into major showdowns. My findings suggest that most Chinese gang violence consists of individual or clique-based activities, either committed by younger members on their own or sanctioned only by their clique.

This study takes exception to Thompson's (1976) view that gang violence in Chinatown was used as a mask for racketeering activities operated by adult organizations in the community. My study found gang members to be very active in providing protection to vice operations in Chinatown; however, this activity was not reported to be a factor in promoting violence. My subjects also did not indicate that their aggression was sanctioned or instigated by operators of vice businesses.

My study also does not lend much support to Takagi and Platt's theory (1978), discussed earlier, regarding gang violence. Careful examination of the data reveals that most of the violent incidents in Chinatown appear to be related to Chinese gangs. Tong members were only involved in a few incidents, either as instigators or victims. Moreover, the "political intimidation of progressive organizations" (Takagi and Platt, 1978: 22) was not mentioned by my respondents as a factor contributing to gang violence. My data suggest that members of non-tong-affiliated gangs were involved in violent acts as frequently as members of tong-affiliated gangs.

Furthermore, information gathered from business owners and gang members suggests that Chinese merchants are rarely assaulted by gang members, which is contrary to the impression given by the media and the police. The merchants in my survey were rarely physically assaulted, even when they refused to comply with gang demands. Even verbal threats were rare when gang members approached business owners for money, goods, or services.

I believe that most violent activities in Chinatown are committed by gang members independent of tongs and other adult organizations, and that these violent incidents are not associated with protection rackets or related to political intimidation. While I recognize that these beliefs are inconsistent with those of earlier researchers (Thompson, 1976; Takagi and Platt, 1978), possibly the passage of time and/or the change of venue may have contributed to these differences of opinion.

In sum, drug use, drug trafficking, tong affiliation, protection rackets, and community politics appear to have little influence on gang violence in New York City's Chinatowns. With the exception of planned attacks that are rare and that characterize turf-expansion violence, most Chinese gang assaults are spontaneous reactions to minor provocations, and they are often carried out on an individual basis. The findings in this study are in accord with Fagan's research (1989) and the reports of the Los Angeles County District Attorney (1992). Both studies found that gang violence was seldom related to drug dealing and other organized crime activities, but was usually fueled by traditional gang conflicts over turf, status, or revenge.

8

The Gang as an Enterprise

Gangs in the late 1980s and early 1990s have been described by researchers as corporations or enterprises formed by young people who are primarily interested in making money (M. Sullivan, 1989; Taylor, 1990; Padilla, 1992). Unlike the neighborhood gangs observed by A. Cohen (1955) and W. Miller (1958), modern era gangs appear to be made up of predominantly utilitarian-oriented, individualistic young people determined to promote their financial well-being through gang participation (Jankowski, 1991). In order to operate efficiently, the structure, norms, values, and recruiting practices of contemporary gangs are relatively similar to those of legitimate business establishments.

As was discussed in chapter 6, Chinese gang members cite money as the most important reason for joining gangs. For them, becoming a gang member signifies *wan shik* or *wan shai kaai*—it is simply an alternative way of "making a living."[1] Members of the Chinese underworld often view themselves as a unique group of people who "come out to make a living" in a social subculture conceptually known as *jiang hu* (Chin, 1990). They view themselves as originally law-abiding citizens who were pushed to the edge by corrupt public officials and greedy landlords or merchants (Li, 1981).

Within the gang subculture, any measure that might generate money is actively explored and exploited. Historically, extortion, gambling, prostitution, and robbery have been some of the most common income-generating enterprises of Chinese gangs.[2] This chapter explores gang involvement in gambling, prostitution, and robbery, plus heroin trafficking and the smuggling of aliens—transnational crimes alleged to be the main activities of Chinese gangs in the 1990s.

Gambling

When the first wave of Chinese immigrants arrived in California in the mid-nineteenth century, they established a Chinatown in San Francisco (R. Lee, 1960; Nee and Nee, 1986). Soon, the community became infested with gambling dens alleged to have been sponsored by tongs and protected by *boo how doy* (hatchetmen), street thugs who worked for the tongs (Gong and Grant, 1930; North, 1944;

Dillon, 1962).[3] The Chinese involvement in gambling was one of the issues focused on in the 1877 U.S. Senate hearings on Chinese immigration and, along with prostitution and opium use, became a catalyst for the Chinese Exclusion Act, which was passed four years after the hearings.[4] This bill prohibited almost all Chinese from entering the United States, and it is the only U.S. immigration statute ever to have targeted a specific ethnic group (Tsai, 1986).

To contemporary observers, most social problems confronting the Chinese American communities seem to be rooted in the gambling industry (Hatfield, 1989). Social ills reported to be rampant in the communities, such as domestic violence, alcoholism, group conflicts, police corruption, heroin trafficking, and gangs, are claimed to be manifestations or consequences of the pervasiveness of gambling in the Chinese neighborhoods (Sung, 1977; Chan and Dao, 1990b; Chin, 1990, 1994; Chin et al., 1990–91).[5] A Chinese merchant in the business survey summed up his observations and feelings about the impact of gambling on the community:

> There are at least 15 major gambling dens in Chinatown. Each den pays at least $30,000 a week in *pai peng* [literally, distributing cakes]. The money is offered to the gangsters who watch the place, to the police who look the other way, and to powerful community leaders who demand that "face" be given. These gambling places each month gross more than 2 million dollars. The money is the income and savings of law-abiding workers. If these are used constructively, like improving the standard of living for Chinatown residents, the community would have been highly developed a long time ago.

There is little information on the prevalence of gambling among Chinese in America. Also, there are no statistics on the number of gambling houses in Chinese communities. Yet, it is assumed that many working-class Chinese like to gamble (Chin, 1990). Furthermore, it is no secret that almost all community associations sponsor one or more gambling operations. These places are called either recreational or social clubs. Many barbershops and retail stores are also involved in operating one or more gambling tables at the rear or in the basement of their business premises and collect a commission for these gambling activities.

There would appear to be at least two reasons for the proliferation of gambling clubs in the Chinese communities of America. First, many working-class Chinese immigrants arrive in the United States alone and need to work long hours in poor working environments. Because of language and cultural barriers, spatial concentration in dense residential and commercial areas, and odd working hours, not many are able to find a respite from the drudgery of work in the recreational activities offered by mainstream society.[6] As a result, most find a reprieve only in community-based gambling establishments that are normally open from noon to dawn, seven days a week. Even those who do not like to gamble may be lured into gambling because of peer pressure.[7]

Second, income from gambling activity is vital for most community associations.[8] Since these organizations need a substantial amount of money to operate, it is doubtful that they could exist without the income derived from gambling.[9] Consequently, the associations have to operate gambling establishments for their survival.[10]

Chinese gangs play an important role in the Chinese community's gambling industry (Chin, 1990). As was mentioned in chapter 7, Chinese gang members are relatively active in gambling and in protecting and guarding gambling establishments. Seventy-eight percent of the respondents in the gang study indicated that their gangs provided security to gambling dens. Among Chinese gang members, the task of protecting gambling dens is known as *tai cheung* (literally, watching a place). Since the gambling dens are at risk of being raided by the police or robbed by gang members, they need people to protect them from both.[11] Gambling houses also need people who can help them scrutinize customers, maintain order within the house, and collect gambling debts (Bresler, 1981). Gangs are well suited for handling these tasks, and their place in the social order of Chinatown gives them access to the operators of gambling dens (Lyman, 1986).

Data from the 62 gang respondents in my study suggest that the gang-gambling relationship has three aspects. First, a gambling establishment may be owned and operated by a group of people who do not belong to a gang. Gambling club owners negotiate with a gang leader for his gang to guard the gambling club for a price. It is not known how much a gang leader might demand from the club, except that the price varies according to the volume and type of gambling in the club.[12] After the two parties reach an agreement, the gang leader will assign the task, through a faction leader, to a group of his followers—normally a clique within the faction. The clique will be paid from $200 to $300 a night for its services. Gang respondents indicated that the income is not provided on a daily basis because the services are required only two or three days a week, for reasons I do not know.

Second, a gambling house may be a joint venture between a gang and a group of investors external to the gang. In this case, the gang leader will not be paid by the house, and he may or may not pay his followers for guarding the establishment.

Third, a gambling den may be owned and operated by a gang leader and an *ah kung* (a tong member who is close to the affiliated gang). No outsiders are invited to invest in or operate the establishment. The gang leader will assign a group of followers to protect the place, and more often than not, the gang members will not be paid for their services.

The data suggest that neither providing protection to gambling establishments nor operating them is a gang business per se. Rather, only a group of gang members participates in these endeavors. The *dai lo* will make the arrangements and instruct a group of followers to be directly involved in these endeavors. Other factions or cliques may have little to do with a particular clique's involvement in a gambling business.

Since gambling was legalized in Atlantic City, the gambling industry in New York City's Chinatowns has been on the decline. Most Chinatown residents now prefer to go to Atlantic City because it is safer and more comfortable to gamble there than in New York's Chinatowns. Besides, the casino industry in Atlantic City has been extremely aggressive in luring Chinese people from the tri-state area of New York, New Jersey, and Connecticut to visit and gamble there.[13]

However, with the dramatic increase in both legal and illegal Chinese immigrants over the past ten years, Chinatown's gambling industry may experience a revival. New immigrants, especially those who are unattached and illegal, are likely to become involved in gambling, but are not likely to visit Atlantic City because of language and cultural barriers. Thus, I believe that many new gambling establishments that cater almost exclusively to illegal immigrants have opened up in the community.

Prostitution

In the late-nineteenth century, authorities claimed that San Francisco's Chinatown was a major commercial sex center frequented by both white and Chinese patrons (Seward, 1881; Wong, 1978–79). Scores of police officers testified at the 1877 U.S. Senate hearings on Chinese immigration that hundreds of Chinese women were imported into the United States to work as prostitutes in a community plagued with brothels (Light, 1974; U.S. Senate, [1877] 1978). The predicaments of these women were vividly described in biographies of Donaldina Cameron, a missionary who spent most of her life rescuing Chinese prostitutes from the hands of the tongs (Wilson, 1974; M. Martin, 1977).

Prior to the mid-1980s, most Asian prostitutes in the United States were believed to be Korean women who had entered the country through fraudulent marriages to U.S. soldiers stationed in South Korea (S. Cohen, 1986). In the mid–1980s, there was an increase in the number of Taiwanese prostitutes working in the United States (Yang, 1985). Most arrived with tourist visas, which allowed them to stay in the country for six months. If these women wanted to, they could apply for an extension enabling them to stay for another six months. However, after the Immigration and Naturalization Service dismantled a Taiwanese prostitution ring in 1986, it tightened the issuance of tourist visas to young Taiwanese women, and the number of Taiwanese prostitutes appears to have declined (Surovell, 1988).[14]

The void was soon filled by Chinese women from Malaysia and China (*Sing Tao Jih Pao*, 1990). The Malaysian Chinese, like the Taiwanese, generally came to the United States as tourists. However, unlike the Taiwanese, they arrived here at their own expense and sought jobs in the community's vice industry. Only a small number of them worked as prostitutes; most were content to make less money working as masseuses. Prostitutes from China were primarily either legal immigrants who work in the vice industry voluntarily or illegal immigrants who were forced into prostitution by those who smuggled them into the country (Kinkead, 1992).

Currently, according to my observations in the field and my understanding of Chinatown, there are four types of Asian-owned prostitution businesses in New York City. The first type is the club. Clubs are similar to brothels: they are visited by men who are interested only in having sex. The clubs normally hire ten to twelve prostitutes and operate from noon to four o'clock in the morning. To prevent robbery and maintain order within the house, the clubs are heavily guarded by gang members with the aid of closed-circuit monitors and layers of steel doors. The media have reported numerous murders and serious assaults inside these clubs. Most of these businesses advertise in the Chinese newspapers and in certain English newspapers simply as clubs. The advertisements inform the readers of the name, business hours, address, and phone number of the establishment.[15] Judging from the advertisements, there are as many as 20 clubs in operation at any one time. Most of these establishments are located where Chinese people congregate, namely, in Manhattan's Chinatown, the downtown area of Manhattan (between 14th Street and Chinatown), the Flushing and Elmhurst sections of Queens, and Eighth Avenue in Brooklyn.

The second type of prostitution establishment is the family-type brothel. The function of these brothels is similar to that of the clubs, except that they operate on a much smaller scale; usually they employ from one to three women. Also, unlike the clubs, the brothels rarely publicize their existence; they place small ads in the classified columns and give no business name or address. There is only a beeper number or a phone number for customers to call in advance to set up a visit. All are located in Manhattan's Chinatown. Some only operate by word of mouth—especially those owned and operated by Fujianese that cater only to Fujianese clients. These places often operate twenty-four hours a day, seven days a week. Recently, there appears to have been an increase in the number of small, family-style brothels in Chinatown (*Sing Tao Jih Pao*, 1993e).

Barbershops constitute the third type of prostitution business. These establishments are similar to the clubs in terms of their business volume, but their major function is to provide massages to clients. Only some of the masseuses work as prostitutes. Barbershops often operate from ten o'clock in the morning to midnight and advertise in the newspapers. Advertisements in the newspapers indicate that from twelve to fifteen such businesses exist in New York City.

Yet another type of Asian prostitution business is associated with some nightclubs. These nightclubs usually hire third-rate singers from Asia to entertain their clients and recruit local Asian women to work as bar girls. If the clients wish, they can check out the bar girls. Since the cost of visiting these places is normally higher than the cost of visiting other types of prostitution houses, the demand is low, and only a few nightclubs in the New York City area operate prostitution businesses.

Law enforcement authorities in New York City believe that the gangs play the role of protectors, operators, and investors in the Asian commercial sex business. They claim that most Asian sex businesses in America are either protected or operated by Chinese gangs. The gangs recruit Asian women either locally or internationally. Prostitutes in these gang-controlled vice enterprises reap huge profits for the gangs (*World Journal*, 1993a).

Most gang respondents (80%) indicated that their gangs provided protection for Asian sex clubs in New York City. A Ghost Shadows member said that his gang owned a club in Chinatown. He said he did not have to pay when he visited the place because his *dai lo* paid for it later. Another gang respondent explained that his major responsibility in guarding massage parlors was to search customers to make sure they were not carrying weapons.

Serious incidents of violence often erupt in Asian-owned vice establishments

(Rabin and Meskil, 1986). Most violent encounters are robbery-related, but some incidents are the result of accidental confrontation between two groups of gang members visiting these places.

It is not known how many Asian women are forced into the commercial sex industry by Chinese gangs. A female subject we interviewed said that some women associates were coerced into working in the vice clubs owned by the gangs. In the media, there have been several reports of Chinese gang members forcing illegal female immigrants, who were predominantly Fujianese, to work in the community's prostitution houses to repay their smuggling debts (Y. Chan, 1993a). However, there is no evidence to suggest that this is a prevalent practice among Chinese gangs.

Armed Robbery

Chinese gangs are also involved in armed robbery. Their targets include legitimate business establishments, such as jewelry stores and restaurants; vice businesses, such as gambling clubs and massage parlors; and residences (Lorch, 1990b; *Sing Tao Jih Pao*, 1991a). The gangs are not known to be active in street or bank robberies.

With the exception of a few souvenir shops catering to non-Chinese tourists, most businesses in the Chinese communities accept only cash. Following the practice in their home countries, most employers in Chinatown also pay their employees in cash. Because so many business establishments in the Chinese communities hold a substantial amount of cash either at the end of a business day or the day prior to paying employee salaries, they are vulnerable to armed robbery.

A significant percentage of the gang respondents in my survey were involved in robbery in the preceding year: 82% had participated in the crime at least once; 70% had committed robbery at least regularly (three times or more a year); and 54% have been frequently involved in hold-ups (12 or more times a year) (see table 7.1).[16]

Nine percent of the business owners ($N = 603$) in the business survey indicated that they had been robbed at least once by Asian youths. Usually victims were not sure whether the predators belonged to gangs, but they were certain that the offenders did not belong to the gangs active in the area surrounding their businesses. Most incidents occurred when there were few or no customers on the business premises. The offenders entered the store, flashed their weapons, announced "robbery," and took the money from the cash register. Sometimes the robbers stole money and personal belongings from the owner and employees. With the exception of one victim, none were physically assaulted.[17]

Most robbery victims (92%) did not resist because the perpetrators were armed. Most (60%) lost between $100 and $1,000 in the robbery incident, but one victim indicated that he had been robbed of $30,000. Most had been victimized either once (63%) or twice (16%) since they started their businesses.

Our data show that, contrary to the implication of the term protection, business establishments paying protection money to gangs were not immune from robbery. In fact, the level of gang extortion was positively associated with robbery (these data are not shown in the tables). Business firms that experienced multiple extortion were more vulnerable to robbery than business firms that were never subject to extortion. In short, complying with extortion demands did not appear to function as a buffer against robbery by Chinese gangs.

An examination of the robbery victims' personal and business characteristics suggests that factors conducive to gang robbery are similar to those associated with gang extortion. In other words, business owners who were well educated and spoke fluent English were less likely to be robbed than those who had little education and did not speak English. Also, business characteristics such as business type and business location were found to be associated with vulnerability to robbery. Among the five categories of businesses, restaurants and retail stores were most vulnerable to robbery, as they were to gang extortion. Business establishments located on East Broadway, Mulberry, the Bowery, and Catherine were more likely to be robbed than business firms situated elsewhere in Manhattan's Chinatown (these data are not shown in the tables).

Although Chinese businesspeople are subjected to extortion mainly by Chinese gangs, they are not robbed only by Chinese gangs. According to my survey of Chinese business owners, Chinese entrepreneurs in New York City are more likely to be robbed by non-Asian than by Asian offenders.

In Manhattan's Chinatown, there are many Chinese-owned jewelry stores along Canal Street (the section between Broadway and the Bowery). Most of these business establishments are located on the street level, and few are protected by security guards. As a result, gang members occasionally rob these stores for cash and jewelry (English, 1995). A successful hold-up of a jewelry store may enable gangs to get away with goods worth tens of thousands of dollars. A group of Born-to-Kill members robbed a jewelry store on Canal Street one evening and left with $350,000 worth of jewelry (*Sing Tao Jih Pao*, 1991b). They were arrested because they forgot to turn on the headlights of the getaway car.

The vice businesses in Manhattan's Chinatown are also often invaded by armed robbers, even though these places are normally heavily guarded. Robbers can easily enter the places by posing as customers. In 1989, a massage parlor located in the community was robbed by seven Chinese youths (*Sing Tao Jih Pao*, 1989). They got away with $4,000 cash and, in the process, raped and assaulted a women employee. Another massage parlor in Chinatown was also robbed by six gunmen who took $10,000 from one of the customers. When a group of gang members robbed a midtown massage parlor, they shot and killed the female manager even though she offered no resistance.

Chinatown gangs, especially the Born-to-Kill and the Fuk Ching, are notorious for their active involvement in residential or home-invasion robberies (Schermerhorn and Hughes, 1984; Badey, 1988; Consoli, 1989; Brown and Davis, 1990; Hannum, 1992). Since many Chinese immigrants, particularly those from Southeast Asia, keep their money and jewelry in their homes, some Chinese gangs have found the invasion of immigrants' homes very lucrative. Typically, heavily armed gang members follow their victim to his or her home, enter it, tie up all of the victim's family members, and then ransack the place for cash and valuables. Should the proceeds not be satisfactory, the gang members might force the victims to go to their business establishments and rob these as well. And some victims might be compelled at gun point to retrieve money from their banks. In some such robberies, the victims have been either sexually assaulted (Brown and Davis, 1990; Burke and O'Rear, 1990) or killed by the perpetrators.

The occurrence of home-invasion robbery is not confined to Manhattan's Chinatown. Wealthy businesspeople living in New Jersey, Long Island, and other suburban areas near New York City have been robbed in their homes by what authorities label "urban terrorists" (Consoli, 1989).

Many illegal Fujianese immigrants in New York City have been victims of home-invasion robberies, committed mainly by Fujianese criminals (*Sing Tao Jih Pao*, 1993d; *World Journal*, 1993e). Some of the streets in Manhattan's Chinatown, namely East Broadway, Eldridge, Forysth, and Allen, and the northeast area of the community are now occupied predominantly by Fujianese merchants and residents (Kinkead, 1992). With the arrival of tens of thousands of illegal Chinese immigrants in New York City in the late 1980s and early 1990s, apartments in Chinatown are in great demand. To save money, a group of seven to ten immigrants will share an apartment with only one or two tiny bedrooms.[18]

The congestion of a large number of undocumented immigrants in an area of not more than a few blocks provides Fujianese criminals with a golden opportunity for home-invasion robbery. First of all, offenders know where to find apartments occupied by groups of illegal immigrants. Second, because offenders and victims are both Fujianese, the former may enter the victims' houses without much difficulty. Third, since there are usually many people living in one apartment, the robbers may be confident that they will not be disappointed with the proceeds. Even if they are not satisfied with the amount of money, they can kidnap one or two victims and force their relatives to pay a large ransom to ensure their release. Fourth, offenders know that the victims are unlikely to report the crime to the police because of their illegal immigration status and fear of retaliation.

Heroin Trafficking

Since their arrival in America, the Chinese have been thought to have been heavily involved in opium use and trafficking (Mark, 1992). In the U.S. Senate hearings on Chinese immigration of 1877, government officials and police officers testified that San Francisco's Chinatown was beleaguered with then-legal opium dens (U.S. Senate, [1877] 1978). It was reported that there were 200 opium dens within the core area (about nine blocks) of the community (A. McLeod, 1947). According to Mark (1992), during the late nineteenth century, a significant number of Chinese businessmen in the San Francisco area were actively involved in the importation and distribution of opium on the West Coast.

Little is known about the role Chinese dealers played in the American drug trade between 1914 and 1965.[19] It is alleged that after the liberalization of the immigration laws in 1965, Chinese criminals, many of them sailors, brought heroin into the United States (Chou, 1993). The seamen turned the heroin over to drug dealers in Chinatown, who sold it in its entirety to middle-level drug dealers of other ethnic groups. The Chinese were not themselves involved in street-level sales.

The Emergence of Chinese in Heroin Trafficking

As was mentioned in chapter 6, most of the gang members we interviewed denied much involvement in either drug use or drug sales. Historically, however, the Chinese have been linked with the illegal heroin trade. For this reason, I discuss this trade briefly and then talk about gang involvement.

After 1983, the amount of heroin imported into the United States from Southeast Asia increased dramatically (Bryant, 1990). In 1984, law enforcement officials claimed that Chinese drug traffickers were responsible for about 20 percent of the heroin imported into this country. They also alleged that 40 percent of the heroin in New York City was of Southeast Asian origin (President's Commission on Organized Crime, 1984).

In 1986, the number of heroin cases involving Chinese offenders began to rise dramatically. Drug enforcement and customs officers took notice of the increase in the number of Chinese heroin couriers arriving in American airports from Hong Kong and Bangkok. Each courier concealed ten to fifteen pounds of high-quality Southeast Asian heroin in luggage, picture frames, and other items, in an attempt to bypass customs checkpoints. Several Chinese drug runners, most of them otherwise legitimate community leaders, business owners, or restaurant and garment factory workers, were arrested at airports in Hong Kong, New York City, Los Angeles, and San Francisco.

In 1987, there was a dramatic change in the importation methods employed by the Chinese (DeStefano, 1988). Instead of using drug couriers, Chinese heroin traffickers began to make use of their expertise in international trade. Large quantities of heroin (from 50 to 100 pounds or more) began to arrive in the seaports of Newark and Elizabeth, New Jersey, and in Chicago, hidden in cargo containers shipped from Asia. The drugs were carefully stuffed in furniture, frozen seafood, and nylon sport bags, in order to evade customs officials (U.S. Senate, 1992).

In addition, Chinese drug traffickers began to stack ten to fifteen pounds of heroin in parcel boxes containing commodities that could conceal the odor of the drug (Lay and Dobson, 1993). The boxes were sent from either Thailand or Hong Kong and arrived in New York City via Oakland, California. Chinese drug traffickers also began to utilize air cargo to smuggle a large amount of heroin into the United States.

In 1987, law enforcement authorities solved more than twenty heroin-trafficking cases involving Chinese importers and seized a record 200 kilograms of 95 percent pure Southeast Asian heroin and millions in drug money (Huang, 1988). Drug enforcement authorities suggested that of all the heroin seized in New York City in 1987, 70 percent was of Southeast Asian origin, compared to 40 percent in 1984 (Koziol, 1988). The purity of the heroin in the streets of New York City rose from 5 percent in the early 1980s to 40 percent in 1987. The American drug enforcement community was overwhelmed with the sudden surge in heroin importation among the Chinese (Stutman, 1987).

Despite law enforcement efforts, Chinese involvement in heroin trafficking continued to increase in 1988 (Kerr, 1987a; Erlanger, 1990). In Chicago, drug enforcement authorities seized 160 pounds of heroin hidden in religious statues arriving from Bangkok. Top-level Chinese smugglers were arrested in New York City for importing several hundred pounds of heroin into the United States. In Boston, 180 pounds of heroin were found inside a bean sprout washing machine shipped from Hong Kong. In the meantime, law enforcement authorities in Asia, especially Thailand and Hong Kong, were stunned by the amount of heroin the Chinese were trying to send to the United States. Thai authorities confiscated 2,800 pounds of heroin destined for New York City (Esposito and McCarthy, 1988), and Hong Kong authorities seized a record 861 kilograms of heroin bound for the United States.

The arrests of major Chinese heroin traffickers continued unabated in 1989. In February, as the result of a worldwide drug enforcement operation known as Operation White Mare, the Organized Crime Drug Enforcement Task Force seized approximately 800 pounds of heroin and $3 million cash in Queens and arrested 38 defendants in the United States, Hong Kong, Canada, and Singapore. The drugs were imported into the United States via Hong Kong, hidden in hundreds of rubber tires for lawn mowers. A Chinatown community leader was indicted for his role as middleman for the foreign-based sellers and the American buyers (Marriott, 1989). Throughout 1989, other Chinese heroin trafficking groups were apprehended by drug enforcement agencies in the United States, Canada, Hong Kong, and Australia (Kinkead, 1992).

By 1990, it was estimated that 45 percent of the heroin smuggled into the United States, and 80 percent of the heroin imported into New York City, was Southeast Asian (U.S. Senate, 1992). By that time, law enforcement authorities in the United States (Bryant, 1990), Canada (Dubro, 1992), Australia (Dobinson, 1992), the Netherlands (Schalks, 1991), and Britain (Black, 1992) claimed that the Chinese dominated the heroin trade in their respective jurisdictions.

In June, 1991, drug enforcement authorities found 1,200 pounds of heroin in a warehouse in Hayward, California (Morain and Hager, 1991). The drugs were imported into the United States from Bangkok via Kaoshiung, Taiwan, in a container. Four Taiwanese merchants residing in California and a Hong Kong citizen were arrested for the crime. So far, it is the largest heroin seizure in the United States, surpassing the 1,000 pounds imported by a Hong Kong businessman in 1988 and the 800 pounds hidden in the rubber tires for lawn mowers in 1989 (Treaster, 1991). (See table 8.1 for a list of the major heroin arrests involving Chinese drug traffickers.)

In 1992 and 1993, many high-level heroin traffickers in New York City's Chinatown were convicted by the United States government, thus putting many Chinese heroin trafficking groups out of business. However, based on the number of arrests made and the huge amount of heroin seized over the past five years, it is

Table 8.1. A List of Major Heroin Arrests in the United States of Chinese Offenders (1986–1992)[a]

Date	Heroin Amount	Transship Point	Arriving Point	Concealed in:	Offenders' Country of Origin	Method
09/86	33 lbs.	Bangkok	Newark Seaport	Furniture	Taiwan	Sea cargo
11/86	10.5 kg	Hong Kong	JFK Airport	Gingsen tea	China	Courier
01/87	15 kg	Bangkok	Elizabeth Seaport	Furniture	Taiwan	Sea cargo
02/87	57 lbs.	Bangkok	Newark Seaport	Furniture	China	Sea cargo
12/87	34 lbs.	Hong Kong	Long Beach	Boat	Hong Kong	Courier
12/87	165 lbs.	Unknown	Unknown	Nylon bags	Hong Kong	Sea cargo
02/88	160 lbs.	Bangkok	Port of Chicago	Statues	Thailand	Sea cargo
02/88	2,821 lbs.	Bangkok	New York City	Rubber bales	Unknown	Sea cargo
03/88	100 lbs.	Hong Kong	New York City	Parcel boxes	Hong Kong	Parcel post
03/88	1,000 lbs.	Bangkok	Seattle, New York	Ice buckets	China	Sea cargo
03/88	7 lbs.	Shanghai	San Francisco	Goldfish	China	Air cargo
03/88	32 kg	Hong Kong	New York City	Tea	Hong Kong	Air cargo
03/88	46 kg	Hong Kong	New York City	Unknown	Hong Kong	Air cargo
04/88	130 lbs.	Hong Kong	San Francisco	Unknown	Hong Kong	Sea cargo
06/88	77 lbs.	Hong Kong	Los Angeles Airport	Can opener	Taiwan	Air cargo
09/88	183 lbs.	Hong Kong	Boston Airport	Bean sprout machine	Hong Kong	Air cargo
02/89	800 lbs.	Hong Kong	New York City	Rubber tires	Hong Kong	Sea cargo
05/89	40 kg	Guangzhou	New York City	Umbrella	China	Sea cargo
10/89	45 kg	Unknown	Chicago Airport	Unknown	China	Air cargo
01/90	18 lbs.	Unknown	Norwalk, CT	Toys	Unknown	Air cargo
01/90	65 kg	Hong Kong	Los Angeles	Lychee cans	Vietnam	Sea cargo
02/90	92 lbs.	Hong Kong	Elizabeth Seaport	Soy sauce	Unknown	Sea cargo
06/91	1,285 lbs.	Taiwan	Oakland	Plastic bags	Taiwan	Sea cargo
03/92	77 lbs.	Singapore	Newark Seaport	Tiles	Singapore	Sea cargo

SOURCE: Official reports and media accounts.

a. Major heroin arrests of Chinese offenders have dramatically decreased since 1993.

fair to say that Chinese traffickers are still one of the most active groups in international heroin trafficking (U.S. Senate, 1992). Recently, Chinese have been arrested not only for importing heroin but also for acting as middlemen (selling a few pounds to dealers of other ethnic groups). There is evidence that Chinese drug dealers work closely with Hispanic dealers and distributors in New York City (U.S. House of Representatives, 1987).

Chinese Gangs and the Heroin Trade

As soon as Chinese were discovered to be active in importing heroin into the United States, law enforcement authorities began to allege that Chinese gangs were responsible for the dramatic upsurge in heroin trafficking (President's Commission on Organized Crime, 1984; U.S. Senate, 1986). Law enforcement authorities charged that gang members, along with tong and triad members, were the main culprits in promoting the heroin trade (Powell, 1989). The media simply accepted the perspectives of the law enforcement authorities and charged Chinese gangs and tongs for the upsurge in the heroin trade (Seper, 1986; Seper and Emery, 1986; DeStefano and Esposito, 1987; Penn, 1990). Journalists often accused Chinese drug traffickers of being members of gangs, tongs, or triad societies, insinuating that there was a conspiracy among these groups to flood the United States with heroin. However, little is known about the nature and extent of Chinese gang involvement in the heroin trade. Although there are anecdotal reports (Green, 1990; Kwong and Miqsqcevic, 1990), no empirical research on this issue has been done.

A careful review of the heroin cases reported in the media that involve Chinese offenders suggests that only a small number of Chinese gang leaders are involved in the trade (Buder, 1988, 1989; Esposito and McCarthy, 1988; Marriott, 1989; Treaster, 1991). Between 1983 and 1993, only three Chinese gang leaders were convicted for heroin trafficking. Ordinary gang members were rarely arrested for drug trafficking.

The first defendant, Michael Yu, alias "Fox," was arrested in March 1988 for importing approximately 100 pounds of heroin into the United States. The 36-year-old, who was one of the leaders of the Flying Dragons, mixed the drugs with herbal medicine and mailed them in boxes from Hong Kong to New York City. Several young Chinese females were recruited by Yu's girlfriend to receive the parcels at their addresses and turn them over to him. Yu paid the receiving parties from $8,000 to $10,000 per box. Each box contained between 15 and 20 pounds of heroin. When the sixth box arrived in Oakland, California, customs officers found the drugs and removed most of them from the box. A sensor was implanted in the box, and a controlled delivery was made. The recipients of the targeted box were arrested, and they led federal authorities to Yu. In this particular incident, 39 Chinese males and females were arrested.

Not only was Yu operating a drug ring independently, he and his girlfriend were also working for another leader of the Flying Dragons, Johnny Eng. After the brutal murder of the gang's leader, Michael Chen, in 1983, Eng became the primary leader of the gang. Federal authorities indicted Eng in two drug cases. The first case, in March 1988, involved the importation in tea boxes of 32 kilos of heroin from Hong Kong to New York City. Fourteen defendants were arrested after the drugs were discovered by customs officials. In the second case, in September 1988, Eng was charged with smuggling 186 pounds of heroin into the United States. The drugs arrived in Boston from Hong Kong, concealed in a bean sprout washing machine especially designed to hide the drugs. A codefendant, a community leader of Boston's Chinatown, was also arrested.

Eng fled to Hong Kong soon after the discovery of the heroin. He was arrested in Hong Kong in August 1989 and was extradited to the United States in October 1991. Michael Yu, the Flying Dragons leader who was convicted for heroin trafficking in the earlier case, became a federal witness in Eng's trial. Eng was convicted on both drug cases and received a 28-year sentence (Lay and Dobson, 1993). Stephen Wong, nicknamed "Tiger Boy," a former leader of the Tung On gang, was convicted in May 1989 for heroin trafficking (DeStafano, 1988).

Although the three Chinese gang leaders mentioned here were convicted for heroin importation and dozens of codefendants were implicated, few, if any, of the codefendants were found to be connected with gangs. This suggests that, at least in these specific incidents, gang leaders were involved in heroin trafficking on their own and the gang as a whole was not involved in the drug trade.

The respondents to my survey indicated that, to the best of their knowledge, only gang leaders and a small proportion of ordinary gang members were involved in the heroin trade. Of the 62 subjects, only 10 (17%) admitted they had participated in the drug business. Most of my respondents were not associated with either the use or the sale of drugs.

Gang members might dissociate themselves from the heroin trade for many reasons. Some do not engage in heroin trafficking because it is prohibited by their *dai los*. One subject said that his *dai lo* was against heroin dealing because he believed it would destroy the gang: "My *dai lo* won't allow us to sell drugs. He does not like it. He said it's a waste of money.[20] Plus, it will ruin us. Our *dai lo* treats us like his own brothers. That's why I like him. He has heart. My *dai lo* is such a good person." Others do not have the money to invest in the heroin business: "My *dai lo* does not get involved in it because he does not have the start-up money." For many, involvement in heroin dealing is too risky, and they refuse to participate even when their *dai lo* encourages them. Three subjects who were asked by their *dai lo* to deal drugs had the following to say about their reluctance to become involved:

Our *dai lo* asked us to, but we didn't want to do it.

I don't touch it. I chose not to do it even when my *dai lo* asked me to do.

My *dai lo* did [deal heroin]. Once, he asked me to do it, but I refused. I am a senior member, and I don't want to sell drugs because it is too risky.

Some gang members became involved in the heroin trade voluntarily. If a gang member is interested in dealing drugs, he can approach a *dai lo* who is actively engaged in drug dealing and ask to participate. A street-level leader described how the process works: "If a *sai lo* [ordinary gang member] is interested in it, I will advise the *sai lo* to talk to the *dai lo*." Those who are willing to participate in the trade are assigned a specific role by their *dai lo*. "We usually have a place to keep the drug. We send a person out on the streets. People will go to him for the drug. We collect money for the *dai lo*."

Some indicated that they sold heroin without the approval or knowledge of their leader. These subjects sold drugs to street dealers of other ethnic groups. One gang member said he sold heroin once because he was desperate for money: "I did it once. I sold it to a black person behind my *dai lo*'s back. I think he was aware of it, but he also knew I needed money. He's a nice guy." Others played the role of deliverymen. One gang member said he often helped his *dai lo* deliver drugs: "I didn't sell, but I have delivered. Not by choice.[21] Two to three of us would go together."

Other respondents talked about being asked by their *dai lo* to deliver drugs to Hispanic, African American, and Asian drug dealers. Although most considered their jobs dangerous, many found it hard to resist the kind of money offered. As a precaution, *dai lo*s often told gang members not to inquire about the contents of the packages they were handling, in case they were arrested.

In brief, the role of Chinese gangs in heroin trafficking is not dissimilar to the role of other ethnic gangs in the cocaine or crack trade. According to a report on gangs and drugs in Los Angeles, gangs are rarely involved in drug dealing on a collective level:

> In truth, traditional street gangs are not well-suited for drug distribution or any other business-like activity. They are weakly organized, prone to unnecessary and unproductive violence and full of brash, conspicuous, untrustworthy individuals who draw unwanted police attention. For all these reasons, big drug operators—those who turn to drug dealing as a serious career—typically deemphasize gang activity or leave altogether. (Los Angeles County District Attorney, 1992: xxii)

Chinese Organized Crime and Heroin

The evidence that Chinese became relatively active in the American heroin trade in the late 1980s is substantial, but three important questions must be answered before an objective assessment of the issue is possible. First, one must ask, How reliable are the law enforcement estimations of the proportion of Southeast Asian heroin among all heroin available in the United States? Some observers question the techniques authorities employ in their estimations. Second, one must ask, What percentage of the Southeast Asian heroin being smuggled into the United States is actually imported by Chinese traffickers? Since Italians, Nigerians, Pakistanis, Israelis, and members of other ethnic groups are also involved in importing heroin from Southeast Asia to America, the increase in the amount of Southeast Asian heroin in the United States should not be automatically interpreted as the work of Chinese traffickers. Recently, a U.S. Department of State report (1994) indicated that Nigerians are responsible for the bulk of the Southeast Asian heroin imported into the United States (Sciolino, 1994). Third, one must ask, Of the Southeast Asian heroin brought into the United States by Chinese traffickers, what proportion is actually imported by members of the gangs, tongs, and triads? Is it possible that most Chinese heroin dealers do not belong to any of these types of organizations?

Unfortunately, little reliable information is available to provide answers to these questions. I can only speculate and provide a tentative answer to the last question. To date, no gang, as an organization, has been indicted for heroin trafficking. However, individual gang members have been arrested for heroin trafficking. The same is true with regard to the tongs and the triads. Thus, as one researcher puts it, the connection between heroin trafficking and Chinese organized crime (gangs, tongs, or triads) is weak at best (Dobinson, 1992). A senior DEA officer also reached the conclusion that most Chinese heroin importers are not members of the Chinese underworld:

> There is a significant class of "freelance" heroin violators within the New York Chinese community. This violator is usually a newly arrived immigrant who becomes aware of the huge profit one can make by successfully smuggling one to three pounds of heroin into the United States. The freelance operation is usually

comprised of a group of blue-collar restaurant or garment workers, one of whom has a connection in Hong Kong and another who has a buyer in New York. This group of "investors" pools their savings to finance one drug smuggling transaction. If successful, they usually invest their profits in a legitimate business and get out of the drug business. (Stutman, 1987: 6–7)

In his testimony at the 1992 U.S. Senate hearings on Asian organized crime, a senior law enforcement official gave a carefully thought-out and reasonable explanation of the connection between Chinese organized crime and heroin trafficking:

We see most of their ventures, their smuggling ventures—whether it is White Mare or some of the other cases—as sort of a joint venture on the part of the players. Some may be triad members; some may be tong members; some may be just simple associate businessmen. And they join on each particular organizational chart for purposes of smuggling that particular load or loads. (U.S. Senate, 1992: 182)

In short, my study supports these analyses, and my results also suggest that gangs, tongs, and triads do not play a leading role in the American heroin trade. Rather, I find evidence which suggests that a new generation of Chinese criminals is emerging on the American crime scene. They appear not to belong to gangs, tongs, or triads; are responsible for the bulk of the heroin imported into the United States; and are more likely than tong and gang members to infiltrate the larger society through drug trafficking, the smuggling of aliens, and money laundering and other types of white-collar crime. They are wealthy, sophisticated, and well connected with associates outside the United States. Further, they are not committed to the rigid triad subcultural norms and values and thus can assemble quickly when criminal opportunities arise and dissolve a criminal operation upon its completion.

Human Smuggling

In 1978, the United States established diplomatic relations with the People's Republic of China. Since then, tens of thousands of Chinese have legally immigrated to the United States (Zhou, 1992). Because of the limited immigration quota for China, only a small number of these Chinese, with family members living in the United States as citizens, have the opportunity to come to America legally.[22] Consequently, some Chinese turn to "snakeheads"—professional smugglers—for help.[23] Between 1978 and June 1989, the media reported that a substantial number of Chinese were arriving in the United States with the assistance of smugglers (Glaberson, 1989). After the June 1989 crackdown by the Chinese government, many students and intellectuals who had participated in the prodemocracy movement in China fled the country to avoid persecution by the government. Moreover, the resurrection of left-wing political leaders after the incident, coupled with rampant corruption among government officials, left many ordinary Chinese, especially those in the coastal areas of southern China, disillusioned by government promises for economic and political reform. Understandably, there was a surge in the number of Chinese who wanted to leave their country (Kamen, 1991; Mydans, 1992). In the aftermath of the assault on the student movement in Beijing, immigration officials in the United States, Taiwan, Hong Kong, Macau, Japan, Australia, Hungary, Italy, the Netherlands, and Canada were alarmed by the dramatic increase in the number of undocumented Chinese residing in their countries (Boyd and Barnes, 1992; Dubro, 1992; Eager, 1992; A. Lee, 1992; Tam, 1992; Stalk, 1993).

The United States ranks high among the choices of destinations for illegal Chinese immigrants. The arrival of large numbers of undocumented Chinese since 1989 has forced New York City's Chinatown, the destination of choice for many illegal immigrants, to expand its territory into Little Italy and the eastern part of the Lower East Side of Manhattan, an area once populated by Jewish immigrants (Loo, 1991; City of New York Department of City Planning, 1992). One estimate suggests that as many as 8,000 Chinese are covertly entering the United States every month (Myers, 1992). According to official estimates, approximately half a million Chinese are now residing in the United States illegally (English, 1991).

There are several ways an illegal Chinese immigrant can enter the United States. One technique is to travel to Mexico or Canada from China and then enter the United States by illegally crossing the border (Glaberson, 1989). The second method involves air travel. Many unauthorized Chinese arrive in Florida from South America by small airplane. Some fly into major American cities via any number of transit points, which can be in any city around the world (Lorch, 1992; Charasdamrong and Kheunkaew, 1992; U.S. Senate, 1992). Between August 1991 and July 1993, a third means, entering the United States by sea, became popular. A large number of Chinese are smuggled into the United States aboard fishing trawlers. In June 1993, a ship called the *Golden Venture*, with more than 260 men and women aboard, became stranded on a New York City beach. Ten passengers drowned while attempting to swim ashore (Fritsch, 1993). In all, between 1991 and 1993, thirty-two ships, with a total of as many as 5,300 Chinese, were found in the waters off Japan, Taiwan, Indonesia, Australia, Singapore, Haiti, Guatemala, El Salvador, Honduras, and the United States (Kamen, 1991; Schemo, 1993a, 1993b; U.S. Immigration and Naturalization Service, 1993) (see table 8.2).

U.S. immigration officials estimate that as many as 4,000 Chinese are temporarily waiting in Bolivia at any one time, ready to be shuttled to the United States by smugglers. Another 4,000 are believed to be awaiting entry into the United States in Panama. Thousands more are in Haiti and other parts of the Caribbean, or in Peru—all waiting anxiously to get into the United States. U.S. officials maintain that the Chinese smuggling rings have connections in 51 countries that are either part of the transportation web or are involved in the manufacture of fraudulent travel documents (Freedman, 1991; Kamen, 1991; Mydans, 1992). According to a senior official, "at any given time, thirty thousand Chinese are stashed away in safe houses around the world, waiting for entry" (Kinkead, 1992: 160).

Unlike Mexican illegal immigrants, who enter the United States at little or no cost (Crewdson, 1983; Jones, 1984; Cornelius, 1989), each illegal Chinese immigrant must pay smugglers about $30,000 for their services (U.S. Senate, 1992). Since thousands of Chinese are smuggled out of their country each year, people trafficking

Table 8.2. Vessels Caught Smuggling Chinese into the United States

Date	Destination	Vessel	Flag	Approx. Number of Passengers
08/31/91	Los Angeles	*I-Mao*	Taiwan	131
01/28/91	Guatemala	*Lo Sing*	Taiwan & China	216
01/31/92	Guatemala	*Chen Fong*	Taiwan	Unknown
02/17/92	Honolulu	*Yun Fong Seong*	Taiwan	930
02/22/92	Honolulu	*Discoverer*	Taiwan	510
02/22/92	Los Angeles	*San Tai*	Taiwan	85
05/25/92	El Salvador	*Cheng Fong*	Taiwan	20
06/18/92	Honolulu	*Lucky*	Belize	119
07/31/92	Guatemala	*Jinn Yin*	Unknown	Unknown
09/08/92	Morehead City, North Carolina	*Chin Wing*	Honduras	150
09/11/92	Los Angeles	*Hong Sang*	Taiwan	158
09/18/92	Honolulu	*Eing Dong Ming*	Taiwan	137
09/22/92	New Bedford	*Unknown*	Unknown	200
10/25/92	Yokohama	*Dai Yuen*	Taiwan	142
12/10/92	Guatemala	*Shann Der*	Unknown	100
12/21/92	San Francisco	*Manyoshi Maru*	Honduras	180
12/27/92	Baja, California	*Sea Star*	Honduras	300
02/13/92	Marshall Is.	*East Wood*	Panama	528
01/10/93	Singapore	*Solas*	Jamaica	128
04/27/93	Baja, California	*Jenn Yang*	Taiwan	306
05/11/93	Honduras	*Mermaid*	Honduras	237
05/12/93	San Diego	*Chin Lung Hsiang*	Honduras	199
05/24/93	San Francisco	*Pai Sheng*	Honduras	171
06/02/93	San Francisco	*Pelican*	United States	120
06/02/93	San Francisco	*Angel*	Unknown	184
06/06/93	New York	*Golden Venture*	Taiwan	296
06/25/93	Indonesia	*Ever Rise*	Honduras	156
07/19/93	Baja, California	*To Ching*	Taiwan	254
07/19/93	Baja, California	*Long Sen*	Taiwan	170
07/19/93	Baja, California	*Sing Li*	China	236
07/28/93	Guatemala	*An Shien*	Taiwan	46
03/15/94	Virginia	*Kuo Long*	Taiwan	110
04/11/94	San Diego	*Jin Yi*	Taiwan	113
Total				5,336

SOURCE: U.S. Immigration and Naturalization Service, Intelligence Division; media accounts.

is a very lucrative business. One case illustrates the point: a 41-year-old Chinese woman convicted of smuggling a large number of Chinese into the United States was alleged to have earned approximately $30 million during her career (Chan and Dao, 1990a). A senior immigration official has estimated that Chinese organized crime groups make more than $1 billion a year from human smuggling operations.

Although many studies on immigration have been conducted, most focus on Mexican immigrants or on the impact of undocumented workers on the American economy (Weintraub, 1984; Cornelius, 1989; Bean et al., 1990; Delgado, 1992). Other than a general report prepared by an immigration lawyer in Philadelphia

(Myers, 1992), there have been no systematic studies of undocumented Chinese in America.[24] Consequently, little is known about the relationship between Chinese gangs and people trafficking, although the connection is claimed to exist by the authorities. Such a connection has also been portrayed and sensationalized in the media—especially in the aftermath of the *Golden Venture* incident, in which a smuggling ship ran aground off New York City and ten passengers drowned.

Chinese Gangs and Human Smuggling

Most illegal immigrants work hard to repay their debts to their snakeheads, but some disputes and conflicts invariably arise. If there is a financial problem between an illegal immigrant and a smuggling ring, it is very unlikely that either party will attempt to solve the problem in the courts. Thus, those who are unable to pay off their debts may be kidnapped or tortured by people who are hired by the smugglers to collect their fees (Kifner, 1991; Lorch, 1991; Strom, 1991).

Apart from possible victimization by smuggling rings, illegal immigrants may also fall prey to Chinese gangs and criminal groups. For example, an illegal immigrant having difficulty repaying smugglers may be recruited by a drug-trafficking group to work as a courier (Chan and Dao, 1990b). Many are also believed to be hired by criminal groups to work as enforcers in their illicit businesses (Kifner, 1991). Female illegal immigrants may end up working as prostitutes, either voluntarily or through coercion when their debtors demand repayment (Y. Chan, 1993a).

The lack of family life among thousands of Chinese illegal immigrants, coupled with limited access to recreational activities within their isolated communities, has led to a proliferation of brothels and gambling dens in New York City's Chinatowns (*China Press*, 1992; *New York Times*, 1993a). This increased demand for illicit goods and services in the Chinese community may have facilitated the expansion of the Chinese underworld.

The intricate ties between crime and illegal immigration have led some law enforcement officials to believe that Chinese triads, tongs, and gangs are involved in the human smuggling business. American officials have claimed that Hong Kong–based triads are responsible for the massive movement of illegal Chinese immigrants to the United States through Hong Kong (U.S. Senate, 1992; Torode, 1993). A smuggler testified that a member of the 14K triad in Hong Kong was involved in human smuggling. Federal agents accused the California-based Wo Hop To triad society of smuggling 85 undocumented Chinese in a boat that reached Long Beach, California. But so far, no triad groups have been indicted for human smuggling.

The tongs, especially the Fukien American Association, have often been implicated in this lucrative business. At the 1992 U.S. Senate hearings on Asian organized crime, a police officer testified that he *believed* tongs were involved:

> Senator Roth: Let me ask you this: During the course of your investigation, did the Major Case Squad uncover any connection between the Fukien American Association and the alien smugglers?
>
> Mr. Pollini: The only thing that I can indicate as far as that, Senator, is when we were conducting our investigation, we conducted extensive surveillance and telephonic surveillance. A majority of the calls that we tracked back came back to the

Fukien American Association, and surveillance led us to subjects of the investigation going in and out of the location freely.

Senator Roth: Can we draw the conclusion that the tong known as the Fukien American Association is in some way connected with the illegal alien smuggling activity?

Mr. Pollini: It is difficult to establish that positively, Senator, but as a result of our investigations, we are under the belief that they are. (U.S. Senate, 1992: 200–201)

Leaders of the Fukien American Association, however, denied that their organization had ever been involved in human smuggling. The president of the association, labeled by journalists as the "commander-in-chief of illegal smuggling," announced at a press conference that his organization

does not have control over certain individual members and therefore can not be held responsible for their illegal activities. It is unjust to blacken the name of the Fukien American Association as a whole based on the behavior of some non-member bad elements which are not under the control of the Association. (Lau, 1993: 5)

Chinese gangs have also been accused of involvement in human smuggling.[25] In 1990, several defendants believed to be members of the Fuk Ching gang were arrested for kidnapping an illegal Fujianese immigrant (Kifner, 1991). Since that incident, many more illegal immigrants have been abducted by Fujianese offenders in the New York City metropolitan area. The victims were kidnapped either because they owed smugglers money or because the kidnappers decided to take advantage of the victims' illegal status. The relatives of the kidnapping victims were forced to pay the kidnappers large sums of money for their release.

Before 1991, law enforcement authorities and the media rarely hinted that Chinese gangs played an important role in the smuggling of Chinese into the United States. In 1991, a *San Francisco Chronicle* article asserted that Asian gangs were deeply involved in human trafficking (Freedman, 1991). In the following years, many media accounts about the involvement of Chinese gangs in human smuggling appeared. Most of the articles claimed that Chinese gangs were helping smugglers to collect smuggling fees in New York City. Gang members would go to the airports or seaports, pick up newly arrived illegal immigrants, keep them in safe houses, and compel them to call their relatives in China or the United States to ask them to pay the smuggling fees. Once the fees were paid, the illegal immigrants were released, and the money was turned over to the smugglers. For their services, the gangs were paid from $1,500 to $2,000 per illegal immigrant. There has been no evidence that gangs are involved in other aspects of human smuggling operations or invest any money in such operations (Strom, 1991).

Between December 1991 and June 1993, many smuggling-related incidents of violence were reported in the media (Nieves, 1993; Torres, 1993). According to the news accounts, undocumented Chinese were badly treated by their captors, and those who were unable to pay the smuggling fees were tortured or sexually abused. The reports indicated that, since each illegal entrant is worth $25,000 or more to the smugglers, gang members often abduct the illegals from the hands of their rivals so that they can later demand a ransom. In one incident, an illegal immigrant was shot to death on bustling East Broadway when an attempt by his relatives to rescue him from the debt collectors went awry. Other reports claimed that many illegal immigrants, even though they did not owe any money to smugglers, would be kidnapped by gang members who thought they were easy prey (Y. Chan, 1993b; Faison, 1993d).

However, it was not until the *Golden Venture* ran aground off New York City in June 1993 that authorities began to mention a particular gang—the Fuk Ching—and implicated it and its leader, Kuo Liang Kay, in the human smuggling operation (Burdman, 1993; Faison, 1993a; Gladwell and Stassen-Berger, 1993; Treaster, 1993a). The gang not only invested money in the purchase of the *Golden Venture* but also was directly involved in recruiting would-be illegal immigrants. The gang supposedly orchestrated the voyage, arranged for local transportation in the United States, and collected the smuggling fees. Thus, after the *Golden Venture* incident, immigration officials and law enforcement authorities began to define some Chinese gangs as service providers to smuggling organizations, as well as criminal groups capable of bringing in hundreds of illegal immigrants on their own (Lay and Dobson, 1993).

In the aftermath of the well-publicized *Golden Venture* incident, law enforcement authorities mounted crackdowns on Chinese gangs that they suspected of being involved in collecting smuggling fees. Members of the White Tigers, the Green Dragons, and the Fuk Ching were arrested and indicted for assisting smugglers in moving people from various border and coastal areas of the United States to New York City and were charged with collecting smuggling fees. None of them, however, was directly charged for participation in the *Golden Venture* incident.[26]

Although tongs and gangs are alleged to be involved in human smuggling, little is known about the extent of their involvement. Also, assuming there is involvement, it is not clear whether the smuggling operations are sponsored by tongs and gangs jointly or if they are carried out by certain tong and gang members on an ad hoc basis. Furthermore, little is known about the structure of the smuggling rings. For example, it is not clear who the other participants are or how people in various parts of the world cooperate in order to move a large number of people through many countries and finally into the United States. There is no doubt that the smugglers are internationally linked, but what is not known is how the links are established and maintained and how the proceeds from the crime are distributed among the participants.

Legitimate Businesses

A report prepared by the Federal Bureau of Investigation in 1988 concluded that "the most developed Chinese organized crime groups are diversifying into a broad range of legitimate businesses" (U.S. Department of Justice, 1988: iv). An experienced police detective from Los Angeles testified before the U.S. Senate in 1992:

> A disturbing trend in Asian organized crime is the increasing involvement of Asian gangs in semi-legitimate businesses. For example, the leaders of the Wah Ching gang in California have insulated themselves from the street level, and are now primarily involved in the entertainment industry and leasing of videotapes. (U.S. Senate, 1992: 157–58)

Thus, according to some law enforcement officials, Chinese gangs are shifting some of their assets and resources from purely criminal operations to legitimate or semilegitimate businesses.

Actually, my research data suggest that Chinese gangs are already relatively active in legitimate businesses. About 77 percent of my gang subjects indicated that their gangs owned or operated legitimate businesses such as restaurants, retail stores, and wholesale supply firms. Other businesses include vegetable stands, car services, factories, banks, ice cream parlors, fish markets, videotape rental stores, and employment agencies.

Wholesale supply businesses in particular are mentioned by both law enforcement authorities and Chinese businesspeople as being vulnerable to gang involvement. A restaurateur testified to the U.S. Senate that he was asked by a gang member to do business with him:

> In the past and recently, our restaurant also has been required to buy vegetables from a gang member. He would get the produce from other merchants and sell it to us at higher prices. Other restaurants in the area were also required to buy their vegetables from the gang for more than they would cost at other produce stores. (U.S. Senate, 1992: 51)

Some restaurant owners we interviewed confirmed the validity of this testimony. They indicated they were buying dried food, rice, and seafood from Chinese gang members under duress; however, some of my respondents did not indicate that they were overcharged by the gangs. One subject said that a gang member actually offered him better prices than his initial legitimate supplier.

Officials also believe the entertainment industry has been penetrated by Chinese gangs (Shelly, 1994). Top-rate entertainers from Hong Kong and Taiwan are believed to be managed by gangs, who set up performance dates in American casinos and nightclubs. Officials claim that a famous Hong Kong actress was invited by a California-based Chinese gang to perform in Las Vegas (U.S. Senate, 1992). After her arrival in Las Vegas, the sponsoring gang not only forced businesspeople in San Francisco's Chinatown to buy show tickets but also ordered the gambling houses in the community to close down for a few days so that gamblers might be persuaded to go to Las Vegas to gamble and attend the show.

It is not clear whether the gang as a whole or the gang leader and a number of his followers are involved in legitimate and semi-legitimate businesses. From my data, it would seem that legitimate businesses are usually owned and operated by a gang leader whose purpose is mainly to promote his self-interest. Ordinary gang members may or may not know about their leader's legitimate business interests, but they are unlikely to be involved in his businesses.

Summary

Chinese gangs or their individual members are involved in income-generating crimes, including extortion, gambling, prostitution, robbery, heroin trafficking, and human smuggling. In addition, they are also involved in certain legitimate businesses. Although most of their activities affect the Chinese communities and American mainstream society negatively, their role in heroin trafficking and human smuggling is of greatest concern to law enforcement authorities. It is safe to say that it was because of alleged Chinese gang involvement in these international crimes that the law enforcement community began to treat gangs as racketeering enterprises.

However, I suggest that the extent of Chinese involvement in heroin trafficking and human smuggling appears to have been exaggerated by a few well-publicized incidents. For example, since the *Golden Venture* tragedy, illegal immigration among Chinese has become a major concern for the immigration authorities. Yet INS data show that in terms of number of illegal immigrants in the United States, China ranks twenty-first on a long list of countries from which the vast majority of illegal migrants come (City of New York Department of City Planning, 1993).[27]

My data—when contrasted with media accounts, which are based on law enforcement news releases—seem to reveal that Chinese gangs are being treated as scapegoats for heroin trafficking and human smuggling operated by Chinese. Although there is evidence that gang members provide services to the heroin traffickers and human smugglers, the extent of their involvement, especially as a group, seems to have been exaggerated. My study suggests that a small number of gang leaders and gang members are the tools of heroin traffickers and human smugglers based in the United States. The gangs appear to have no significant long-term association with smugglers based in Asia. Moreover, and this point cannot be emphasized too strongly, many young criminals working for the smugglers in the United States are not affiliated with gangs. The police and the media have customarily labeled all young Fujianese males arrested for collecting smuggling fees as members of the Fuk Ching gang, although many loosely knit Fujianese groups that are not associated with the Fuk Ching gang exist in the Chinese community. We can conclude that law enforcement authorities are either improperly using the word gang or not investigating these freelance criminals' backgrounds thoroughly enough.

There are many similarities between heroin trafficking and human smuggling: both are transnational crimes involving many countries; both are very lucrative; both involve gang members in the United States as service providers; both appear to be dominated by a unique group of people who are well traveled, posses international links, and are familiar with the Golden Triangle,[28] the main source of heroin and the major exit point for many undocumented Chinese; and both are considered victimless crimes, at least by the Chinese offenders, and consequently not much stigma is attached to engaging in them. Smugglers view both crimes simply as lucrative business activities. Although a number of law enforcement authorities have suggested that many Chinese offenders are involved in both heroin trafficking and human smuggling, there is no reliable information to support this contention at this time.

9

Controlling Chinese Gangs

According to Spergel (1990), there are four basic strategies for dealing with youth gangs: local community organization or neighborhood mobilization; the provision of social and economic opportunities; youth outreach or street gang work; and the suppression and incarceration of gang members. In New York City's Chinatowns, organized responses to Chinese gangs have primarily involved suppression and incarceration of gang members. The first two strategies mentioned by Spergel have never been implemented.[1] The third strategy, youth outreach or street gang work, is almost nonexistent. Although there is a youth outreach program, called Project Reach, that operates on the outskirts of Manhattan's Chinatown, it only deals with a limited number of at-risk youths from various ethnic groups. The program's main purpose is to provide tutoring, counseling, and recreational activities to high school students after school, and it appears to have limited, if any, impact on the Chinese gang problem. Another youth program, named Turn a New Leaf, which is sponsored by the Asian Americans Communications group and is located in Queens, is reported to be actively involved in helping hard-core Chinese gang members. However, the efficacy of the program has not been confirmed (*World Journal*, 1994c).

This chapter examines the evolving role of law enforcement authorities in combating Chinese gangs and the levels of gang control attempted by local police, federal agencies, and foreign authorities. Also, some of the major problems encountered by law enforcement agencies in containing Chinese gangs will be explored. (All citations to "personal interview" refer to interviews with law enforcement personnel and community leaders who wish to remain anonymous.)

Local Law Enforcement Agencies

New York City is divided into 113 precincts. A precinct is a police command subdivision; it carries out law enforcement functions such as patrol work, safety and traffic control, and criminal investigations within its territory. The precincts are supported by borough commands, divisions of detective units, specialized bureaus, and task forces organized to cope with crime problems that extend beyond the scope and capacity of the local precincts.

The New York City Police Department (NYPD) bears the major responsibility for antigang efforts at the local level. The Fifth and Seventh Precincts in Manhattan, the 109th Precinct in Flushing, Queens, and the 66th Precinct in Brooklyn are most affected by Chinese gang activities.

Manhattan

The core areas of Manhattan's Chinatown are patrolled by the Fifth Precinct of the NYPD. This precinct covers the major streets of Chinatown, such as Mott, Bayard, Pell, the Bowery, and Canal. The Fifth Precinct also serves some parts of the Italian community north of Canal Street and the Puerto Rican community at the southern border of Chinatown. The precinct's area is bounded by Allen Street on the east, Broadway on the west, East Houston Street on the north, and Frankfurt Street on the south.

The Fifth Precinct is considered to be extremely knowledgeable about Chinese gang activities in the tri-state (New York, New Jersey, and Connecticut) area. Police officers and detectives from across the country and Canada often seek help from the Fifth Precinct when they believe that crimes in their jurisdictions were committed by gang members or associates of gangs in Manhattan's Chinatown. Of the 140 police officers assigned to the precinct, only 20 (14%) are of Chinese descent (Newman, 1992). This means that police communication with a predominantly Chinese-speaking community is difficult. Moreover, the ability of the NYPD to address crime control and public order issues is diminished because the non-Chinese officers often do not understand Chinese customs.

In the late 1970s, the Fifth precinct established a Special Task Force (STF), which was funded by the city government, to deal exclusively with Chinese gangs. The task force, which was staffed with 25 uniformed police officers, was primarily involved in detection, surveillance, and community affairs. The duty of investigation was left to detectives in the Fifth Precinct. Members of the STF took pictures of gang members on a routine basis in order to be able to identify them. According to a police officer assigned to the STF:

> With these photographs we can identify all the gang members. We can immediately tell "who is who" by the picture and to which gang he belongs. If you were seen with a gang member inside an automobile, a photograph would be taken of you and also the license plate of the car would be taken. The information collected will be processed and then put in our intelligence files. (*Canal Magazine*, 1979)

A decade later, in 1980, the Fifth Precinct set up a new police strike force to deal with the outbreak of gang violence. Some of the members of the unit were drawn from the STF; but unlike the STF, the new strike force focused primarily on investigation and arrest (Buder, 1980).

Three years later, the strike force was reorganized as the Asian Gang Intelligence Unit. Since its formation, the Asian Gang Intelligence Unit has been instrumental in solving numerous gang murders in the community and it also plays a vital role in the surveillance of gang activities. In 10 years, two Chinese American police officers from the unit have arrested many gang members active in the community, and their presence in the community has not only worked as a deterrent to gangs but also encouraged Chinese community residents to approach the police when they are victimized.[2] The Asian Gang Intelligence Unit is currently staffed with one sergeant and five police officers, two of whom are Chinese-Americans (*World Journal*, 1994a).

Also, within the Fifth Precinct, there are more than 100 nonpaid, civilian block watchers who are members of the Chinese community. Each of them is given a code, and when they see something suspicious, they call the police immediately. Also, many Chinatown merchants and residents volunteer to work as auxiliary police. While auxiliary police wear the same type of uniform as the regular police, they do not arrest criminals or carry weapons. Currently, there are 150 auxiliary police in the Fifth Precinct, most of whom are Chinese (Newman, 1992).

Community involvement has been a goal of the most recent antigang strategies in the Fifth Precinct. To this end, the precinct has developed a community outreach organization—the Chinatown Project—which offers local residents aid and assistance in discussing their problems with non-Chinese-speaking police officers and other government officials. The primary aim is to help local residents communicate with the police. The organization also alerts the community to the social services that municipal agencies provide (for example, victim's assistance services).

Every month, the captain of the Fifth Precinct meets with community leaders and merchants, informs them of the crime rate in the community, and encourages them to express their concerns. These monthly meetings are held at the precinct or the offices of the Chinese Consolidated Benevolent Association (CCBA), an umbrella community organization.

The Seventh Precinct is located on the eastern outskirts of Manhattan's Chinatown. Since the late 1980s, tens of thousands of Fujianese immigrants, both legal and illegal, have settled within the Seventh Precinct's command. Since then, the Fuk Ching gang has become involved in a bloody power struggle with the neighboring Tung On gang, and it has allegedly initiated smuggling-related violence, which is reportedly rampant within the Fujianese community. As a result of the Fuk Ching's presence, law enforcement efforts in policing Chinese gangs have changed dramatically. Within the past few years, the precinct has been actively involved in raiding gambling clubs and massage parlors located within its command. Recently, some of the Fifth Precinct's officers who are familiar with Chinese gangs have been transferred to the Seventh Precinct.

In addition, the Manhattan Detective Task Force contains an Oriental Gang Unit (or the Jade Squad) which works closely with the prosecutors of the Manhattan District Attorney's Office. The Jade Squad, which was established in October 1981 and was staffed with a sergeant and four detectives, played a crucial role in making the first Racketeer Influenced and Corrupt Organizations Act (RICO) case against the Ghost Shadows (Leng, 1984). At its peak, in 1984, the squad had eight detectives (Faso and Meskil, 1984). Although the squad functioned under the auspices of the Manhattan District Attorney's Office, it was active in the investigation of Chinese gang crime citywide. The unit played a vital role in controlling Chinese gangs in the 1980s, but it has sharply reduced its activities in the 1990s due to program cutbacks (U.S. Senate, 1992).

In the 1990s, the NYPD reorganized its intelligence-gathering operations on street gang activity. A gang unit was formed to centralize data gathering on street gangs of every ethnic and racial group in the entire city. Within the Intelligence Division's Principal Gang Unit, ethnic and racial specialists evaluate reports of incidents and precinct observation reports on street gang activity. Should one area experience a dramatic rise in street crime among specific groups, the unit can deploy specialist officers to investigate and affect arrests.

Queens

The Chinese population in Queens resides mostly in areas patrolled by the 109th and 110th police precincts. These areas comprise two sections of Queens—Flushing and Jackson Heights. Many Chinese residents of Flushing and Jackson Heights speak Mandarin instead of Cantonese (D. Martin, 1988), and Chinese merchants and residents of Queens are reported to be wealthier, better educated, and more assimilated into the mainstream society, and to speak better English, than their counterparts in Manhattan's Chinatown (Chen, 1992). Flushing is part of the NYPD's 109th district; Jackson Heights lies in the jurisdiction of 110th Precinct.

The 109th Precinct, in which Flushing is located, is experiencing an increase of gang crime (R. Sullivan, 1992). To cope with a surge in extortion and gang violence in the borough, Queens District Attorney Richard Brown established a Queens Asian Crime Investigation Unit in May 1991 (*World Journal*, 1992b). The unit, which operates out of the 109th Precinct, is headed by a sergeant who is in command of three Chinese and one Korean detective. The unit, like the Fifth Precinct's Asian Gang Intelligence Unit, has been highly acclaimed for its effectiveness in dealing with Chinese gangs (*Sing Tao Jih Pao*, 1993b). The unit moved to Long Island City in June 1994 as part of a plan for relocating all NYPD special units for logistical reasons. Brown also formed an Asian Gangs Special Unit in his office to prosecute Chinese gang offenders. The prosecution unit works closely with the 109th Precinct's Asian Crime Investigation Unit.

Brooklyn

Brooklyn has also experienced a growth in Chinese gang crimes, especially in the borough's Chinatown, which is located along Eighth Avenue (*Sing Tao Jih Pao*, 1992d; 1993c). Most of the area is covered by the 66th and 72nd Precincts.

An Asian Unit was established in 1990 within the NYPD's Brooklyn Robbery Squad to deal with crimes involving Asian offenders and victims (*World Journal*, 1993d). One Asian-American detective is assigned to the unit.

Citywide Programs

The NYPD has organized a Principal Gang Unit (PGU) within its Intelligence Division. One of the PGU's main functions is to create a gang database from citywide arrest reports, probation documents, surveillance and undercover work, and personal interviews with street gang members. Its other functions include the collection of demographic information, such as date of birth, gender, race, ethnicity, physical description, arrest record, gang affiliation, place of origin, and criminal history, on street gang members. The PGU also serves as an investigative arm of the NYPD's Intelligence Division and as a training unit for officers in precincts in which gang activity is especially chronic.

The PGU was formed in response to the serious problem street gangs pose in certain communities of New York City. It is developing new reporting forms and updating its database by soliciting information from every precinct in the city and from every city agency that is involved in youth crime work.

The seriousness of the gang problem is reflected in the fact that youth gang information and intelligence have been shifted from the Chief of Patrol Division to the Intelligence Division in the department. According to Sergeant Michael Collins, the head of the PGU: "The gang problem has gotten worse. Our role is to define the gang problem and help the department develop strategies to confront it" (personal interview).

With the increase in kidnapping of illegal Fujianese immigrants by Chinese gang members, the NYPD's Major Case Squad has come to play an important role in coping with Chinese gangs (Y. Chan, 1993b). Since 1992, the squad has solved several well-publicized kidnapping cases involving Fujianese offenders and victims.

Finally, the Morals Division of the NYPD is responsible for controlling gambling and prostitution in the Chinese community. The division has occasionally carried out high-profile raids against well-established gambling dens and massage parlors in the community, with or without the assistance of the local police precincts (*Sing Tao Jih Pao*, 1992b).

Federal Law Enforcement Agencies

The American law enforcement community has often viewed Chinese gangs as "organized gangs" rather than "street gangs" (U.S. Department of Justice, 1985, 1988; U.S. Senate, 1992). Because so many Chinese gangs are affiliated with members of adult crime groups that are involved in national or international crimes, federal law enforcement agencies have frequently joined local police in the investigation and suppression of Chinese gangs (Dobson, 1993). The Federal Bureau of Investigation (FBI), Drug Enforcement Administration (DEA), and Immigration and Naturalization Service (INS) are the three federal agencies most active in curbing Chinese gangs and their links to organized crime groups.

Federal Bureau of Investigation

A report on Asian organized crime prepared by the U.S. Department of Justice in 1988 concluded that "the capabilities and priorities of local law enforcement are not well-matched with the national and international activities of some COC [Chinese organized crime] groups" (iv). In response to these findings, several federal agencies, especially the FBI, have become actively involved in the investigation of Chinese gangs (*Sing Tao Jih Pao*, 1991c).

In 1989, under the auspices of the Organized Crime Strike Force, the FBI's New York Branch formed an Anti-Asian Gang Task Force. Currently, 27 federal agents, including four Asian Americans, work in the task force (*World Journal*, 1992a). The unit is not only active in investigating heroin trafficking among Chinese but also instrumental in scrutinizing gang-related kidnappings and murders. It has also played a vital role in the RICO indictments against the Green Dragons and the Fuk Ching gangs (Dannen, 1992; Faison, 1993b).

FBI agents in San Francisco, Los Angeles, Seattle, Washington, D.C., and Boston are also active in investigating Chinese gang crimes in their jurisdictions (U.S. Senate, 1992).

Drug Enforcement Administration

The DEA plays a major role in investigating heroin trafficking among Chinese. In response to a significant increase in the amount of Southeast Asian heroin entering the United States in the early 1980s, the DEA in New York City established a special unit in 1985 known as Group 41. Since its inception, the unit, along with prosecutors in the federal district court, has convicted some of the major heroin traffickers of Chinese origin (Kerr, 1987b). The unit consists of ten federal agents.

Immigration and Naturalization Service

Within the INS Investigation Division, there are three units to cope with gangs in general and alien smuggling in particular (U.S. Senate, 1992). The Interagency Violence Gang Task Force deals with gang-related violence, regardless of the ethnicity of the gangs. The Anti-smuggling Unit investigates specific smuggling syndicates. The unit has approximately 300 agents who work full-time in anti-smuggling efforts, and approximately 25 percent of their cases are related to Chinese organized crime groups (U.S. Senate, 1992). The Interagency Chinese Boat Smuggling Task Force deals exclusively with boat smuggling among Chinese. All three units are located in the headquarters of the INS in Washington, D.C. In addition, the INS Investigation Division has initiated a special Asian Crime Task Force (the ACT team) to focus primarily on Chinese organized crime (U.S. Senate, 1992).

Other Federal Agency Involvement

The Bureau of Alcohol, Tobacco, and Firearms (ATF) within the U.S. Department of Treasury became involved in policing Chinese crime groups when heroin traffickers were found to be importing firearms into the United States (*World Journal*, 1988). The ATF participated in several joint operations with the FBI and DEA to crack down on Chinese gangs and organized crime groups. Another Treasury Department agency, the U.S. Customs Service, has also been active in controlling

Chinese crime, especially heroin trafficking and the smuggling of goods and aliens into the United States.

According to Dombrink and Song (1992), other federal agencies such as the U.S. Postal Service, the Internal Revenue Service (IRS), and the Department of Labor are involved to some degree in investigation of Chinese organized crime activities. Due to the surge in alien smuggling among Chinese, the Department of State has become concerned with Chinese organized crime (Wallis and Lewis, 1993), and it plays an important role in negotiating with China on matters such as the deportation of illegal aliens.

In addition, in some jurisdictions, joint task forces have been formed to cope with Chinese gangs. For example, the Asian Organized Crime Unit was established in 1992 in the Washington, D.C., area to deal with Asian crime. The unit includes 10 full-time and part-time investigators from the FBI, the INS, the Virginia State Police, and the Fairfax County and Arlington County police departments. Also, there are two interagency programs on the federal level that deal with Asian gangs, among other crime groups: the Organized Crime Drug Enforcement Task Force (OCDETF) and the Organized Crime and Racketeering Strike Force (OCRS) of the U.S. Department of Justice.

Investigating and Prosecuting Chinese Gangs

The NYPD has not adopted all-out gang suppression tactics in which police saturate a neighborhood and conduct street sweeps and round-ups.[3] Gang members are not sought out and arrested without good cause. Instead, the NYPD has developed a tradition of close association and interaction with local community groups in dealing with gang problems (Orrick, 1990). Precinct-level specialized units target the most active and violent gangs and emphasize rapport and frequent contact with them. Police often work in plain clothes and conduct informal interviews on the street so that gang members are aware they are under constant surveillance.

The Fifth Precinct Asian Gang Intelligence Unit, the Oriental Gang Unit of the Manhattan Detective Task Force, and the Principal Gang Unit of the Intelligence Division monitor gang members daily and maintain a large photo file of those associated with massage parlors and gambling establishments and of those engaged in extortion activities (personal interview). Regular contact with gang members enables local police to identify gang members by their associations, criminal records, and street reputations. The subtleties of the police approach are effective. Despite the presumed low level of internal gang cohesion, a strategy of harassment and explicit confrontational techniques might actually serve to strengthen the gangs. According to police specialists, despite their ties to the tongs and vice activities in the Chinese community, many gangs define themselves by their enemies; and for the gangs, the NYPD would constitute a unifying opponent. Thus, policies under which individuals are openly and aggressively confronted because of their gang membership may achieve the opposite effect of what is intended—they may solidify cohesive gang bonds rather than weaken them.

Most NYPD specialized units are small (consisting of several officers and detectives) and are not comparable to the antigang units in other large cities such as Los Angeles and Chicago that are plagued with street gang problems (Spergel, 1990; Los Angeles County District Attorney, 1992). In brief, the NYPD specialized units are primarily engaged in intelligence gathering and subtle patrolling and do not engage in active gang suppression or gang intervention tactics, which are part of community-based policing strategies in other locales. Aggressive tactics are used by the NYPD, along with federal law enforcement agents, only when a particular gang is under investigation.

Thus, whenever a major violent incident erupts, an increased number of police officers will be seen patrolling the community—especially known gang turfs—in an effort to deter the gangs and frustrate retaliatory aggression. If the police wish to put additional pressure on the gangs, they attack the community-based vice industry by raiding gambling clubs and massage parlors, on the assumption that operators of these businesses will restrain gangs from further violence, albeit temporarily (*Centre Daily News*, 1986). If the local precincts need additional help, the NYPD headquarters can summon all Chinese-speaking police officers in the city to report to the local precincts as a stopgap measure (*World Journal*, 1985a).

In general, from the interviews with law enforcement authorities, I ascertained that both local law enforcement authorities and federal agencies have employed the following methods to collect information on Chinese gang members and to suppress gang activities:

1. *Street gang informants.* Former gang members are cultivated as informants and regularly consult with both local and federal authorities, sometimes as part of their probation status. This method has been used successfully in RICO cases against the Ghost Shadows, the Green Dragons, the Born-to-Kill, and the Tung On.
2. *Undercover law enforcement operations.* To infiltrate the gangs and collect vital information about their criminal activities, Asian American law enforcement officers often pose as potential buyers in DEA and FBI drug cases (Bolden, 1990; Kwong and Miqsqcevic, 1990), as potential investors in INS prostitution cases (Surovell, 1988), or as aspiring gang members (Kaplan, 1992).
3. *Hot lines.* The local police and the FBI, with the help of the local Chinese media, have often asked Chinatown residents to report certain types of crime to a special hot line. Also, on the eves of major Chinese holidays, local police often notify the community business sector to be on the alert for gang extortion and urge them to call the police if they are approached by gang members for money. Such notices are usually distributed in the community and published in the local Chinese media.[4]
4. *Police street patrols.* Members of the Asian Gang Intelligence Unit of the Fifth Precinct occasionally stop and search suspicious-looking youths. This has resulted in the arrests of gang members for weapons possession.[5]
5. *Electronic surveillance.* The gang's apartments are put under surveillance, gang members' movements around the apartments are videotaped, and their phone conversations are taped. This method was utilized by the FBI in the case against the Green Dragons.
6. *Roadblocks.* Occasionally, authorities in the tri-state area of New York, New Jersey, and Connecticut set up highway checkpoints to deal with highly mobile Chinese

gang members who are involved in home-invasion crimes or commercial robbery. (*World Journal*, 1985b)

Cooperation among Federal and Local Agencies

Until fairly recently, Chinese street gangs were not a federal priority (Chin, 1990). Because of their alleged ties to drug traffickers, gangs have now come to the attention of federal agencies. However, the real work of dealing with the gangs on a daily basis has been left to local police. Federal investigators have had little training or experience with street gangs. Their professional background and jurisdictional responsibilities tend to be in narcotics and organized crime. Their tactics— wiretapping, electronic surveillance, infiltration, and long-term investigations— are typically effective against organized crime groups and drug traffickers. Moreover, federal investigative priorities focus on the nexus between gangs and drugs. Thus, to the extent that federal law enforcement agencies are involved with street gangs, their experience tends to be limited to the *dai lo*s, or gang leaders. In joint operations with local police and organized crime units, federal agencies cooperate, but leave the initiatives of launching investigations to the local police. It is at the precinct level then that the impetus and stimulus for joint task force operations begins.

According to Catherine Palmer, an Assistant United States Attorney active in RICO prosecutions against Chinese street gangs and drug traffickers, the NYPD plays an important role in many cases and investigations involving both the DEA and FBI. In discussing several prosecutions of street gang members, Palmer noted that:

> Precincts are where most of the underlying crimes originated, so we could not have done anything without [the cooperation of] the NYPD. The problem is that different agencies answer to different political and jurisdictional entities. The police answer to the Commissioner, the FBI to Washington, and so on. The way it works is on the personal level: we get to know some police officers and work closely together. . . . It's not going to come together at the top. (personal interview)

In contrast to federal agencies, state and local law enforcement offices do not focus on the connection between Chinese street gangs and narcotics (personal interview). Instead, they concentrate on local criminal activities that fall within their areas of jurisdiction and responsibility. As a result, there are problems of cooperation among different levels of law enforcement. Closer, more intensive working liaisons between them are desirable for a number of reasons. Though somewhat inexperienced in dealing with local street gangs, federal prosecutors operate in a court system that facilitates prosecutions more efficiently than that of their state counterparts (personal interview). In many cases, federal law makes it easier to deny bail and thereby remove dangerous gang members from the street. Also, federal penalties are usually stiffer than state and local penalties for similar crimes, and federal sentences must be served in full without probation or parole. The latter dimension of federal prosecutions was bolstered in 1986 by the passage of the Minimum Mandatory Sentencing law, which dictates that offenders must serve a minimum amount of time for their crimes. The U.S. Marshal's Witness Security Program and the RICO laws are also incentives for offender cooperation.

Differences between federal and local law enforcement tools to combat street gangs hinge on RICO, the most potent weapon in the law enforcement armory (Blakey, 1994). According to Palmer:

> RICO is an effective tool because it enables you to get at the organization as a whole. Also, and as importantly, it helps us to make cases because it ordinarily involves many substantive charges in an indictment against an organization. When you're dealing with reluctant witnesses, it is especially helpful. Usually, an extortion victim is one of many; there are numerous witnesses and some gang members who cooperate with us against the gang. Too many people are testifying. . . . Who will the gang go after? The gang is soured on their own members who turn state's evidence. The State [local, New York Organized Crime Control Act legislation] does not have the advantage we have: they need corroboration for an accomplice's claims, we don't. (Personal interview)

Between 1985 and 1994, fifteen Chinese crime groups were indicted as racketeering enterprises (see table 9.1). The first RICO case was mounted against the

Table 9.1. RICO Indictments of Chinese Gangs, Tongs, Triads, and Other Crime Groups (1985–1994)

Year	Name	Number of Defendants	Major Charges	Law Enforcement Agencies Involved[a]	Results
1985	Ghost Shadows	25	Murder	NYPD, FBI	Pled guilty
1986	Shih Hsiao Poa	3	Prostitution	INS	Convicted
1986	United Bamboo	9	Drug dealing	NYPD, FBI	Convicted
1990	On Leong	33	Gambling	FBI, IRS	Hung jury
1990	Green Dragons	7	Murder	NYPD, FBI	Convicted
1991	Born-to-Kill	8	Murder	NYPD, ATF	Convicted
1993	Fuk Ching	20	Murder	NYPD, FBI	Pled guilty
1993	Wo Hop To	19	Arson	SFPD, FBI, ATF, RHKP	Pending[c]
1993	Tung On Assoc., Tsung Tsin Assoc., and Tung On gang	15	Murder	NYPD, DEA, ATF	Convicted[b]
1993	White Tigers	17	Murder	NYPD, DEA	Pending[c]
1994	Ping On	15	Murder	FBI, DEA	Pending
1994	Ghost Shadows	21	Murder	FBI, DEA	Pending[c]
1994	Flying Dragons	33	Murder	FBI, DEA	Pending[c]

a. NYPD = New York City Police Department; SFPD = San Francisco Police Department; ATF = Bureau of Alcohol, Tobacco, and Firearms; FBI = Federal Bureau of Investigation; DEA = Drug Enforcement Administration; IRS = Internal Revenue Service; INS = Immigration and Naturalization Service; RHKP = Royal Hong Kong Police.

b. A leader of the Tsung Tsin Association is to be tried separately.

c. Some of the defendants have pled guilty.

Ghost Shadows. The gang was indicted in 1985, after the NYPD, the Jade Squad of the Manhattan District Attorney's Office, and the FBI had worked together for two years collecting evidence on the gang's criminal activities. The 85-count indictment included 13 murders and numerous incidents of attempted murder, robbery, extortion, kidnapping, bribery, and illegal gambling (U.S. District Court, Southern District of New York, 1985a, 1985b). In May 1986, most of the defendants pleaded guilty and received the maximum sentence of 25 years.

In 1986, a RICO case was brought against the Taiwan-based United Bamboo gang. Nine United Bamboo members in California, Texas, and New York were charged with leading a racketeering enterprise that was involved in many serious crimes. The FBI was able to infiltrate the gang by getting two undercover agents formally inducted into the gang. At the trial, all the defendants were found guilty of racketeering activities (U.S. District Court, Southern District of New York, 1985c; Kaplan, 1992).

In 1990, after a witness in a criminal case involving the Green Dragons was abducted and killed, the New York City office of the FBI, along with the NYPD, began to build a RICO case against the Green Dragons. With the assistance of four Green Dragons members who agreed to work as informers, the investigation—which included wiretaps on telephones used by the gang members, as well as extensive surveillance—resulted in the arrests of sixteen gang members in November 1990. A search of two of the gang members' homes resulted in the seizure of 29 firearms, including one Uzi machine gun and one Uzi machine pistol. Seven of the gang members arrested were indicted under RICO for seven murders, three kidnappings, and many cases of extortion (U.S. District Court, Eastern District of New York, 1990). In 1992, all seven were found guilty by a jury and were sentenced to life imprisonment. However, the primary leader of the gang is still at-large; he is believed to be hiding in China (Dannen, 1992; Dao, 1992; Lubasch, 1992).

Approximately three months after the *Golden Venture* incident, the FBI and the NYPD's Major Case Squad arrested twenty leaders and members of the Fuk Ching gang (Faison, 1993b). The gang was charged with being a racketeering enterprise that was heavily involved in extortion, kidnapping, human smuggling, and murder. The leader of the gang was arrested in Hong Kong and extradited to the United States to stand trial (Faison, 1993c).

The Wo Hop To, a crime group based in California, was the center of attention at the 1991 Senate hearings on Asian organized crime (U.S. Senate, 1992). The organization, which American law enforcement officials labeled the first triad society to have been transplanted from Hong Kong to America, was alleged to have been in the process of becoming a "super gang" by consolidating various Chinese gangs on the West Coast under its umbrella. However, in late 1993, the FBI, the ATF, the San Francisco Police Department's Asian Gang Task Force, the Royal Hong Kong Police (RHKP), and state and local law enforcement authorities in California worked together in a joint operation that resulted in the arrest and indictment of nineteen Wo Hop To leaders and members. The primary leader of the gang was later arrested in Hong Kong and extradited to the United States to face numerous charges (Rosenfeld, 1993).

Except for a 1990 case against the On Leong, all RICO indictments against

Chinese gangs have proved successful. However, even after they have been con-victed as racketeering enterprises and their core leaders and members have been imprisoned, gangs such as the Ghost Shadows, the Green Dragons, and the Born-to-Kill have been able to regroup and survive the federal assaults (*Sing Tao Jih Pao*, 1994). Thus, it appears that RICO indictmments can only put the gangs out of business temporarily but cannot dismantle or eliminate them.

Public Hearings

Over the past ten years, the numerous public hearings on the emergence of Chinese gangs and organized crime conducted by the United States government and its various agencies have drawn attention to the severity of the problem (Raab, 1984; *World Journal*, 1990b; *Sing Tao Jih Pao*, 1992c). The first hearings on Asian organized crime were sponsored in 1984 by the President's Commission on Orga-nized Crime. In the three days of hearings, dozens of law enforcement officers, crime experts, victims of Chinese gangs, and former gang members described the structure and activities of Chinese, Japanese, and Vietnamese gangs and organized crime groups in America and Asia (President's Commission on Organized Crime, 1984). Several alleged Asian crime bosses were subpoenaed by the commission to appear at the hearings, but none complied. The alleged leader of Boston's Ping On gang was sentenced to jail for resisting the court order, and the then president of the On Leong Merchant Association left the United States and went to Asia.

The 1984 hearings were well publicized. They made the headlines of the major English-language newspapers across the nation for several days and were heavily covered by the Chinese media. Tong and gang involvement in violence, extortion, drug trafficking, gambling, prostitution, and money laundering—issues rarely discussed openly in the local Chinese media—became the talk of the Chinese community.

In 1986, the U.S. Senate Permanent Subcommittee on Investigations conducted hearings on emerging criminal groups in the United States. Chinese gangs and organized crime groups, along with Nigerian drug trafficking groups, were the focus of these hearings (U.S. Senate, 1986). From testimony provided mainly by subcom-mittee staff members and local law enforcement officials, it was apparent that the subcommittee was concerned with the possible transplantation of Hong Kong–based triad societies to the United States when the colony is returned to China in 1997.

The U.S. House of Representatives' Select Committee on Narcotics Abuse and Control conducted hearings in 1987 at John F. Kennedy International Airport in New York City on emerging international heroin groups. At the hearings, several prosecutors and senior law enforcement officers from the FBI, the DEA, the INS, the U.S. Customs Service, and the Port Authority of New York/New Jersey testified that the Chinese were emerging as the dominant group in Southeast Asian heroin trafficking. One senior official stated that:

> There is indisputable evidence to indicate that Chinese are the major suppliers to traditional organized crime, to black distribution groups and to Hispanic organi-zations. I know of no other group which regularly imports heroin into the New

York area with the degree of frequency and quantities as the Chinese. (U.S. House of Representatives, 1987: 3)

In the late 1980s, the alleged connections between Chinese crime groups in America and Hong Kong–based triad societies became a major concern for the U.S. law enforcement community (U.S. Senate, 1992). The continued involvement of Chinese in heroin trafficking and the increase in Chinese human smuggling prompted the U.S. Senate Permanent Subcommittee on Investigations to hold another session devoted to Asian organized crime in 1991. Many senior government and law enforcement officials, subcommittee staff members, victims of gang extortion, heroin traffickers, and former gang members were invited to testify. Several reputed Asian crime leaders were subpoenaed. They appeared before the U.S. Senate, but all invoked their Fifth Amendment rights and declined to answer any questions that might incriminate them (U.S. Senate, 1992).

International Cooperation

With the increase in transnational crime, the need for international cooperation and the internationalization of U.S. law enforcement efforts is becoming immensely important (Nadelmann, 1993). Crimes that may not usually be internationally linked may involve people abroad if they are committed by Chinese crime groups or Chinese gang leaders acting on their own accord. For example, a gang may kidnap a victim in the United States and demand that the victim's relatives in his or her native country pay ransom. For American authorities, the successful investigation and prosecution of these transnational crimes very much depends on the cooperation of law enforcement agencies abroad.

Since 1984, U.S. law enforcement agencies have been working closely with authorities in Canada and Hong Kong, in joint operations against Asian crime groups. For example, in 1988, the FBI, the DEA, the ATF, the U.S. Customs Service, and the RHKP participated in a joint operation known as "Operation Bamboo Dragon." With the aid of the RHKP, an American undercover agent infiltrated a major international drug ring. The operation resulted in the arrest of more than forty defendants in America and Hong Kong (Bolden, 1990). A year later, the FBI, the DEA, the U.S. Customs Service, the Royal Canadian Mounted Police (RCMP), the RHKP's Narcotics Bureau, and police in Singapore joined forces in an international operation code-named "Operation White Mare," which was initiated by the U.S. Organized Crime Drug Enforcement Task Force. It proved very successful: dozens of drug traffickers were arrested in the United States and Hong Kong, and 800 pounds of heroin were seized in New York City, as were millions of dollars of drug money (Marriott, 1989; Kinkead, 1992).

Encouraged by the successes in international cooperation, the DEA has proposed a new operation, named "White Lotus," which is intended to fight the growing threat from Southeast Asian heroin that continues to flood the United States. If the project is approved, it will include a New York-based international task force made up of experts from the United States, Hong Kong, Thailand, Singapore, Australia, Malaysia, and several European countries including Britain.

This will enable the pooling of knowledge and experience in combating Chinese gang activity (Marsh, 1992a).

Currently, the DEA, the FBI, the U.S. Customs Service, and the INS have offices in Hong Kong and Thailand. The DEA also has offices in Korea, Malaysia, the Philippines, and Singapore (Nadelmann, 1993). The ability to interact with foreign law enforcement agencies on a permanent and regular basis enables American law enforcement agencies to solicit better cooperation and better quality information from foreign agencies.

The American law enforcement community also requires the support of other nations in arresting and extraditing Chinese criminals who flee the United States to avoid prosecution. Over the past ten years, the U.S. government has had success in prosecuting several major criminal organizations because dozens of key defendants, after fleeing, were extradited back to the United States by foreign authorities. Had these arrangements been jeopardized in any way, many indictments against Chinese gangs in America would have collapsed.

Even countries that have no extradition treaty with the United States are asked by U.S. authorities for aid in combating Chinese gangs (U.S. Senate, 1992). For example, because it was urged to do so by the FBI, the Taiwan government arrested a Ghost Shadows leader for overstaying his tourist visa and placed him on a flight destined for New York City, where he was immediately arrested upon arrival at JFK Airport (*Centre Daily News*, 1985b).

To promote international cooperation, the U.S. law enforcement community has sponsored numerous international conferences on Asian organized crime. The purpose of these conferences is to provide opportunities for Asian crime investigators from around the globe to meet regularly on an informal basis so they can establish close working relationships with foreign colleagues. One major conference, the International Asian Organized Crime Conference, was established in 1978. At its 15th annual meeting, held in Las Vegas in 1993, more than a thousand law enforcement officers from 26 countries participated.[6]

Problems Encountered by Law Enforcement Authorities

Over the past 10 years, the activities of violent gangs, heroin trafficking groups, and human smuggling rings have been impeded, at least to a certain extent, by a determined law enforcement response (Kamen, 1993). However, major problems still persist, and the law enforcement community faces a challenge in overcoming them. Next, I will examine the problems associated with controlling Chinese gangs at all three levels of law enforcement: local, federal, and international. Since many impediments are shared by both local and federal law enforcement authorities, those two levels of law enforcement will be examined together.

Local and Federal

Some of the major problems encountered by law enforcement officials in dealing with Chinese gangs include a lack of understanding of the gangs and their community, an insufficient number of Chinese-speaking police officers, poor community relations, limited resources, and intra-agency and interagency conflicts.

LACK OF UNDERSTANDING

In dealing with Chinese gangs and organized crime, law enforcement authorities are hampered by their lack of understanding of Chinese communities and Chinese customs in general, and Chinese gangs in particular. As was discussed in chapter 1, the social processes of gang formation, the characteristics of gang structure, and the patterns of gang activities cannot be adequately understood unless the historical, social, economic, and political aspects of the community are fully comprehended. Chinese communities in the United States are complex sub-societies in which individual and group conflicts are widespread because of the underlying diversities among the Chinese population in terms of country of origin, political orientation, economic position, immigration status, group affiliation, and ethnic identity. If they do not have a clear understanding of how certain adult organizations and youth groups in the Chinese community are affected by ethnic, economic, and political tensions, law enforcement agencies may not be able to develop an effective long-term strategy for controlling Chinese gangs. A former member of the Wah Ching gang in San Francisco concluded that "the police cannot solve the problems of the gangs because they know absolutely nothing about Chinatown and how to deal with the people there" (Pak, 1972).

Their lack of understanding of the gang situation in particular has often misled authorities into labeling all Chinese youth crimes as gang crimes. Whenever a group of youthful Chinese offenders are arrested for heinous crimes, the police—either out of ignorance or from a need to provide a simple explanation—conclude that the youthful offenders are members of a gang, and the offense is defined as gang related (Song and Dombrink, 1993). Joe Fong, a former leader of the Joe Fong gang in San Francisco, had the following to say about police tendencies to blame gangs for whatever went awry in the Chinese community:

> If the moon had a hole in it, they would say that the Joe Fong gang did it. It is an easy solution to anything—something that the pubic will buy because the media had conditioned them to it. You have a shooting, mention Joe Fong's name and then it fits into a picture. You have something like the Golden Dragon [murders]? Mention Joe Fong and you have an easy way to explain it. (Ramirez and Hatfield, 1977: 1)

The point Joe Fong made can be substantiated with examples. For instance, when dozens of non-Asian customers and employees in an electronics store in Sacramento, California were taken hostage by a group of young Asians in 1991, authorities and the media readily denounced the incident as a bold move by Asian gangs to spread mayhem into the mainstream society. Only after the incident ended in a bloody shootout between police and the perpetrators did the authorities come to realize that the offenders were not members of a gang and their motives were nothing like those speculated by the frenzied media (Song and Dombrink, 1993). Likewise, when the sister of a notorious Tung On gang leader was abducted, both local and federal officials hastily concluded that she had been kidnapped by her brother's rivals. An all-out effort was mounted by the authorities to pressure the gangs in the community to release the victim (Rosario and Santangelo, 1986). Gambling clubs and massage parlors were forced to shut down, and a large number of gang members were harassed. Only after the victim's body was found in the backyard of her apartment complex did the authorities discover that the crime had been committed by a mentally deranged neighbor with no gang connections. The Chinese community was furious with the way the police handled the case (*World Journal*, February 21, 1986), and it has had an adverse impact on victim willingness to report kidnappings to the authorities in similar incidents that have occurred since then.

A police officer summarized the dilemma by admitting the following about Chinese gangs: "Quite frankly, we don't understand them and they don't understand us" (Layton, 1991).

LACK OF CHINESE-SPEAKING OFFICERS

The language problem affects all levels of law enforcement concerned with crime in Asian communities. This may be merely a generational problem, because the current influx of immigrants is so large that English-speaking Chinese appear to be a minority within the ethnic community. What seems more likely is that most of those involved in criminal activities are immigrants and this exacerbates crime control in general and intelligence-gathering in particular. Specifically, victims and witnesses of crimes who do not speak English are not easily able to cooperate with police investigations. More generally, Chinese community members with little or no English-language skills are unlikely to approach police with problems or report crimes. Presently, no law enforcement agency has a sufficient number of Chinese-speaking personnel to adequately handle the demands of investigations and information collection.

As the Chinese population continues to expand, as it is expected to (City of New York Department of City Planning, 1992; Zhou, 1992), the language barrier may become acute. Increasingly, immigrants are coming from regions of China and Southeast Asia where dialects other than Cantonese are spoken (Mandarin, Fujianese, Hakka, and Vietnamese, for example). Even if a sufficient number of Cantonese-speaking officers are recruited, they may not be equipped to handle the language and communication problems that may occur as a result of new immigration trends.[7]

In 1995, there were about 25,000 police officers in the New York City Police Department, but only 275 of them were Asian. Some Asian police officers, if they were born in the United States, may not speak Mandarin or any Chinese dialect, and those who do speak Chinese may not willingly accept assignments to work in the Chinese communities because of concerns for their family's safety (*World Journal*, 1985a). Although the NYPD is interested in recruiting more Asian police officers, it is widely believed that Asians are generally reluctant to become involved in police work. Moreover, some Asians who are interested in police work may not be qualified because they are not American citizens. As a result, both local and federal agencies have been frustrated in finding Asian recruits.

Similar problems exist in various federal law enforcement agencies. In 1995, among the more than 9,700 FBI agents across the country, only 158 are of Asian descent. The DEA has about 300 agents working in its New York City office in 1995, but only two are Chinese. In a recent recruitment drive by the DEA, of 700 applicants, not one was an Asian American. Likewise, within the INS Investigation Division, there are only a limited number of Fujianese-speaking agents, even though the agency is overwhelmed by the influx of illegal Fujianese immigrants.

The lack of Chinese-speaking police officers and federal agents makes it extremely difficult for the U.S. law enforcement community to investigate and prosecute crimes involving Chinese offenders and victims. First, investigators are compelled to find an interpreter to help them communicate with the offenders and the victims, and more often than not, an interpreter is hard to come by. Second, without being able to speak their language, police officers may not be able to build rapport with the offenders or the victims. Third, if law enforcement authorities have to rely on interpreters to communicate, misunderstandings between the two parties can easily occur when one misreads the other's demeanor or gestures. To put it simply, the American criminal justice system is not adequately equipped to communicate with members of the Chinese immigrant community.

In summary, a significant problem law enforcements agencies face is their failure to recruit Chinese-speaking men and women. Most think that an increase in the number of Chinese-speaking officers, even if they are not ethnically identifiable as Chinese or Asian, will do much to generate and inspire trust among Chinese communities. An increase in the number of Chinese-speaking police officers may help allay fear and weaken stereotypes of the police as venal, corrupt, and racist. With more police officers who are ethnically identifiable as Chinese participating in patrol units in the communities and in investigative roles, prejudices against law enforcement may diminish; likewise, prejudices among police officers about the Chinese may be challenged. In any event, I believe the recruitment of more Chinese-speaking officers and officers who are ethnically identifiable as Chinese to be a positive step toward improving cooperation and trust between the Chinese communities and criminal justice agencies.

POOR COMMUNITY RELATIONS

In the United States, relations between local precincts and Chinese communities can scarcely be described as ideal. Chinese immigrants in general, and community leaders and merchants in particular, appear to have little confidence in the police because they believe the police are not doing their best to protect Chinese crime victims (*World Journal*, 1990a). For instance, in 1993, after a Fujianese restaurateur was gunned down by a group of teenagers in the Bronx and robbed of nineteen dollars, members of the Fujianese community marched in protest at the NYPD's headquarters. They called for more police protection for immigrants, particularly for restaurant workers who make their living in high-crime neighborhoods (*New York Times*, 1993b).

Members of Chinese communities often feel antagonized by law enforcement authorities' pointed remarks about crimes in their communities. For example, an official in San Francisco publicly claimed that people in that city's Chinatown were actually protecting the smugglers of illegal Chinese immigrants by not reporting to the authorities what they knew about human smuggling operations (*Sing Tao Jih Pao*, 1993a). Naturally, the residents of the community were offended and irritated by the official's statement.

On the other hand, local police officers are frustrated in their dealings with Chinese communities in general, and Chinese victims in particular (*Centre Daily News*, 1985a). The police believe that the Chinese are rather uncooperative when it comes to police investigations. In the aftermath of an incident of serious gang warfare, when police officers were unable to collect any information from the more than several dozen Chinese people present at the crime scene, a police captain blasted the community with these harsh words:

> Chinese people are the most uncooperative ethnic group pertaining to police investigations. I believe if the incident had occurred in other ethnic communities, there would be at least one person willing to provide information to the police. Here, there is no witness at all. All our information comes from our own investigation, the victims, and the informants. Our biggest obstacle in fighting the gangs is the community's uncooperative attitude. Our task is to help and protect the community, but if they do not support us, we do not know where to start our job! (*Centre Daily News*, 1985a)

Police investigators have been frustrated by the reluctance of Chinese victims to testify in court. On many occasions, suspects are set free because Chinese victims fail to appear at the trial to testify, prompting a police captain to ask the question, "Are Chinese people willing to be victimized forever?" (*World Journal*, 1992c). Thus, it is not unusual for the authorities to detain a Chinese witness or victim to ensure that he or she will not disappear before the trial (*Bergen Record*, 1991).

LIMITED RESOURCES

Some observers claim that law enforcement authorities are staging a war without an army against Chinese crime groups. According to a special narcotics prosecutor:

> The federal war on Asian organized crime is a rhetorical one. We are fighting the drug war as best we can, but the view in Washington is that it should be financed locally; that's a very stupid view. They should provide more resources locally. They should also provide more resources to federal law enforcement. (DeStafano and Esposito, 1988: 8)

In the aftermath of the well-publicized *Golden Venture* incident, the White House allocated more than $170 million to antismuggling efforts, but when the incident faded from the front pages, the money originally intended for antismuggling efforts was reallocated to the border patrol division of the INS (Faison, 1994).

Citywide, the NYPD is understaffed. And while drug problems and violence are making urgent claims on police resources, the department is further threatened by the fiscal crisis in the city.

INTRA-AGENCY AND INTERAGENCY POWER STRUGGLES

As Chinese gangs have become more diverse in size, ethnicity, and criminal behavior, law enforcement problems have been compounded. There are the problems of coordination, and jurisdictional disputes among law enforcement groups of an inter- and intraorganizational nature. As the Chinese population spreads across the city and settles in all five boroughs, and as the youth gangs locate themselves in various enclaves and communities, the number of law enforcement agencies at the local, state, and federal levels has also expanded. This has created coordination problems and interagency disputes of one kind or another (U.S. Senate, 1992). Thus, the turf war problem associated with the activities of criminal gangs is matched, so to speak, by bureaucratic struggles that involve the commitment of resources and manpower among cooperating agencies, information sharing, and the determination of priorities, including which agencies should lead investigations, handle surveillance, and make arrests (Freedman, 1991).

Information sharing within the police department, in the investigative units of the district attorney's offices, and with federal agencies is often problematic (personal interview). Internal priorities and the status of investigations in which sensitive information, informants, or undercover operations may be jeopardized by dissemination outside the agency lay at the root of the difficulties in such joint operations.

The NYPD units do provide information on street gang activities to the FBI, the DEA, the ATF, and the New York State Police. The exchange of information is not always reciprocal or friendly, however (personal interview). Federal practice generally entails informational exchanges on a person-to-person rather than an agency-to-agency basis.

To overcome these obstacles, some public officials have proposed that permanent interagency joint task forces be formed. Daniel Rinzel, chief counsel to the U.S. Senate's Permanent Subcommittee on Investigations, suggested the following:

> We have in the course of our investigation visited a number of cities. Generally speaking, it seems that a task force approach, that is, an investigative unit with representatives from the FBI as well as perhaps from other agencies like the INS or local police, which have different jurisdictional and different information bases, can be most successful in attacking these Asian organized crime groups in various cities around the country. (U.S. Senate, 1992: 27)

Critics, however, say that such task forces tend to blow minor local cases out of proportion by taking them through the federal court system in the hope of obtaining speedy guilty verdicts and longer sentences. According to one critic, by creating such task forces, federal officials "waste a lot of money. Then they have to justify it, and they've got to go out and build something." Another opponent said, "I don't know if we have to create dragons for the dragon slayers" (R. Howe, 1993).

International

Because of differences in language, culture, legal systems, political ideology, and even time zones, cooperation between American and foreign law enforcement agencies can be haphazard. The "Goldfish Case" illustrates how a seemingly groundbreaking international joint operation could turn into a disaster for American and Chinese authorities.

In 1988, Chinese authorities in Shanghai intercepted approximately seven pounds of heroin stuffed in condoms which were tucked inside the bodies of 140 goldfish. The drug-laden fish, which were six to nine inches long, were stitched back together and packaged with 1,000 live fish in large plastic bags filled with water. Chinese authorities allowed the shipment to proceed to San Francisco by plane as intended, but they secretly put a Shanghai police officer and a DEA agent aboard the flight. When the packages arrived in San Francisco, DEA and U.S. Customs agents confiscated most of the heroin-stuffed goldfish. DEA agents left one fish full of narcotics in each of the boxes and attached electronic monitoring devices onto two boxes before resealing the packages. Three Chinese from the Bay Area were arrested after they picked up the packages and delivered them to a goldfish store. Several defendants were also arrested in Shanghai and Hong Kong.

In 1990, the Chinese authorities allowed one of the Shanghai conspirators, Mr. Wang, to come to the United States to testify at the trial of the American defendants. During the trial, the witness asked for political asylum on the grounds that the Chinese authorities had tortured him to obtain a confession, that they had urged him to provide false testimony at the trial, and that he could be executed if sent back to China. When the U.S. government accepted his application, five Chinese police officers who had accompanied the witness to the United States left the court in protest and flew back to China. Consequently, the judge for the case declared a mistrial.

The Chinese authorities were furious. The Foreign Ministry demanded Wang's immediate return and accused the United States of disregarding international law and China's judicial autonomy. The deputy commissioner of the Public Security Bureau protested angrily that they "could never have imagined that a superpower like the United States would actually accept a criminal" (*World Journal*, 1991). The level of cooperation on narcotics cases dropped considerably thereafter because, as one China expert put it, "The Goldfish Case has been one great big pain in the neck for everyone. Everyone from [the] DEA or anywhere in Government has had this thing thrown in their faces by the Chinese" (Hays, 1994). Assistant Secretary of State Melvyn Levitsky had the following to say to the Senate Judiciary Committee on the impact of the Goldfish Case on international drug enforcement operations:

> I regret to say the seemingly intractable problem of the "Goldfish Case" continues to be an irritant and barrier to Sino-US narcotics co-operation. The Chinese officials also wanted to increase co-operation but held fast to the principle that improved co-operation was not possible until we upheld our agreement to return the witness to China. We have explained that our options are limited by constitutional and legal procedures. (Marsh, 1992b: 3)

The Chinese allegedly maintained their anger for years, and according to Hays (1994), the case "has brought joint drug enforcement efforts to a standstill at a time when China is a major conduit for heroin bound for the United States. The events have also cast a pall over other Chinese-American criminal justice and diplomatic ventures." Although Wang's application for asylum was denied by the INS, he appealed his case, and it is now pending. A federal judge has ordered that Wang not be deported because American officials violated his constitutional rights. The three defendants at whose trial he was to testify later pleaded guilty to lesser charges (Dobson, 1992).

Besides unexpected twists and turns in international cooperation, another major problem facing the American law enforcement community is the lack of formal diplomatic relations between the United States and Taiwan. As a result, no extradition treaty exists between the two countries. Since many Chinese criminals take advantage of this situation by fleeing to Taiwan, the American government is now actively working to find a way to establish extradition agreements with the Taiwan government (U.S. Senate, 1993). Since a number of Taiwan fugitives are residing in the United States, the Taiwan authorities are also anxious to have some sort of extradition protocol with the United States.

Although American federal agencies have sponsored numerous regional and international meetings in order to establish an international network among investigators of Chinese gangs and organized crime, full international cooperation is hampered by either existing legislative constraints or diplomatic concerns. Senator William Roth of Delaware, a member of the U.S. Senate's Committee on Governmental Affairs, introduced to Congress in 1993 a bill entitled the "International Organized Crime Control Act." The bill was written after the 1991 Senate hearings on Asian organized crime. As a result of the hearings, the Committee on Governmental Affairs concluded that there was "little evidence that either U.S. or foreign law enforcement entities are currently equipped to meet the challenge" of international criminal organizations. Senator Roth proposed, among other things, to establish "a mechanism to enforce sanctions under the Foreign Assistance Act against those countries which fail to cooperate with U.S. law enforcement efforts against international organized crime," "to enhance penalties for crimes typically perpetrated by Asian crime groups and their members, including alien smuggling," to require "federal law enforcement agencies to report on efforts to establish task forces and hire former Royal Hong Kong Police officers," and to ask for "negotiation of extradition and mutual legal assistance agreements with Taiwan under the Taiwan Relations Act" (U.S. Senate, 1993).

As Nadelmann (1993) suggests, international law enforcement cooperation may be circumvented by international politics. For example, when former President Bush ordered the INS not to deport any Chinese nationals in the United States in the aftermath of the Tiananmen Square massacre, the ability of the INS to control the massive arrival of illegal immigrants from China was significantly undermined (U.S. Senate, 1992). The current attack on the Chinese government for violation of human rights has also put a damper on Sino-U.S. law-enforcement cooperation. The complexities of the political conflicts between Hong Kong and China, and between Taiwan and China, also create problems and circumscribe the extent of cooperation among them.

Finally, insensitivity to foreign regulations by American authorities working in foreign-based liaison offices could frustrate international cooperation. In the aftermath of the grounding of an alien smuggling ship near New York City, the INS, under pressure from the White House, became very aggressive in intercepting human trafficking vessels before they arrived in the United States (Clairborne, 1993). In their haste to uncover a ship of illegal immigrants, INS officers in Hong Kong inspected a ship in July 1993 without being accompanied by Hong Kong authorities. The move angered Hong Kong police officials because the INS's actions could have upset covert operations by needlessly putting local shipping agents on guard. According to a local detective, "We just don't understand what they expect to get from all this by themselves. They have absolutely no authority here, so they will have to be very, very careful if they start doing things alone" (Torode, 1993).

Similar incidents have occurred in U.S. relations with Taiwan and China. Recently, law enforcement authorities in the United States and Taiwan established a cordial relationship. However, when a U.S. government report on alien smuggling accused high-ranking Taiwan police officers of being major snakeheads (alien smugglers) and the Department of State alleged that Taiwan was becoming a major transshipment point for heroin trafficking, efforts to form a close framework for cooperative law enforcement projects were impeded.

Likewise, Chinese authorities have expressed dismay over the American law enforcement community's indiscreet use of the words "China White" to describe Southeast Asian heroin that is actually produced outside of China (Lam, 1992). The Chinese also claim that they were, and are, victims of international heroin trafficking, and resent being labeled as a "major heroin transit point." They feel they are being doubly victimized. Chinese authorities strongly resent the fact that their efforts in curbing the drug trade have been grossly ignored and unappreciated by American authorities (Lam, 1992). Both Chinese and Taiwanese law enforcement agencies view the harsh and unfair criticisms of American public officials as nothing less than a disincentive for enhanced cooperation with American federal agencies.

Summary and Recommendations

Government knowledge of the Chinese gang situation has greatly improved over the past few years. If we compare the current criminal justice system's understanding of Chinese gangs, as revealed in our interviews with law enforcement officials, with governmental reports prepared in the early 1970s (Attorney General of California, 1972; State of California, 1973), or even with reports written as recently as the mid–1980s (U.S. Department of Justice, 1985; U.S. Senate, 1986), it is apparent that law enforcement authorities possess a more comprehensive picture of the activity and structure of Chinese gangs and tongs. This may be the result of successful prosecutions of several Chinese gangs and drug trafficking groups, in which local and federal law enforcement authorities worked together and were assisted by gang members who turned informants.

This chapter suggests that law enforcement efforts at curbing the criminal activity of Chinese gangs have been somewhat effective, but nowhere near what they must and should to be to ensure a level of safety and freedom from the nuisances and occasional violence that the gangs impose on the Chinese community. There are four levels of analysis and action at which the problem of gang extortion and illegal gang activity might be curbed: (1) through law enforcement efforts, (2) within the business sector itself, (3) on the community level, and (4) through policy-making.

Law Enforcement

In view of the changing patterns of Chinese criminality in the United States, there are at least seven issues that should be of concern to criminal justice practitioners. First, there is a need to effectively control crime in the Chinese community by attacking gang leaders, tongs, and other criminally influenced adult organizations. The attempt to eradicate crime in Chinatowns by focusing on gangs while neglecting the moral and financial support structure of the adult organizations could prove futile. For example, the RICO conviction of the Ghost Shadows gang in 1985 had little impact because the gang quickly regrouped under the auspices of the On Leong Association, an adult organization. Therefore, tong leaders and members who are associated with gangs should be targeted for arrest and prosecution. However, in the process of aggressively going after gang-affiliated tong members, precautions must be taken to avoid incriminating law-abiding tong members.

Also, investigations should focus squarely on gang leaders. Concerted efforts should be made to seek conspiracy convictions for gang leaders not present during the commission of crimes. RICO indictments of entire gang organizations should continue unabated. Besides tongs and street gangs, other Chinese crime groups, including triads and heroin and human smuggling groups, should be of concern to law enforcement agencies. Police officers and federal agents should be keenly aware of which type of crime group they are dealing with in a particular criminal case.

Second, relations between the police and the Chinese community must be vastly improved because the current tensions between law enforcement authorities and Chinatown residents are palpable and harmful to both. There are several channels through which relations can be improved:

1. More Chinese police officers and federal agents should be recruited and given career opportunities with the understanding that they will have to work in Chinatown. Efforts should be made to recruit immigrant Chinese with experience in criminal justice—especially those who are used to dealing with Chinese gangs in their country of origin. This could be achieved by waiving the current citizenship requirements for new recruits. This would enable the police force and federal agencies to enlist the services of Chinese who speak a variety of Chinese dialects. The language barrier and other cultural impediments are at the root of the tensions between the law enforcement agencies and the community at large. A concerted effort should also be made to promote Asian police officers to command ranks in Chinatown precincts. The Chinese community is likely to be more responsive to a Chinese precinct chief than to a non-Chinese.

2. The NYPD should encourage non-Chinese police officers to learn basic Mandarin, Cantonese, and Fujianese by offering free language classes. There has been a dramatic increase in the number of Fujianese immigrants in the United States, and consequently, human smuggling and kidnapping among Fujianese are on the rise. Unfortunately, law enforcement agencies are not equipped to cope with the ethnic and linguistic subcultural characteristics of the Fujianese.

3. The training for non-Chinese police officers assigned to Chinatowns should include instruction in the culture of the community so that officers become familiar with Chinese customs, norms, and beliefs. For instance, this would help police officers examine why Chinatown business owners and residents are wary of approaching law enforcement authorities, and thus help them find ways to alleviate the Chinese community's concerns.

4. New business-permit holders should be asked to tour police stations and meet with police officers in order to strengthen ties between the police and the community. The Chinatown Project and monthly meetings between senior police officers and business owners would facilitate the process and encourage trust and a willingness to report crime. Understanding each other's values, customs, and needs can only enhance cooperation between the police and the business sector of the community.

5. Police should undertake a positive image campaign both to help recruit police officers and to expose Chinatown youths, adults, and business owners to "friendly" police officers who are there to help them.

Third, the Immigration and Naturalization Service should begin to play a more active role in controlling Chinese gangs and organized crime. It should increase its efforts in preventing foreign criminals from entering the United States and denying them the opportunity to become permanent residents or citizens, and it should promptly deport noncitizens who are convicted of felonies. Deportation could be one of the most effective deterrents for offenders who are not U.S. citizens.

Fourth, problems within and among law enforcement agencies ought to be resolved in order to enhance their cooperative efforts. Since it is clear that in the past many interagency joint operations were extremely successful in investigating Chinese gangs, more joint ventures among local and federal law enforcement agencies are likely to be fruitful.

Fifth, there is an increased need to combat the Chinese crime problem through cooperation with law enforcement authorities abroad. Over the past several years, it has become apparent that many crimes in the Chinese American communities, especially drug trafficking, money laundering, and human smuggling, are linked to Chinese communities in Asia. Also, Chinese gang members and other fugitives have had a tendency to flee to Asia when sought by American law enforcement authorities. Consequently, the key to success in controlling Chinese organized crime in the United States may depend on how closely the American criminal justice system is able to work with law enforcement agencies in Asia. Deportation, extradition, joint operations, and intelligence sharing among law enforcement authorities from various countries should be carried out routinely. In order to achieve these goals, extradition treaties must be instated— especially between countries that do not have formal diplomatic relations. Also, U.S. authorities should be more culturally sensitive in dealing with foreign law enforcement agencies.

The sixth measure involves the protection of Chinese witnesses. Occasionally, Chinese witnesses have been murdered by gang members after agreeing to testify against the gangs. Undoubtedly, these killings have put a chill on victims' willingness to cooperate with the criminal justice system. As a result, the authorities should make an all-out effort to avoid similar incidents from occurring again, through wider use of the Witness Security Program.

Finally, efforts to cope with Chinese gang involvement in transnational crimes should not be emphasized at the expense of curbing crimes within the community such as extortion, robbery, prostitution, and illegal gambling. It is within the community that Chinese gangs establish their strongholds and generate their power. The prevalence and persistence of gang extortion erodes the Chinese community's confidence in the police and creates an atmosphere of lawlessness and intimidation. Moreover, gang leaders and chronic offenders who have emerged as major figures in federal and international crimes are nurtured and trained in the fields of community crimes such as extortion, protection rackets, and armed robbery. As a proactive and preventive measure, law enforcement strategies must attack the criminal environment in which future heroin traffickers and human smugglers are raised and empowered.

The Business Community and Its Prerogatives

Chinese businesspeople can, and should, play an important role in curbing gang activities in their community. They might begin by taking steps to decrease the potential for gang extortion, such as encouraging their customers to pay for goods and services with credit cards rather than cash. Another preventive measure would entail discouraging Chinese gangs from selling items such as tangerines and moon cakes to potential victims—plant and bakery stores should devise a means to stop selling large quantities of these items to customers with whom they are not familiar and/or demand that large sales be made by credit card or purchase order only. Chinese merchant associations could lead the way in helping businesses structure and implement these changes away from "cash only" business practices.

Both attempted and completed extortion—regardless of how insignificant the amount of money involved—ought to be reported to the police. Likewise, the police should encourage business owners to resist extortion, and let it be known that gang retaliation is rare.

Eventually, Chinese businesspeople must address community issues. They must learn that, although they may not be significantly hurt by gang extortion in the short term, the persistence of gangs in the community and the negative image associated with gang violence will eventually lead to a decline in their businesses. I believe there are good reasons for business owners to play a more vigorous role in community affairs. Offering financial support for community youth programs and job opportunities to community youths will improve their image; actually, business owners are already "donating" money, under coercion, to the gangs on a regular basis, so they might as well provide funds to develop recreational facilities or vocational programs serving at-risk youths and, in the process, help themselves by reducing the number of gang activities.

Above all, the business community should seek to inform newcomers about how the American criminal justice system works. Chinese-language booklets containing basic information about federal and local commercial laws affecting business operations and information about the structure and operation of the criminal justice system, along with the addresses and telephone numbers of relevant law enforcement agencies, should be produced and made available to Chinese merchants. The pamphlets could be disseminated by the police as part of the positive image campaign already mentioned.

Community-Level Activities

The key to controlling the gang problem in American Chinatowns may not be just the adoption and implementation of aggressive law enforcement measures, or the cooperation of the business community with government agencies. As long as individual and group conflicts, be they economic, political, or cultural, remain rampant in Chinese American communities, gangs will develop and persist. Also, as long as a strong demand persists within Chinatowns for illicit services such as gambling, prostitution, and human smuggling, gangs will emerge to provide or protect these services. Accordingly, in order to contain the formation of street gangs, there is a need to reduce individual and group conflicts and the demand for illicit services. There are large numbers of unattached males in the Chinese community, and if nothing is done to provide recreational activities and outlets for them, illegal recreational services will continue to flourish no matter how outraged the society at large is.

Specifically, social service providers should intervene before at-risk youths become gang members. For instance, there are no well-established youth programs in the Chinese community that provide alternative role models and gathering places and activities for Chinese adolescents. Recreational facilities for Chinatown youths are either nonexistent or poorly maintained. Although there are several well-financed social service agencies that operate in the community, none of them has been aggressive in developing programs for troubled youths. The passivity of the social service agencies is unacceptable but understandable since the gang problem in Chinatown is not merely a youth phenomenon but is entangled with powerful community associations such as the tongs. Currently, the situation is so desperate that if a Chinatown youth became detached from school and family, he would likely become associated with a gang or tong, in absence of other alternatives.

Also, immigrants, or at least business owners, should be strongly encouraged to learn English. According to my findings, Chinese in the United States who are fluent in English are less likely to be approached by or become victims of gangs than those who are not fluent. Further, language facility accelerates their integration into society and familiarizes them with American customs and values, including reporting crimes to the police.

Finally, the community needs to become educated about the seriousness of crimes such as heroin trafficking and human smuggling. Currently, there is not much stigma associated with these crimes, and that enables criminals to operate their illicit operations in Chinatown with relative ease, free from negative informal social sanctions.

Policy Initiatives

Finally, there are several policy initiatives that must be undertaken to curb Chinese gang activity. The first involves illegal immigration. Obviously, illegal immigrants are less likely than legal immigrants to learn English and rapidly adapt to American culture. Because of their lack of integration and acculturation, they are likely to become victims of Chinese gang activity. Moreover, they are also likely to be the prime consumers of illegal services, such as gambling and prostitution, and the source of strong demands for these illegal services, which, in turn, fuel gang enterprises. Though it may seem radical, I believe that drastic changes in immigration policy are needed to accommodate the large number of illegal immigrants already in the United States and to help them become legal.

A second policy that needs to be initiated has to do with unlicensed businesses. Within the commercial sectors of Chinatowns throughout the United States, there are a substantial number of unlicensed businesses. These businesses are the most vulnerable to gang victimization because they are candidates for blackmail and their owners are the least likely to approach the police for help. The U.S. cities in which Chinatowns are located need to crackdown on these illegal businesses and better educate potential business owners about how to operate their businesses legally.

A third policy that could have an impact on gang formation involves discouraging tong membership. This policy initiative could involve a cooperative effort between public and private sector social service agencies and law enforcement representatives to tackle the problem of gang formation at its roots. It should involve a publicity campaign that would point out the hazards of tong membership. What seems most important at this juncture is to develop alternatives to the tongs and gangs as mechanisms for conflict resolution.

It is important that U.S. and foreign law enforcement and government officials not be fooled by the massive deception under way in Chinatown by the tongs. Tongs, which are gang affiliated, have been successful for years in convincing outsiders that they are actually patriotic benevolent associations. Until quite recently, they have been fiercely anti-Communist and have been morally and financially supported by those in powerful positions who share their ideology. It is time for this moral and financial support to stop and for supporters to recognize the role these organizations play in the crime scene in the Chinese community.

NOTES

Chapter 1

1. It is important to note that of the hundreds of community organizations in New York City's Chinatowns, only six are alleged to be affiliated with street gangs. Furthermore, only a few members of these gang-affiliated adult establishments are associated with gangs.

2. Tongs are fraternal associations that were originally formed by Chinese immigrants in the United States in the late 1850s as self-help groups (Liu, 1981; H. Lee, 1989; Ma, 1990). The word *tong* means "hall" or "gathering place" (Dillon, 1962). Because of their pervasive and consistent involvement in illegal gambling, prostitution, opium trafficking, and violence, the tongs are considered by American law enforcement authorities to be criminal enterprises (Ashbury, 1928; Gong and Grant, 1930). However, the tongs, like the family and district associations, provide many needed services to immigrants who could not otherwise obtain help (U.S. Senate, 1992). Over the past 150 years, more than 30 tongs were formed in the United States, predominantly on the west and east coasts (U.S. Department of Justice, 1988). These associations became places for members to socialize, to seek help, and to gamble. Working-class Chinese who do not gamble join the associations because they want someplace to turn to if they need help. Businessmen join the associations mainly for protection. Most association members are law-abiding employed people who visit the associations only once in a while to meet friends and gamble; otherwise, they have little to do with the associations. But some members are closely identified with the associations—they are either full-time employees of the associations, or they are retired or unemployed. Among them, quite a few are young, tough teenagers who have nowhere to go and nothing to look forward to. They become the strong-arms of the associations. Most tong organizations have a president, a vice president, a secretary, a treasurer, an auditor, and several elders and public relations administrators (Chin, 1990; U.S. Senate, 1992). Branches may be found in cities where there is a large number of Chinese. Each branch has a ruling body resembling its headquarters organization staff that includes a president, a secretary, a treasurer, an auditor, and several staff members (Chin, 1990). Since the 1960s, most tongs have abandoned the name tong and have renamed their associations because the word tong evokes unpleasant memories of the infamous tong wars (Glick, 1941; Glick and Hong, 1947; C. Lee, 1974; Minke, 1974).

3. In the United States and Canada, most Chinese immigrants live in urban areas and congregate in areas known as "Chinatowns" (Liu, 1981; Kwong, 1987; Loo, 1991; Kinkead, 1992; Zhou, 1992). The size of each Chinatown varies from city to city. Some are mainly commercial districts where Chinese restaurants, gift shops, grocery stores, and theaters are

located. Few Chinese live within the vicinity. Some larger Chinatowns are both commercial and residential. These communities have their own schools, social service agencies, post offices, hospitals, and banks. The areas are so well established that Chinese residents rarely need to leave the communities to fulfill their needs. These Chinatowns are "Chinese societies" within American society.

4. Unless otherwise indicated, I will use "China" to denote the People's Republic of China, and "Taiwan" to denote the Republic of China. China considers Taiwan as part of China, not an independent country. Hong Kong is a seaport located on the coast of southern China. Following the Opium War (1840–1842), China was forced to cede Hong Kong to the British. The colony will be returned to China by the British in 1997.

5. In this book, one of the Chinatown gangs being discussed is the Born-to-Kill (BTK). Since most BTK members are either Vietnamese or Chinese from Vietnam, many Chinatown observers and journalists view the gang as a Vietnamese gang. Thus, throughout this book, the BTK will be referred to as a Vietnamese gang. However, because many BTK members are Vietnamese Chinese, and the gang is an important component of the Chinatown underworld, I would like to make it clear that I generally mean to include the BTK when I use the words Chinese gangs in this volume. The oldest immigrant group, the Toisanese (or Taishanese), is primarily comprised of people from four relatively poor districts of Guangdong Province. The Cantonese, mostly from the city of Guangzhou and its surrounding area, including Hong Kong, are considered the most sophisticated and wealthy Chinese immigrants. The Hakka (meaning "guest") are the descendants of a group of people who emigrated from northern China to Guangdong Province many generations ago. The Fujianese come from the vicinity of Fuzhou City of Fujian Province and constitute the fastest-growing group in New York's Chinatown.

6. Sun Yat-sen is hailed as the founding father of the Republic of China because he was the principal political architect of the revolution that ousted the Qing dynasty.

7. The Chinese Consolidated Benevolent Association (CCBA) is considered the informal government of Chinatown (C. Wu, 1993). Almost all Chinatowns have their own CCBAs. The president of the CCBA is known as the mayor of Chinatown and normally is the most politically visible figure within the community. His major responsibilities include representing the community in almost all external affairs, maintaining close relationships with the government of Taiwan, arbitrating all kinds of personal and organizational conflicts within the community, maintaining close ties with local police in order to deter crime, and providing economic assistance and language programs for newly arrived immigrants.

8. In Manhattan's Chinatown, rents for both commercial and residential property are high (Scardino, 1986). Annual rent for the most expensive retail space in Chinatown is $275 per square foot, compared to $400 for Fifth Avenue and $255 for Madison Avenue. A one-bedroom apartment costs approximately $700 monthly, plus $5,000–$8,000 *fong dai cheen* (key money) up front for getting the lease. Despite the high rents, the apartments in Chinatown are small and poorly maintained (Kinkead, 1992). Since the decision by the British to cede Hong Kong to China in 1997, huge amounts of investment dollars from the colony have poured into New York's Chinese community over the past several years, further energizing the community's economy (Kwong, 1987; Farolino, 1987).

9. In China, there are more than 100 Chinese ethnic groups, and each has its own dialect, although there is only one written language (Chinese). The official spoken language, which is called *guo yu* or *pu tong hua* in Chinese, is called Mandarin in English.

10. When the Chih Kung Tong was first established, in 1850, its major political goal was to overthrow the Qing dynasty (1644–1911) and restore the Ming emperor. Later, the Chih Kung Tong and the Chinese revolutionary organization in Tokyo worked together to

establish a financial support center that collected money from overseas Chinese to aid the revolutionary army in China. The center's ability to provide desperately needed financial aid to Chinese soldiers played a pivotal role in the struggle against the Qing government (Ma, 1990).

11. The On Leong Merchant Association was formed in 1894, in Boston, by a Chih Kung Tong member. Ten years later, the On Leong headquarters moved to New York City. Law enforcement authorities have alleged that On Leong leaders have links with Chinese gang members. In 1990, leaders of the On Leong in New York, Chicago, and Houston were indicted in Chicago for racketeering activities (Kinkead, 1992). Thirty-three core members of the On Leong were arrested, close to a half million dollars of gambling money was confiscated, and the building owned by the Chicago On Leong was forfeited. The case ended in a hung jury, and the On Leong has remained a powerful organization in the Chinese community.

12. The Hip Sing Association was formed in 1855. Its headquarters are located in Manhattan's Chinatown. Benny Eng (or Ong) was the Permanent Chief Adviser of the Hip Sing and was also the leader of the Chih Kung Tong. Little is known about Eng, except that he was imprisoned for murder in 1936 and was paroled eighteen years later. He had been arrested for assault, robbery, gambling, and drug offenses before his 1936 conviction for murder. In 1976, he was sentenced to prison for bribery (Daly, 1983; Meskil, 1989). He died in 1994, at the age of 87 (McFadden, 1994).

13. Hakka immigrants from two areas of Guangdong Province, Tung Kuang and Po On, formed the Tung On Association. Federal agents believe that the association is active in running gambling operations in Chinatown and that it is connected with a Hong Kong–based organized crime group. Both the association and its affiliated gang were indicted as racketeering enterprises by federal authorities in 1993 and were convicted in 1995 (Fried, 1993, 1995).

14. The Tsung Tsin Association was established in 1918. Members of the association are predominantly Hakka, an ethnic group that migrated to southern China from northern China during a period of war and famine. The Tsung Tsin's headquarters is only a few buildings away from the Tung On's, and like the Tung On, the Tsung Tsin is heavily involved in gambling activities. The physical proximity of the two Hakka associations has enabled the Tung On gang to provide protection for the gambling operations of both associations. In 1993, a leader of the association was indicted, along with leaders of the Tung On Association, for involvement in racketeering activities.

15. The Fukien American Association is perhaps the fastest-growing organization in New York City's Chinatown. With the dramatic influx of both legal and illegal Fujianese migrants in the past decade (Myers, 1992), the association, which was established in 1942, is now in control of the newly expanded areas east and north of Chinatown. Members of the association are allegedly active in human smuggling, promoting gambling and prostitution, and heroin trafficking.

16. According to Thrasher (1927), the formation of gangs in interstitial areas was the result of young people's spontaneous organizational response to the weakness of social controls in their community. Through conflict and negative societal reactions, loosely knit play groups developed into more solidified, group-conscious street gangs. Shaw and McKay (1942) attributed the development of delinquency, including youth gangs, to social disorganization in the inner-city areas of Chicago. Due to poverty, high population mobility, and ethnic heterogeneity, certain urban areas are structurally and culturally disintegrated. Cloward and Ohlin (1960) concluded that adult groups play a limited role in the formation of youth gangs, and claimed that different types of gangs reflect the characteristics of the community and the accessibility of illegal opportunities that are largely determined by

adult criminal activity. Suttles (1968), like Thrasher, found that inner-city youths formed street-corner groups to help them communicate with one another in minority communities where the norms and values of the dominant society might not be applicable in interpersonal relationships. Gangs provided lower-class adolescents with a mechanism to identify themselves, to protect themselves from a hostile environment, and to socialize with other peer groups and the wider society. According to Vigil (1988), gangs emerged in the Latino barrios of Southern California and the Southwest within a specific cultural context. Because of the uniqueness of barrio life, low socioeconomic status, street socialization and enculturation, and problematic development of self-identity, the subculture of the *cholo*—a distinctive street style of dress, speech, gestures, tattoos, and graffiti— became a way of life within the barrio. Jankowski (1991), unlike Thrasher, claims that gangs provide members with a competitive advantage in obtaining material resources within a highly competitive lower-class community. According to this theory, gangs are developed by defiant individuals who want to promote their life chances, and their capability to do so largely depends on the gang's ability to establish a symbiotic relationship with the community in which it thrives.

Chapter 2

1. The National Crime Victimization Survey (NCVS) is conducted annually by the Bureau of the Census and the Bureau of Justice Statistics. It measures personal victimization by interviewing individuals about their experiences as victims. However, it has no specific category for Chinese Americans. Until recently there was no designation for Asians in general. Nor is the NCVS compatible with measurements of victimization that occur primarily in the context of business. Commercial crimes might not be reported in victimization surveys that sample by household and are skewed toward victimization that occurs in residential or noncommercial contexts. NCVS items mention loss of personal property—an ambiguous term for crimes committed in a business milieu—or personal injury, also an ambiguous concept if only threats are made or violence is targeted at property. Also, the crimes that typify victimization of Chinese business owners, primarily demands for protection and other forms of extortion, are not included as standard items that are aggregated in analyses of survey data. Moreover, lack of proficiency in English limits the participation of many Chinese households. Because of narrow sample frames, the commercial version of the NCVS provided limited comparisons of different types of businesses, and the base rates were often too low to provide meaningful analyses. The commercial component of the NCVS was therefore halted in the mid-1970s (Garofalo, 1990).

Constructing sample frames for a survey of Chinese businesses is further complicated by the large number of undocumented immigrants, the informality of many businesses, and the rapid opening and moving of businesses within an area. Finally, the NCVS does not capture the complexity of multiple incidents of victimization of individuals or businesses. Unlike either personal or commercial victimization of non-Chinese businesses, in which repeated victimization of the same individual is rare, extortion and victimization of Chinese businesses appear to be lengthy processes with continuous interaction between victim and offender and repeated incidents of victimization (Chin, 1990). The NCVS is not designed to measure or describe such continuous patterns of victimization. There are also gaps in official statistics describing patterns of victimization or the characteristics of victims. Statistics on reported crimes are usually kept by police precincts or substations and are then compiled in citywide reports. The affected ethnic communities do not keep their own data on such incidents. In New York City, the Fifth, Seventh, and Thirteenth Precincts overlap in Manhattan's Chinatown. Other ethnic groups reside in each precinct, and this complicates efforts to measure crimes committed against Chinese businesses. Calculating crime rates is complicated by the same factors that are problematic for sampling businesses: the underreporting of crimes by Chinese merchants or Chinese citizens, coupled with the informality of many businesses. These complications may lead to biased estimates and systematic undercounts.

2. The Chinatown in Manhattan is a well-established social, political, and commercial center. It is located on the Lower East Side of Manhattan and is bordered by City Hall, Little Italy, and the East River. It was established in the 1850s and developed from a few stores on Mott Street into the largest Chinese settlement in the United States. Approximately 70,000 Chinese residents now live in the vicinity, and the population is growing rapidly as a result of China's open-door policy and of political instability in Hong Kong. Residents are mostly working-class, Cantonese- or Fujianese-speaking immigrants from China or Hong Kong (Kwong, 1987; Loo, 1991; Zhou, 1992; Epstein, 1993). The Chinatown in Queens is located in Flushing, where approximately 86,000 Chinese have settled along Main Street and the No. 7 subway line, which runs through Jackson Heights and Elmhurst. Residents are predominantly new immigrants from Taiwan and Korea (Chen, 1992). Brooklyn's Chinatown is situated along Eighth Avenue (between 50th and 63rd Streets) in Sunset Park and neighboring Sheephead Bay and Bensonhurst. It is connected to Manhattan's Chinatown by the N and B subway lines, which serve as social and economic lifelines between the two communities (M. Howe, 1987; Smith, 1988; Gladwell, 1993). According to the 1990 census, approximately 68,000 Chinese lived in Brooklyn.

3. The *Chinese Business Guide and Directory* is the only classified directory of Chinese businesses in the New York City area, and it is widely circulated among Chinese people there. More than 5,000 firms were listed in the 1989–90 edition of the *Directory*—most of them small and medium-sized businesses located in the five boroughs of New York City or in New Jersey, Connecticut, and Long Island. Except for small take-out Chinese restaurants and large international firms, most Chinese-owned businesses were listed in the *Directory* (Key Publications, 1990).

4. I intended to interview only Chinese business owners because I assumed that Chinese gangs only victimize Chinese. Therefore, after the sample was drawn, I made an effort to exclude businesses that were apparently owned by non-Chinese or that were known to the research team to be owned by non-Chinese. Still, there were a number of non-Chinese firms that eluded my scrutiny.

5. I initially planned to interview about 50 subjects from Brooklyn's Chinatown. Because the commercial center of Brooklyn's Chinatown is relatively small, only about 100 firms from the area were listed in the *Directory*. As a result, only 36 businesses from Brooklyn's Chinatown were included in the original target sample. Of these 36 firms, 19 were interviewed. A decision was made to interview some of the stores located in the area that were not included in the original sample. The interviewers were instructed to approach one of the 10 business types selected for the study. Eventually, an additional 23 businesses in Brooklyn's Chinatown were interviewed. A comparison between sampled and nonsampled businesses in Brooklyn's Chinatown indicates no difference in terms of subjects' characteristics, such as age, sex, country of origin, length of residence in the United States, English proficiency, and education level. Also, there was no difference in terms of business characteristics, such as business type, firm age, and firm size.

6. For example, a restaurant owner offered the following explanation for the gangs' demand for money:

> There is nothing wrong with asking for protection money. Some people donate money to the church regularly. Would you say that the church is involved in racketeering activity? It's the same with extortion. We all give lucky money to our children during Chinese

New Year. Could you say that our children are extorting money from us? This is nothing more than a Chinese custom. Yes, we also bought certain items from the gangs for a price higher than the market value, but isn't that what Macy's is doing? It is also true that gang members came to eat and asked for a discount, but my friends did that, too. What's the difference?

7. Pilot test results indicated that: (1) respondents were easily distracted; (2) owners seemed reluctant to talk about certain aspects of their business and personal life, such as their immigration status, the number of employees working for them, and the profitability of the business; (3) businesspersons reacted poorly when questions were presented in a formal and literal fashion; and (4) owners wished to talk about other forms of victimization to which they were exposed in addition to gang or organized crime victimization.

8. Questions pertaining to the subjects' immigration status, place of residence, and kinship ties were removed from the questionnaire because of the pretest. Also, subjects were not asked about the number of employees, size, hours, or profitability of their businesses. Instead, interviewers were asked to provide their own assessments and observations about these personal and business characteristics. The majority of the questions about the subjects' personal and business attributes contained in the original survey protocol remained intact after the pretest.

9. For safety reasons, interviewers were asked to comply with the instructions whenever possible. (1) Do not do fieldwork late at night. (2) Always carry the interviewer identification card issued by Rutgers University. (3) Conduct the interview only at the subject's business premises. (4) Always sit facing the entrance; if youths who appear to be gang members walk in, you may stop the interview and figure out who they are before resuming the interview. (5) Always carry a manila file folder or a newspaper to hide the questionnaire if you need to do so. (6) If subjects mention any particular person by name during the interview, try to stop them by reminding them that names are not necessary. If they prefer, they may use a pseudonym. (7) Do not provide subjects with personal addresses or phone numbers. If they want to know more about the study or the results of the study, suggest that they contact one of the investigators. (8) Do not discuss the interviewing job with classmates, friends, or colleagues. Under no circumstances should the names and locations of respondents be disclosed to those not related to the project. (9) If people who look like gang members appear near the premises, the interview may be terminated. You can excuse yourself and leave the premises immediately. Tell the subject that you have something to do and will contact him/her later for another appointment.

10. For example, on one occasion, when a film company came to Chinatown to shoot a movie about the Chinese underworld without securing the community leaders' support in advance, an uproar erupted. The company was forced to build a Chinatown set elsewhere, at a cost of millions of dollars.

11. Although $20 is a rather modest stipend, many store owners openly acknowledged the implicit respect and gratitude conveyed by this gesture. An envelope containing the stipend was placed discreetly on the table at the beginning of the interview, shortly after the informed consent statement was read to the respondent. I do not think this practice could have significantly affected the randomness of my sample, the honesty of my subjects, or the reliability of my data.

12. Interviewers were given the following instructions on phone contact. (1) Take notice of the type of business before making the phone call. If it is a restaurant, do not call during lunch or dinner hours. The best time to call a restaurant is in the morning (between 10:00 and 11:30 A.M.), in the late afternoon (between 2:30 and 5:00 P.M.), or in late evening (after 10:00 P.M.). (2) Do not ask for the owner immediately when the call is answered

(some owners are reluctant to identify themselves as owners when they are talking to a stranger over the phone). Identify yourself to the person who answers the phone and vaguely describe what you are doing. Then ask to speak to the owner. (3) Make sure that the business owner is of Chinese descent during the phone contact. Otherwise, do not make an appointment for the interview. Politely excuse yourself and enter a note under "Comment" on the sample list. (4) Do not take a "no" from the owner easily. Try your best to persuade the owner to grant you an interview. However, you should not push too hard for an appointment. It is up to your good judgment how persistently you should press for an interview. If the subject refuses to be interviewed, you may consider calling him again a few days later. The owner may change his/her mind.

13. Since very few merchants report gang intimidation to the police and only victims who are heavily extorted or threatened are likely to contact law enforcement authorities, the police do not maintain any systematic data on gang extortion in the Chinese community. Consequently, it is impossible to cross-validate the reliability of the survey data with official statistics.

14. Subjects for the follow-up interview had to meet the following criteria: (1) they had to have indicated that they were willing to be interviewed again and (2) they had to have experienced at least three types (out of the six types, four forms of extortion plus robbery and burglary, included in the business survey) of victimization. Prior to the field interview, a letter of notification in both English and Chinese was written and mailed to the subjects who met the above two criteria.

15. The recruiter was paid $50 per subject, both for his recruitment and for his protective role as bodyguard for members of the research team.

16. Subjects were asked to indicate what their positions were in the gangs, and their self-reported gang ranks were cross-validated by their roles in extortion and other gang activities.

17. When a subject indicated that he or she was more comfortable communicating in (either Mandarin or Cantonese), the Chinese questionnaire was used, and the interview was conducted in the dialect the subject was familiar with.

18. None of the subjects had any contact with the interviewer prior to the study. To prevent the subjects from viewing the interviewer as an authoritative figure, they were not informed that the interviewer was a school counselor.

19. It is not clear why the subjects were reluctant to talk about their involvement in burglary, but not other crimes, such as robbery and extortion. From informal discussions with the respondents and from examining the oaths and rules of Chinese gangs (Chin, 1990), it appears that burglary is considered a lowly act within the subculture of Chinese gangs. Respondents may have been reluctant to reveal the number of people in their gangs and the amount of money their gangs earned because they viewed such information as gang business and did not want to betray their organizations. Some, especially the ordinary members, appeared to have very little knowledge about these aspects of gang composition. As a result, these questions were excluded after the first few interviews.

20. Five subjects indicated they would like to remain anonymous.

21. These organizations were chosen because (1) some are alleged to be affiliated with gangs, and I wanted to find out how these organizations would respond to the allegation; (2) some are reported to be involved in either gambling or loan-sharking activities; (3) some serve as umbrella organizations for either the whole or a substantial segment of the community; and (4) some are professional, social service, or advocacy organizations serving the Chinese community.

22. To protect the identity of the subjects, the names of the community organizations that participated in the study are not disclosed.

Chapter 3

1. Respondents in the study distinguished between protection and lucky money, although the New York State Penal Code does not. To maintain consistency in reporting on criminal behavior and its consequences, the distinctions in community definitions of extortionate activity neither violate the spirit of the law nor distort the reporting of results. Such community distinctions, which lack significant differences and legal consequences, do not confuse the descriptions of crime patterns and their prevalence in the Chinese communities.

2. Many Chinese people believe harmony is a prerequisite for success and happiness because they are deeply influenced by Chinese sayings such as "Everything go well for a harmonious family" and "Harmony breeds wealth."

3. For Chinese, "face" is equivalent to respect. To "give face" to someone means to respect that person, and to "not give face" means to disrespect. Under most circumstances, "face giving," or the lack of it, is reciprocal. To "save someone's face" is to try to not embarrass that person. People who are rich and powerful are considered to "have face." A person who behaves inappropriately is viewed as someone who "throws away one's face," meaning the person has no self-respect (Bloodworth, 1965).

4. Respondents provided information for the lifetime of a business at its current address and in its current form.

5. Since the sample is nonrandom, the personal and business characteristics of the subjects may not be generalizable to the entire Chinese business population of New York City.

6. Since most Chinese immigrants have limited financial resources, it is common for them to invite close friends or relatives to become business partners. These business partners not only invest money but also are involved in operating the business. This way, investors will be assured of a share in the profits, if there are any, as well as of a job and a regular salary.

7. My data suggest that most victimization occurs at the hands of Chinese gang members. Nearly all protection demands and forced sales incidents were perpetrated by persons identified by the victims as gang members. Nearly nine out of 10 incidents of forced sales and eight in 10 protection demands were attributed to gang members. Some victims could not identify all the perpetrators as gang members, although fewer than 5 percent said that gang members were *not* involved. As a result, all extortion activities reported by the respondents may be considered examples of gang extortion.

8. The Chinese have their own calendar, which is somewhat different from the Roman calendar. Chinese New Year is celebrated either at the end of January or in early February. During the New Year, Chinese people visit their relatives and friends, indulge in lavish dinners, hand out *hung bao* (a red envelope with cash inside) to children, and gamble. Firecrackers and tangerine plants are two indispensable items—the former to drive away evil spirits, and the latter to generate good luck. The Mid-Autumn Festival, which is observed in September, is a popular celebration. The two main activities during the festival are gazing at the moon and eating mooncakes.

9. Normal extortion can be defined as routine extortion against legitimate business owners. There are other extortion incidents that can be defined as abnormal if the motivation for extortion is not limited to monetary and material gains or if the victims are owners of illegitimate businesses (Chin, 1990). For example, a person may be extorted for thousands of dollars because he or she owes money to a gambling house. Also, operators of illegal businesses such as massage parlors may be asked to pay as much as $1,200 a month for protection.

10. Other threats reported by victims included the following: "We will take the money from the cash register"; "We will come back to rob you"; "We will burn down your store and kill you"; "We will rob or extort your customers"; and "There will be troubles for you."

11. Respondents were not asked whether they had to buy items from, or provide free goods or services to, more than one gang.

12. The On Leong Merchant Association is located one street away from Little Italy, and Chinese business activities within the Italian neighborhood are mainly under the influence of the On Leong Merchant Association.

13. We need to be cautious when designating a specific street as the turf of a particular gang. Some Chinatown streets are controlled by more than one gang. For example, the eastern section of Canal Street (east of the Bowery) is controlled by the Fuk Ching, the middle section (between the Bowery and Baxter) by the Ghost Shadows, and the western section (west of Baxter) by the Born-to-Kill. Other streets with more than one gang in control include East Broadway, Hester, and Grand.

14. Sometimes gang members did insist that they should be paid the asking price. In one incident, a gang member asked a business owner to pay $360 lucky money for the opening of his business. The owner asked the offender to return the next day and paid him $20 when he came. The offender said, "The amount of money is too small, it violates the rules. I cannot violate the rules, so I am not going to accept it." He showed up on the following day, and the owner paid him $360.

Chapter 4

1. In Hong Kong, protection money is called *taw dei fai* (territory fee) or *heung yau cheen* (incense oil money) (Zhang, 1984).

2. The actual name of the gang is not provided because I am concerned with the safety of the victim. Was I to provide the name of the gang (along with the amount of money being asked for), I might expose the victim's identity and thus place him in jeopardy. Throughout this chapter, if I am uncertain whether the revelation of a gang's name might expose the victim's identity, I do not disclose the gang's name.

3. Gang members may or may not telephone a new business firm prior their appearance at the business premises. One gang member stated his gang normally calls before he and his fellow gang members show up for the money: "We mainly target newly opened stores or well-to-do stores. We usually call the store owner and ask him to prepare to pay regularly, and then we'll show up at the store and collect the money."

4. On many occasions, gang members do not reveal their gang affiliation. Instead, they simply tell the owner which street they are from. Because most merchants in the community know which gangs control which streets, mentioning the street name is equivalent to identifying the gang. In this case, the owner would have known that the extortionists belonged to the Ghost Shadows.

5. More often than not, the gang members do not elaborate much and simply demand protection money from a business owner. However, sometimes gang members give the following explanations for why victims should pay:

Everyone in this area pays protection money to us. It has been like this for several decades. Now, please do not defy this tradition.

Every Chinese who owns a store in Chinatown has to pay protection money. You are no exception.

6. The following account was given by a merchant who readily accepted the reality of extortion in Chinatown:

Before I opened this take-out restaurant, not only had I heard a lot about gang extortion, I even saw gang members extorting money from a friend's restaurant. My friend told me that if I am willing to pay, everything will be all right. Therefore, I was prepared. When they showed up, I just paid.

7. Apparently this "contractual" term applies only to members of the gang who receive protection money from the business owner. My data suggest that gang leaders generally have little desire or ability to enforce this term. Thus, being "protected" by a gang does not necessarily ensure that a business owner will not be exploited in other ways by members of that gang. Moreover, even if this term is closely observed by members of the gang "protecting" the business owner, the business owner is still subject to victimization by members of other gangs.

8. A community leader explained why certain businesses are more vulnerable to gang extortion: "Many barbershops in Chinatown operate illegal massage services. Because these businesses are not legitimate, they would not call the police. Even if gang members rob everybody inside the shop, the owner would not call the police."

9. One owner explained how he avoided paying protection money by taking the initiative:

I used to own a business on Mott Street, and I've been active in Chinatown for a long time. I know the gangs' big brothers, and I know how the gangs operate. That's why when I opened this store in 1986, I informed the big brothers before the business started, invited them to come and collect lucky money during the opening ceremony. I also asked them to tell their little brothers not to come for protection money. We gave face to one another.

10. According to a merchant who hired a former gang leader to negotiate for him, it was like "asking a tiger to get rid of a wolf." A community leader explained how he and his association sometimes helped business members strike a deal with the gangs:

We help them find the troublemakers. After we did, we help the owners negotiate. This is the most effective way because the victim pays less and the offender won't be too rude to the victim in the process. Let's say a member of our association was asked by a gang to pay $3,000 grand opening ceremony money, and we help him to reduce it to $500 or $1,000. Gang members usually do not want to make it a mess [by refusing the offer] because they want "face."

11. According to a merchant who claimed to be extremely familiar with the Chinese underworld's "face-giving" protocols, the key to dealing effectively with gangs is knowing how to give face:

It's very important for a person to know how to give face to others. Gangsters are also human beings. If you respect them, they respect you too. Of course, one cannot be too soft, otherwise, they will exploit you. For instance, if the little brothers come to sell items during Chinese holidays, I will pay them some money just to get rid of them. If they come at other times, I refuse. However, if they appear during the Chinese New Year bare-handed, they won't get any money from me. I will tell them, "My name is XXX. Go back and tell your big brother I didn't give you face today; he will explain to you why." Since I opened my business in 1986, nobody has ever come to my store to create problems. Once, a gang member and his girlfriend came to have dinner and said he would pay later. I waited until both of them left the store, then I went out and asked the gang member to come back inside the store with me. I asked the girl to wait outside. I told him, "I have given you enough face, don't ever come back to eat for free." He paid the bill, even though I didn't insist. I know how to *jo yan* [meaning, to behave like a human being], so very few people come bother me.

12. A three-digit amount. To protect the identity of the restaurant, the exact figure is not revealed.

13. The English word "triad" means a triangle of heaven, earth, and man (Chesneaux, 1972). Triad societies are considered to be the largest, most dangerous, and best organized crime groups in the world (Posner, 1988; Booth, 1991; Black, 1992; Chin, 1995). These secret societies were formed in China three centuries ago by patriots in order to fight against the oppressive and corrupt Qing dynasty (1644–1911). When the Qing dynasty collapsed and the Republic of China was established in 1911, some triad societies became involved in criminal activities (Morgan, 1960). According to one source, there are currently 160,000 triad members in Hong Kong, who belong to more than 50 societies (M. Chang, 1991). In Hong Kong, triads appear to be in control of most illegitimate enterprises and of some legitimate businesses as well (Fight Crime Committee, 1986). However, triad activities are not limited to Hong Kong; law enforcement agencies in North America, Europe, and Southeast Asia report that triad activities are increasing in their jurisdictions (O'Callaghan, 1978; President's Commission on Organized Crime, 1984; U.S. Senate, 1992). In 1997, Hong Kong will be returned to China. The political uncertainty in Hong Kong has made law enforcement authorities in the United States, Canada, Australia, and other countries deeply concerned that triad groups might transfer their operations abroad (Kaplan at al., 1986; Grace and Guido, 1988).

14. To protect the identity of the subject, the actual amount of the payments is not stated. I can only reveal that the monthly payment was less than $100.

15. Although some stores in Manhattan's Chinatown may change owners, the payment to the gangs does not change. The new owners simply continue to pay the same amount to the same gang as the former owners.

16. According to data from the business survey, sometimes (22% of the time) gang members do not give a reason.

17. The number 1, pronounced *yat* in Cantonese, signifies *yat lo*, meaning "all the way," and eight signifies "prosperity" because it is pronounced *bat*, which sounds like the word for prosperity—*faat*.

18. The number 4 is pronounced *sei* in Cantonese, which is similar to the Cantonese pronunciation of the word for "dead."

19. As mentioned earlier, the tangerine plant is considered a cultural necessity for the Chinese New Year celebration, in every Chinese household and place of business. The pronunciation of the Chinese word for "tangerine" is similar to that of the word for "good fortune."

20. The roles of the faction *dai lo*s and the *ah kung*s will be discussed in chapter 6.

21. During the interviews, street-level *dai lo*s often talked proudly of how many stores they "own." This means that they are completely in charge of collecting money from these stores and decide how to distribute the proceeds from them.

22. If a street-level *dai lo* goes along with his gang members to collect money from stores that are not "owned" by him, he will take only a small portion of the money.

23. I do not have data on how a faction *dai lo* of a tong-affiliated gang may share the money from extortion with the *dai dai lo*.

24. It is not clear whether the store owner meant that both tong members and gang members are crooked or that they both came to extort money from him.

Chapter 5

1. During the Chinese New Year, as was explained in chapter 3, it is customary for Chinese parents to give *hung bao* (red envelopes) containing brand new bills to their children and relatives who are single. Employers may also offer *hung bao* to their employ-

ees. During this time of the year, children and young adults often playfully greet a person older than themselves by saying, "*Kung hei faat tsoi, hung bao loh loi*" ("Prosperity to you, *hung bao* to me").

2. The tangerine is called *kat* in Cantonese and *ji* in Mandarin. These words are pronounced the same as the word "good luck" in both Cantonese and Mandarin. The tangerine is therefore one of the major decorative items during the Chinese New Year.

3. The data suggest that telling gang members that the owner of the business is not around is one of the most common tactics used by merchants to deflect extortionists. Some merchants told the gang members that the owner was on vacation in Asia and was unlikely to be back for several months.

4. Most Chinese gods or spiritual figures are considered to be friendly and to bring good fortune to people. A few ferocious gods, however, symbolize disaster; these gods are generally known as *wan shan*. One way to deal with *wan shan* is to offer them food and ask them to go away.

5. A "dry partner" is someone who need not invest any money, but is entitled to share a certain percentage of the profits.

6. Multivariate analysis utilizing the logistic regression model was conducted to examine the relationship between subjects' personal and business characteristics and their resistance to attempted gang extortion. In the model, I found that business type was significantly related to resistance, whereas educational level of the subject and neighborhood of the business were marginally significant. No other personal and business characteristics were found to be significant.

7. It should be noted that the crime reporting rates in the NCVS data and in this study are not completely compatible. In the NCVS, respondents were asked whether they reported their victimizations in 1990 to the police. In my study, Chinese business owners were asked whether they had *ever* reported gang extortion to law enforcement authorities during the lifetime of their current business. The reporting rate for Chinese victims of extortion might have been lower if the time frame had been limited to one year.

8. For Chinatown restaurateurs, contacting the police for a crime they consider not serious could result in serious consequences, even if the gangs do not retaliate. A community leader explained why:

> They [merchants] are afraid to let people know [about their being victimized by gangs] because they are afraid that customers will not dare to patronize their restaurants. There are so many restaurants in Chinatown; if word spreads that your restaurant is in trouble with a gang, customers are not going to come to enjoy your food and risk their lives. I can't think of one restaurant in Chinatown that is that much appealing not to lose their customers over this.

Also, Chinatown merchants are concerned that if people in the community know that their stores are being victimized, they might have difficulty in selling their businesses in the future.

9. One subject indicated he would definitely not contact the police because he was afraid he might be killed by the gangs: "They didn't demand us not to report to the police. We will not report it anyway. Never ever ask me to testify at court. A while ago, a store owner on Canal Street testified, and he was retaliated against. He was shot to death."

10. Logistic regression analysis was conducted to determine the nature of the association between personal and business characteristics and reporting behavior in a multivariate relationship. I found that gang threat was still the most significant variable in predicting reporting behavior, and the profitability of the business (not included in the bivariate

analysis) and the subject's sex were marginally significant. No other variables were significant in predicting the subjects' reporting behavior.

11. I did not ask the respondents why they thought the police were fair or unfair.

12. Some business establishments in Manhattan's Chinatown exhibit a certificate of membership in either the Hip Sing Association or the On Leong Association, at the entrance or behind the counter. Some stores display pictures showing the leaders of these two organizations with the store owners. The certificate and the picture are there to inform any would-be perpetrators that the store or the owner is well-connected with the leadership of either the Hip Sing or the On Leong.

Chapter 6

1. I am not sure whether a female associate can hang out with more than one gang. According to some subjects, it is all right to do so; however, others indicated that it is not permitted.

2. The word *po* is Cantonese slang. It means hanging out in the streets. The word for play is also Chinese underworld slang. As Toy (1992a) pointed out, in San Francisco's Chinatown, joining a gang is known as "coming out to play." New York City's Chinese gang members also often used the phrase "coming out to play" to indicate their participation in the gangs and their commitment to the norms and values attached to "play."

3. *Guan Gong*, an army general also known as the God of War, was a ferocious warrior during the period of the Three Kingdoms (A.D. 221–265). The general personified values cherished by the Chinese underclass—especially loyalty and righteousness.

4. Non-tong-affiliated gangs are gangs that have no connection with tongs. Later in this chapter, I will discuss the similarities and differences between tong-affiliated and non-tong-affiliated gangs.

5. Since respondents were extremely reluctant to indicate how many members belonged to their gangs and the few who were willing to provide estimations appeared to be guessing, the question was dropped after the first fifteen interviews. Most subjects knew only how many members belonged to the particular factions with which they were associated, but not the number of members of the whole gang.

6. Intragang violence will be discussed in detail in chapter 7.

7. For example, a faction leader may have to decide which clique to use when he is asked by the primary leader to guard a gambling place. The faction leader and clique members, when offered such opportunities, will gain a stable income from the operators of the club. Faction leaders also try to win the trust of the top leader in order to gain other lucrative contracts. However, the key leader's decision to ask a faction to provide services, especially such services as protecting gambling establishments and prostitution houses, may be predetermined by the locality of the vice operation and not by the relationship between the primary leader and the faction leaders.

8. The Toy (1992b) and Joe (1994) articles were based on the same data set, which was based on a major ethnographic study of gangs in San Francisco, conducted by the Institute of Scientific Analysis.

9. According to the 1993 federal indictment of the Tung On Association, the Tsung Tsin Association, and the Tung On gang, the titles for the various positions that exist within the alliance between the adult organization and gang are somewhat different from the Hip Sing–Flying Dragons connection. In the Tung On Association–Tsung Tsin Association–Tung On gang alliance, the presidents of the two adult organizations are known as *dai dai lo*, the highest leader of the gang is known as *dai lo*, and the deputy leader is known as *dai ma* (big horse) (Fried, 1993).

10. Efforts to disguise the links between tong members and the gang is evident in this

episode. When the gang leader was arrested for heroin trafficking, the Hip Sing Association immediately denied any connection between itself and the gang leader and erased his name from the list of its nationwide office that had already been prepared for the media. As a result, when the list, which had more than thirty names on it, appeared in the media, no name was listed under the position of national manager.

11. According to Chin (1990), *jiang hu* (literally, rivers and lakes) denotes lack of roots. People referred to as *jiang hu* are involved in exploiting and intimidating the rich and powerful and in providing illegal services such as protection, gambling, and prostitution. They believe they are making a living in an alternative way—a way that is justifiable because it redistributes wealth that is unevenly distributed in an imperfect world.

12. According to a leader of an association affiliated with a gang, it used to be that everybody in Chinatown knew who the *ah kungs* were, but not anymore. These people now make a concerted effort to hide their identities.

Chapter 7

1. The definition of a gang-related incident is controversial (Klein and Maxson, 1989). Journalists and police in the Chinese community appear to use the relatively loose definition adopted by the Los Angeles Police Department and the Los Angeles Sheriff's Department in defining gang-related incidents (Maxson and Klein, 1990): that is, if either a victim or an offender in a violent confrontation is a gang member, then the incident is considered gang related.

2. Although violent episodes in the Chinese community that involve multiple victims or bystanders are often well publicized in the American media, most Chinese gang warfare is only reported in the Chinese media. Even so, the Chinese media normally cover only incidents in which one or more victims are killed or seriously wounded. Thus, most minor gang clashes in the Chinese community go unnoticed.

3. I searched New York City's English-language newspapers (mainly the *New York Times*, the *Daily News*, the *New York Post*, and *New York Newsday*) and its Chinese-language newspapers (including *World Journal, China Times, Sing Tao Jih Pao,* and *Centre Daily News*) and found that 304 incidents of Chinese gang-related violence were reported in the media between 1968 and 1992.

4. If a respondent indicated that he had left the gang, the interviewer asked him to provide estimates for the year prior to his dissociation from the gang. Comparisons between active and former gang members in the sample show that there are no significant differences between the two groups in terms of their involvement in violence and other criminal activities for a particular year, with the exception that active gang members were more involved in selling items to business owners than were former gang members. As a result, active gang status was not controlled for in the analysis of Chinese gang members' involvement in violence and other criminal activities.

5. As was mentioned in chapter 2, my gang sample is not a random sample. As a result, my findings may not be generalizable to the entire Chinese gang population.

6. Data collected from the interviews with Chinese business owners indicate that the prevalence of theft of goods and services was lower than that of forced sales and asking for lucky money. However, in the data collected from interviews with gang members, the respondents said the form of extortion they most often engaged in was asking for free or discounted goods and services. Likewise, although forced sales was reported by business subjects to be the most prevalent type of extortion, gang subjects reported that they were least likely to be involved in this type of extortion. This discrepancy may be easy to explain: a small number of gang members may be forcing owners to buy unwanted items and may be doing so at a very high rate.

7. As was noted earlier in this book, not all Chinese gangs are affiliated with adult organizations. Also, many adult organizations deny being affiliated with gangs and/or participating in illicit activities.

8. Members of the Vietnamese Born-to-Kill (BTK) were often accused of extorting money from store owners outside their turf and ignoring the gang rule of not stepping into other gangs' territories. Perhaps for this reason, the second-in-command of BTK was shot to death in BTK's turf by rival gang members. BTK members not only orchestrated a high-profile funeral for their deceased leader but also decided to have the motorcade pass through core areas of Chinatown not in their turf, in protest. When the mourners arrived at the cemetery in Linden, New Jersey, for the burial, three heavily armed men fired at them. Twenty-three young males and females were wounded (English, 1995). The authorities theorized that BTK's intentional encroachment on other gangs' territories in an unusual way angered their rivals and led to the shootings in the cemetery (Lorch, 1990a).

9. Although this respondent linked these issues, I counted them as separate motives in my survey.

10. Robbery and robbery-related violence will be discussed in detail in the following chapter.

11. This issue will be discussed in the following chapter.

Chapter 8

1. *Wan shik* means "finding food," and *wan shai kaai*, "finding a world of one's own."

2. Within the Chinese criminal subculture, burglary is probably the most unpopular type of crime. Members of the subculture often claim that anybody with some level of self-respect would never be involved in stealing. Among certain groups, prostitution is prohibited because it is looked down on as "eating soft rice" (men relying on the sale of women's sexual favors to support themselves financially). Others are reluctant to have anything to do with "powder" (heroin) because they either see it as a risky business or as something that could destroy many lives. For these reasons, members of the subculture have historically been most inclined to exploit businesspeople.

3. They were called hatchetmen because they often used hatchets in street fights.

4. A police officer testified at the hearings as follows about the prevalence of gambling among Chinese in California:

> I think there are more professional gamblers in proportion to the population of the Chinese than any other class of people in the world except Indians; but Indians are not professional gamblers, they are general gamblers. Really, more Chinamen seem to live off the receipts of gambling houses, and by being connected and attached to them, seeming to have no other business, than any other class of people. . . . I think it is a natural passion with them—that nothing could cure them. I do not believe that there is a Chinese individual in the State of California today who does not gamble more or less. I may be mistaken as to one or two. (U.S. Senate, [1877] 1978: 223–24)

5. For many community associations, gambling creates internal power struggles. Ordinary members of the community associations often accuse their leaders of embezzling or mishandling income from association-sponsored gambling activities.

6. Many working-class Chinese immigrants are employed by restaurants and garment factories. These jobs normally require them to work 12 hours or more a day (from 10:00 A.M. to 11:00 P.M.), six days a week. Most restaurant workers are not allowed to take their weekly day off on the weekends.

7. When Chinese visit their family or district associations in Chinatown, there is little for them to do except gamble. They can hang out on the premises, read newspapers, and

chat with others, but they will be considered by others who are there to gamble as squares or outsiders. It is difficult, if not impossible, for any conscientious person to visit the associations frequently and refrain from gambling because gambling is the only activity going on in these organizations.

8. Sponsoring a gambling establishment, even a modest one, can be lucrative. The house normally collects 5 percent of the winning bets.

9. Operating expenses may include rent, maintenance fees, water and electricity bills, purchase of household items such as paper towels and cups, and costs for an annual dinner.

10. Only a few wealthy family or district organizations that own many properties in the community do not need to rely on gambling income. Rents from the properties can cover their operational expenses.

11. In fact, gambling houses in Chinatown are rarely raided by law enforcement authorities. In the past, the police were compelled to launch assaults on the gambling industry only in the aftermath of well-publicized incidents of violence in Chinatown (*Centre Daily News*, 1986).

12. One gang subject disclosed that his clique collected $100 to $200 a week from a small gambling den and over $1,000 a week from a relatively large gambling house. Another respondent indicated that his *dai lo* received $3,000 to $4,000 a month from a gambling establishment.

13. Buses from Chinatown to Atlantic City offer passengers excellent deals. Not only are the bus fares low, but also free gambling chips and food coupons are offered to the bus passengers upon their arrival in Atlantic City. During major holidays, at least 200 buses per day leave Chinatown for Atlantic City. The casino industry is successful in luring ordinary, as well as high-stakes, Chinese gamblers. During major festivals, it is also not unusual to observe many limousines parked in the narrow streets of Chinatown, waiting to take business owners and their families to Atlantic City. While the businesspeople gamble at the baccarat tables, their families will be enjoying, for free, the performances of top-rated entertainers from Hong Kong in the casinos' ballrooms. Casino-industry spokesmen have indicated that Asians make up about 1 percent of the gamblers in Atlantic City, but account for as much as 10 percent of the revenues (Millman, 1985).

14. The Immigration and Naturalization Service (INS) arrested a Taiwanese woman by the name of Shih Hsiao Poa and her daughter for importing more than 50 women from abroad to work at massage parlors in San Francisco, Denver, and New York City (Lubasch, 1986). Shih Hsiao Poa's son-in-law, the owner of a Taiwan-based travel agency, was responsible for recruiting women in Taiwan. In a conversation with an INS undercover agent who posed as a potential investor, Shih Hsiao Poa said, "If a girl wants to come here, my son has her sign a contract. This is her agreement that she will pay back all her travel expenses after she has earned them by working for me. Every month, we are getting visas issued from the Taiwanese U.S. Consulate, where my son has a connection inside. We give the girls money to buy the airplane tickets, money to settle their families down" (Surovell, 1988: 42). Shih Hsiao Poa was convicted for racketeering activities, but there was no evidence that her prostitution ring was affiliated with Chinese gangs.

15. To attract customers, these clubs often stress in their advertisements that they provide a large number of beautiful women from a variety of Asian countries, safety, and high-standard facilities. In order to underscore the safety issue, one club emphasized that it was protected by Italian people, perhaps implying a mafia connection.

16. Since I did not ask the respondents to describe the characteristics of their targets, I do not know if they were mainly involved in commercial or residential robbery.

17. As might be expected, media reports of robbery incidents reflect much more

violent incidents of the crime. For example, in robbery-related shootouts in Los Angeles's Chinatown, a police officer and two offenders were killed; a jeweler was shot to death in a failed robbery incident in Manhattan's Chinatown; and while robbing a business firm in Manhattan's Chinatown, a member of the Born-to-Kill accidentally shot and killed his companion (Lorch, 1990b).

18. With the arrival of many legal and illegal Chinese immigrants over the past several years, residential rent in Chinatown has skyrocketed. A poorly maintained two-bedroom apartment may cost between $700 and $1,000 per month. Normally, the bedrooms are extremely small; some of them are converted walk-in closets or storage rooms. Most of these apartments do not have bathrooms, so a make-shift bathroom is constructed in the kitchen or the living room. Seven to ten illegal immigrants may share such an apartment, each paying from $100 to $150 a month in rent. In these apartments, hot water and heat are not available on a daily basis. Illegal immigrants tolerate this abuse by their landlords because they like the proximity of these apartments to their workplace.

19. However, the Chinese involvement in the heroin trade in Southeast Asia is well-documented by McCoy (1973).

20. He probably meant that if they invested money in a risky heroin deal, there was a good chance of being caught and that would have resulted in the loss of the money.

21. He probably meant that he did not want to do it, but he could not resist the money he would be paid for his services.

22. The annual immigration quota for China is currently set at 20,000.

23. In Chinese American communities, illegal immigrants are called *ren she* (human snakes), and smugglers, *she tou* (snakeheads). Smuggling is known as "digging snakes."

24. According to Myers, most illegal Chinese immigrants are working-class Fujianese married males:

> The aliens being smuggled overwhelmingly originate in Fujian Province, PRC [the People's Republic of China]. Ninety-eight percent are married males and 96% have one or more children. The vast majority, 87%, held low-skilled jobs in China with farming and unskilled factory labor being the majority occupations. (1992: 2)

25. Of the 62 gang members I interviewed, none mentioned that they or their gangs were involved in human smuggling. It should be noted that the sample included only one member of the Fuk Ching, the gang alleged to be the most active in alien smuggling.

26. Before the *Golden Venture* arrived in New York City, Fuk Ching leader Kuo Liang Kay (nickname "Ah Kay") went back to China. He was arrested in Hong Kong in August 1993, after the well-publicized tragedy had occurred (Faison, 1993b). He was extradited back to the United States to stand trial for ordering his followers to kill a rival Fuk Ching leader. The intended victim was unharmed in the incident (although two of his followers were mistakenly murdered), and he retaliated by killing five Fuk Ching members who had been Ah Kay's followers. Two of the victims were Ah Kay's natural brothers (Hanley, 1993).

27. According to data released by the INS, in 1992 there were about 1 million Mexicans, 298,000 Salvadorans, 121,000 Guatemalans, 104,000 Canadians, 102,000 Poles, and 101,000 Filipinos living illegally in the United States. The agency estimated that there were not more than 30,000 illegal Chinese immigrants.

28. The Golden Triangle in Southeast Asia is the area in which the borders of Myanmar (formerly Burma), Laos, and Thailand meet. It is considered to be one of the world's major opium-producing area (U.S. Department of State, 1993). Western drug experts estimate

that the area, which is controlled by opium warlords and ethnic insurgent groups, produced 2,797 metric tons of opium in 1993 (U.S. Department of State, 1994).

Chapter 9

1. In the late 1970s, a social worker did attempt to mobilize the community to seek financial assistance from the local government for the creation of a vocational training program for Chinese gang members. He persuaded rival gang leaders engaged in violence to get together and announce a truce. However, the social worker's appeal for government funding was not successful, and the peaceful coexistence among the gangs lasted for only a few weeks. Frustrated, he left his job and opened a travel agency in Chinatown. Later, he was shot to death in his office by an unknown gunman (*World Journal*, 1980b).

2. However, the two were recently promoted to sergeant and transferred to other precincts. It is not clear how this might affect the effectiveness of the unit.

3. For the past decade, the Los Angeles police department has implemented gang suppression techniques such as these in confronting the city's large and violent ghetto gangs. On a regular basis, police saturate an area in which gang violence, murder, and drive-by shootings frequently occur. Everyone on the street suspected of belonging to a gang is arrested, strip-searched, and jailed.

4. The following is an example of one such notice. It is a letter from a police chief to business owners in San Francisco's Chinatown urging them to confer with authorities if anyone tries to extort money from them (Crittenden, 1985):

Dear Merchant:

The Mayor and myself wish to work with your community to preclude any extortion activity during the upcoming Chinese New Year's celebration.

In the past, young gang members have attempted to extort money by displaying red envelopes and soliciting contributions. Many merchants have complained regarding this illegal activity and the Mayor's Office and the Police Department wish to help eliminate this problem.

Any person being victimized should notify the Gang Task Force of the San Francisco Police Department, 553-1401.

Cornelius P. Murphy
Chief of Police

5. This method of policing, however, could have constitutional implications.

6. Although the number of participants reached an all-time high, the 1993 meeting was not without controversy. For the first time, China sent a delegate to the meeting. However, on the eve of the meeting, the Chinese delegate found out that the sponsoring agency, the FBI, allowed members of the Taiwan delegation to use "R.O.C." (Republic of China) in identifying themselves. The Chinese delegates withdrew from the conference in protest. China wanted the Taiwan delegation to identify itself as "Chinese Taipei," a name commonly used to distinguish Taiwan in international events such as the Olympics.

7. Most Chinese immigrants speak Mandarin, the official language of China, Taiwan, and Singapore. However, there are a substantial number of Chinese, especially the elderly, who only communicate in their own dialects. The most frequently spoken dialects among Chinese in the United States are Toisanese, Cantonese, Taiwanese, Fujianese, Hakka, and Chiu Chow. With the exception of those who come from Beijing, most Chinese immigrants speak one or more dialects, and they tend to prefer to communicate in their own dialect among their own people. Thus, the ability to communicate in another person's dialect is the easiest way to establish an immediate rapport.

GLOSSARY

Chinese words and phrases listed here contain Cantonese, Mandarin, and Toisanese. Letters in brackets indicate the language or dialect of the words and phrases: C for Cantonese, M for Mandarin, and T for Toisanese. Mandarin words are transliterated in the pinyin style. Since Cantonese and Toisanese have no standardized transliteration style, the author adopted the style of Fritz Chang's "A Cantonese-English Dictionary of Cantonese Gang Slang" (unpublished report, 1995) and Roy Cowles's *The Cantonese Speaker's Dictionary* (Hong Kong: Hong Kong University Press, 1965).

ah kung [C] (grandfather):   A tong member who is considered a leader by the members of the gang affiliated with that tong
bai tai zi [M] (setting a table):   Treating rival gang members to a lavish dinner to redress grievances and soothe ill feelings
bat [C] (eight):   Eight
boo how doy [T] (hatchetman):   Hoodlums hired by the tongs in San Francisco's Chinatown during the mid-nineteenth and early twentieth century to guard the vice businesses in the community
cha cheen [C] (tea money):   Extortion money
dai dai lo [C] (big big brother):   Primary gang leader
dai lo [C] (big brother):   Gang leader
dai ma [C] (big horse):   Gang leader
faat [C] (prosper):   Prosperity
fong dai cheen [C] (key money):   Front money for getting a real-estate lease
gai so [C] (street money):   Protection money
Guan Gong [M] (General Guan):   A ferocious warrior who personified values cherished by the Chinese underclass
guan xi [M] (relationship):   Personal relationship; good connection
guo yu [M] (national language):   Mandarin, the official spoken language in China
heung yau cheen [C] (incense oil money):   Protection money
hoi moon dai kat [C] (good fortune once the door is opened):   Best of luck to you on the opening day of your business
hung bao [C] (red envelope containing cash):   Within the Chinese gang context, it means extortion money

jiang hu [M] (rivers and lakes):   A Chinese criminal subculture also known as the
    "dark society"

jo yan [C] (to behave like a human being):   To know and follow Chinese norms
    and rules regulating social interactions

kat [C] (tangerine):   Symbol of good luck

kong so [C] (negotiation):   Negotiation

kung hei faat tsoi, hung bao loh loi [C] (prosperity to you, *hung bao* to
    me):   Prosperity to you, *hung bao* to me

lei shi [C] (good for business):   Lucky money or extortion money

leng jai [C] (little kids):   Ordinary gang member

log kaak [C] (no character):   Cheating

ma jai [C] (little horse):   Ordinary gang member

pai peng [C] (distributing cakes):   Protection money offered by gambling houses

po [C] (hanging out):   Hanging out

po oo fai [C] (protection fees):   Protection money

pu tong hua [M] (general language):   Mandarin, the official spoken language in
    China

ren she [M] (human snake):   Illegal immigrant

saam lo [C] (third brother):   Low-level gang leader

sai lo [C] (little brother):   Ordinary gang member

sei [C] (four):   Bad luck (many Chinese do not like the number four because its
    pronunciation is similar to that of the word for "dead")

she tou [M] (snakehead):   Human smuggler

shik pa wong faan [C] (eating the villain's meal):   Eating without paying

shuk foo [C] (uncle):   A tong member who is considered a leader by members of
    the gang affiliated with that tong

soi jaw [C] (hit by misfortunes):   Being killed, arrested, or jailed

tai cheung [C] (watching a place):   Guarding gambling places

tai pa wong hei [C] (watching the villain's movie):   Entering a theater without
    ticket

taw dei fai [C] (territory fees):   Protection money

wan shai kaai [C] (finding a world of one's own):   Making a living

wan shan [C] (god of plague):   God of misfortune

wan shik [C] (finding food):   Making a living

Wo Ping Huey [T] (Peace Committee):   A committee established in the early
    twentieth century by Chinese community leaders to quell tong wars

yat lo faat [C] (prosperity all the way):   Prosperity all the way

yee lo [C] (second brother):   Low-level gang leader

yum cha [C] (drink tea):   Eating

BIBLIOGRAPHY

In English

Adler, Patricia A. 1985. *Wheeling and Dealing*. New York: Columbia University Press.

Aldrich, Howard E. 1979. *Organizations and Environments*. Englewood Cliffs, N.J.: Prentice-Hall.

Allen, Glen, and Lynne Thomas. 1987. "Orphans of war." *Toronto Magazine*, March: 34–57.

Ashbury, Herbert. 1928. *The Gangs of New York*. New York: Paragon House.

Attorney General of California. 1972. *Proceedings of the Conference on Chinese Gang Problems*. Sacramento, Calif.: California Organized Crime and Criminal Intelligence Branch.

Badey, James R. 1988. *Dragons and Tigers*. Loomis, Calif.: Palmer Enterprises.

Barth, Gunther. 1964. *Bitter Strength: A History of Chinese in the United States*. Cambridge: Harvard University Press.

Beach, Walter G. 1932. *Oriental Crime in California*. Stanford: Stanford University Press.

Bean, Frank, Barry Edmonston, and Jeffrey Passel (Eds.). 1990. *Undocumented Migration to the United States*. Washington, D.C.: Urban Institute Press.

Bergen Record. 1991. "Robbery victim held to ensure testimony." May 26: A3.

Black, David. 1992. *Triad Takeover: A Terrifying Account of the Spread of Triad Crime in the West*. London: Sidgwick and Jackson.

Blakey, Robert. 1994. "RICO: The federal experience (criminal and civil) and an analysis of attacks against the statute." In Robert Kelly, Ko-lin Chin, and Rufus Schatzberg (Eds.), *Handbook of Organized Crime in the United States*. Westport, Conn.: Greenwood.

Bloodworth, Dennis. 1965. *The Chinese Looking Glass*. New York: Farrar, Straus and Giroux.

Blumenthal, Ralph. 1982. "Gunmen firing wildly kill 3 in Chinatown bar." *New York Times*, December 24: A1.

Blumer, Herbert. 1971. "Social problems as collective behavior." *Social Problems* 18: 298–306.

Blumstein, Alfred, David P. Farrington, and Soumyo Moitra. 1985. "Delinquency careers: Innocents, desisters, and persisters." In Michael Tonry and Norval Morris (Eds.), *Crime and Justice: An Annual Review of Research*. Chicago: University of Chicago Press.

Bolden, Charles. 1990. "Sting in a dragon's tale." *South China Morning Post Spectrum*, September 2: 1.

Booth, Martin. *The Triads*. 1991. New York: St. Martin's.

Bourgois, Philippe. 1989. "In search of Horatio Agler: Culture and ideology in the crack economy." *Contemporary Drug Problems* (winter): 619–50.

Bowles, Pete. 1993. "Asian gang sweep; Chinatown biz bigs busted." *New York Newsday*, December 10: 29.

Boyd, Alan, and William Barnes. 1992. "Thailand an open door for illegal passages." *South China Morning Post*, June 22: 6.

Bresler, Fenton. 1981. *The Chinese Mafia*. New York: Stein and Day.

Breslin, Jimmy. 1983. "The toughest gangster on Pell Street." *New York Daily News*, March 15: 4.

Brown, DeNee L., and Patricia Davis. 1990. "Home-invasion victim tells of threats." *Washington Post*, October 9: B1.

Bryan, John. 1973. "Inside the Chinese gangs of S.F." *San Francisco Phoenix*, April 19: 1.

Bryant, Robert M. 1990. "Chinese organized crime making major inroads in smuggling heroin to U.S." *Organized Crime Digest* 11, no. 17: 1–6.

Buder, Leonard. 1980. "Special force is assigned on Chinatown shootings." *New York Times*, January 20: L35.

———. 1988. "Top U.S. target in heroin trade seized at hotel." *New York Times*, March 15: B5.

———. 1989. "Biggest heroin distributor seized, U.S. agents say." *New York Times*, October 20: B3.

Burdman, Pamela. 1993. "How gangsters cash in on human smuggling." *San Francisco Chronicle*, April 28: A1.

Bureau of Justice Statistics. 1992. *Criminal Victimization in the United States, 1990*. Washington, D.C.: U.S. Department of Justice.

Burke, Todd W., and Charles E. O'Rear. 1990. "Home invaders: Asian gangs in America." *Police Studies* 13 (winter): 154–56.

Burt, R. S. 1987. "Social contagion and innovation: Cohesion versus structural equivalence." *American Journal of Sociology* 92 (May): 1287–1335.

Butterfield, Fox. 1985. "The shifting picture of crime by U.S. Vietnamese." *New York Times*, January 21: A1.

———. 1986. "Chinese crime network reported moving into areas of U.S." *New York Times*, November 30: A30.

———. 1989. "A new gang's violent role in Chinatown." *New York Times*, March 4: 29.

———. 1991. "Killing of 5 in Boston's Chinatown raises fears of Asian gang wars." *New York Times*, January 15: B6.

Canal Magazine. 1978. "Interview with Nicky Louie." December 8: 1.

———. 1979. "A conversation with the Special Task Force." March 10: 16.

Chan, Joseph Hing-kwok. 1975. *Gang Delinquency in New York City's Chinatown*. Master's thesis, West Virginia University.

Chan, Ying. 1993a. "Forced into sex slavery." *New York Daily News*, May 17: 7.

———. 1993b. "Kidnap spree: Smuggling stymied, Fuk Ching adapts." *New York Daily News*, September 25, 1993: 4.

Chan, Ying, and James Dao. 1990a. "Merchants of misery." *New York Daily News*, September 24: 7.

———. 1990b. "A tale of 2 immigrants." *New York Daily News*, September 24: 21.

Chang, Henri. 1972. "Die today, die tomorrow: The rise and fall of Chinatown gangs." *Bridge Magazine* 2, no. 2: 10–15.

Charasdamrong, Prasong, and Subin Kheunkaew. 1992. "Smuggling human beings: A lucrative racket that poses a threat to national security." *Bangkok Post*, July 19: 10.

Chen, Hsiang-shui. 1992. *Chinatown No More: Taiwan Immigrants in Contemporary New York*. Ithaca: Cornell University Press.

Chernow, Ron. 1973. "Chinatown, their Chinatown: The truth behind the facade." *New York Magazine*, June 11: 39–45.

Chesneaux, Jean. 1972. *Popular Movements and Secret Societies in China, 1840–1950*. Stanford: Stanford University Press.

Chin, Ko-lin. 1986. *Chinese Triad Societies, Tongs, Organized Crime, and Street Gangs in Asia and the United States*. Ph.D. dissertation, University of Pennsylvania.

———. 1990. *Chinese Subculture and Criminality*. Westport, Conn.: Greenwood.

———. 1994. "Out-of-town brides: International marriage and wife abuse among Chinese immigrants." *Journal of Comparative Family Studies* 25 (spring): 53–69.

———. 1995. "Triad societies in Hong Kong." *Transnational Organized Crime* 1 (spring): 47–64.

Chin, Ko-lin, T. M. Lai, and Martin Rouse. 1990–91. "Social adjustment and alcoholism among Chinese in New York City." *International Journal of the Addictions* 25, nos. 5A and 6A: 711–32.

Ching, Frank. 1971. "Peking gains favor with Chinese in U.S." *New York Times*, February 22: A1.

———. 1974a. "Street crime casts a pall of fear over Chinatown." *New York Times*, January 19: L16.

———. 1974b. "Crime in New York's Chinatown." *Bridge Magazine*, 3, no. 2: 11–14.

City of New York Department of City Planning. 1992. *The Newest New Yorkers: An Analysis of Immigration into New York City during the 1980s*. New York: City of New York.

———. 1993. *Estimates of Undocumented Aliens as of October 1992: Data from the U.S. Immigration and Naturalization Service compiled by the Population Division*. New York: City of New York.

Clairborne, William. 1993. "U.S., Mexico end impasse on Chinese; Migrants on ships will be sent home." *Washington Post*, July 15: A1.

Cloward, Richard A., and Lloyd E. Ohlin. 1960. *Delinquency and Opportunity*. New York: Free Press.

Cohen, Albert. 1955. *Delinquent Boys*. New York: Free Press.

Cohen, Sharon. 1986. "Fighting a shadowy foreign trade in sex." *Bergen Record*, September 26: A1.

Conly, Catherine, Patricia Kelly, Paul Mahanna, and Lynn Warner. 1993. *Street Gangs: Current Knowledge and Strategies*. Washington, D.C.: Government Printing Office.

Consoli, Jim. 1989. "Asian homes targets of robberies." *Bergen Record*, January 26: B1.

Cornelius, Wayne A. 1989. "Impact of the 1986 U.S. immigration law on emigration from rural Mexican sending communities." *Population and Development Review* 15, no. 4: 689–705.

Crewdson, John. 1983. *The Tarnished Door*. New York: Times Books.

Crittenden, Anthony R. 1985. *An overview of the Asian Crime Groups Problem in California*. Sacramento Department of Justice, State of California.

Daly, Michael. 1983. "The war for Chinatown." *New York Magazine*, February 14: 31–38.

Dannen, Frederic. 1992. "Revenge of the Green Dragons." *New Yorker*, November 16: 76–99.

Dao, James. 1992. "Asian street gangs emerging as new underworld." *New York Times*, April 1: A1.

Delgado, Hector. 1992. *New Immigrants, Old Unions*. Philadelphia: Temple University Press.

DeStefano, Anthony. 1988. "The Asian connection: A new main line to U.S." *New York Newsday*, February 14: 5.

DeStefano, Anthony, and Richard Esposito. 1987. "Asian gangs move into drugs." *New York Newsday*, September 16: 7.

———. 1988. "U.S. declares war without an army." *New York Newsday*, February 14: 8.

Dillon, Richard H. 1962. *The Hatchet Men: The Story of the Tong Wars in San Francisco's Chinatown*. New York: Coward-McCann.

Dobinson, Ian. 1992. "The Chinese connection: Heroin trafficking between Australia and South-east Asia." *Criminal Organizations* 7, no. 2: 1–7.

Dobson, Chris. 1992. "Goldfish drug case success." *South China Morning Post*, October 18: 3.

———. 1993. "The woman who took on Khun Sa." *South China Morning Post*, April 18: 4.

Dombrink, John, and John Huey-long Song. 1992. "Asian Racketeering in America: Emerging Groups, Organized Crime, and Legal Control." Unpublished final report submitted to the National Institute of Justice.

Douglas, William. 1988. "Febs nab 6 men on heroin charges." *New York Newsday*, February 22: 4.

Dubro, James. 1992. *Dragons of Crime: Inside the Asian Underworld*. Markham, Ont.: Octopus.

Eager, Marita. 1992. "Patten in tough stand against illegals." *South China Morning Post*, July 18: 3.

Egan, Cy. 1971. "7 wounded, 1 held in Chinatown clash." *New York Post*, February 24: 7.

Emch, Tom. 1973. "The Chinatown murders." *San Francisco Sunday Examiner and Chronicle*, September 9, 6–14.

Emery, Julie. 1990. "Wah Mee sentence to be appealed." *Seattle Times*, October 28: B2.

English, T. J. 1991. "Slaving away: Chinese illegals oppressed at home, exploited here." *Smithsonian*, February: 12–14.

———. 1995. *Born to Kill*. New York: William Morrow.

Epstein, Jason. 1993. "A taste of success." *New Yorker*, April 19: 50–56.

Erlanger, Steven. 1990. "Southeast Asia is now no. 1 source of U.S. heroin." *New York Times*, February 11: A26.

Esposito, Richard, and Sheryl McCarthy. 1988. "Record heroin bust sends agent searching in NY." *New York Newsday*, February 14: 5.

Fagan, Jeffrey. 1989. "The social organization of drug use and drug dealing among urban gangs." *Criminology* 27, no. 4: 633–67.

———. 1990. "Social processes of drug use and delinquency among youth gangs." In Ronald Huff (Ed.), *Gangs in America*. Newbury Park, Calif.: Sage.

Fagan, Jeffrey, Elizabeth Piper, and Melinda Moore. 1986. "Violent delinquents and urban youths." *Criminology* 24, no. 3: 439–71.

Faison, Seth. 1991. "Raiders seize 10 as leaders of 'Kill' gang." *New York Times*, August 13: B1.

———. 1993a. "Alien-smuggling suspect eluded immigration net." *New York Times*, June 10: A1.

———. 1993b. "Gang leader is arrested in Hong Kong." *New York Times*, August 29: 29.

———. 1993c. "13 indicted in plot to smuggle aliens." *New York Times*, September 1: A17.

———. 1993d. "Kidnappings tied to fall of a gang." *New York Times*, October 5: B1.

———. 1994. "U.S. officials fear ship is new smuggling wave: Freighter unloaded illegal Chinese aliens." *New York Times*, April 7: B3.

Farolino, Audrey. 1988. "Hong Kong help$ Chinatown grow." *New York Post*, October 20: 58.

Faso, Frank, and Paul Meskil. 1984. "Chinese gangs spreading terror." *New York Daily News*, April 22: 1.

———. 1985. "A fed indictment hits 25 members of Chinatown mob." *New York Daily News*, February 19: 3.

Fight Crime Committee. 1986. *A Discussion Document on Options for Changes in the Law and in the Administration of the Law to Counter the Triad Problem*. Hong Kong: Fight Crime Committee, Security Branch.

Fraser, C. Gerald. 1991. "18–shot killing a defense act, a jury decides." *New York Times*, July 5: B3.

Freedman, Dan. 1991. "Asian gangs turn to smuggling people." *San Francisco Examiner*, December 30: A7.

Fried, Joseph. 1993. "2 businessmen indicted as heads of a crime gang in Chinatown." *New York Times*, December 10: B7.

———. 1995. "Tong leader in Chinatown is convicted." *New York Times*, Janaury 18: B3.

Fritsch, Jane. 1993. "One failed voyage illustrates flow of Chinese immigration." *New York Times*, June 7: A1.

Garfinkel, Harold. 1956. "Conditions of successful degradation ceremonies." *American Journal of Sociology* 61 (March): 420–24.

Garofalo, James. 1979. *The Police and Public Opinion: An Analysis of Victimization and Attitude Data from 13 American Cities*. Washington, D.C.: Government Printing Office.

———. 1990. "The national crime survey, 1973–1986: Strengths and limitations of a very large data set." In Doris L. MacKenzie, Phyllis Jo Baunach, and Roy R. Roberg (Eds.), *Measuring Crime: Large-Scale, Long Range Efforts*. Albany: State University of New York Press.

Glaberson, William. 1989. "6 seized in smuggling Asians into New York." *New York Times*, May 5: B3.

Gladwell, Malcolm. 1993. "Rebirth in New York: Neighborhoods growing again in the city where new immigrants are planting roots." *Washington Post*, September 18: A1.

Gladwell, Malcolm, and Rachel Stassen-Berger. 1993. "Human cargo is hugely profitable to New York's Chinese underworld." *Washington Post*, June 7: A10.

Glick, Carl. 1941. *Shake Hands with the Dragon*. New York: McGraw-Hill.

Glick, Carl, and Sheng-hwa Hong. 1947. *Swords of Silence: Chinese Secret Societies, Past and Present*. New York: Whittlesey House.

Gold, Allan R. 1991. "Leader of Chinatown group slain." *New York Times*, March 21: B2.

Gong, Ying Eng, and Bruce Grant. 1930. *Tong War!* New York: N. L. Brown.

Gould, Terry. 1988. "Who killed Bob Moeini?" *Vancouver Sun Magazine*, May: 49–56.

Grace, Michael, and John Guido. 1988. *Hong Kong 1997: Its Impact on Chinese Organized Crime in the United States*. Washington, D.C.: U.S. Department of State, Foreign Service Institute.

Green, Norman. 1990. "The white powder ghost." *New York Newsday*, October 24: 9.

Gusfield, Joseph. 1981. *The Culture of Public Problems*. Chicago: University of Chicago Press.

Hagedorn, John. 1988. *People and Folks*. Chicago: Lakeview.

Hanley, Robert. 1993. "Gang killings laid to fight over power: Alien smuggling called root of Teaneck battle." *New York Times*, May 26: B1.

Hannum, Phil. 1992. *Nightmare: Vietnamese Home Invasion Robberies*. Falls Church, Va.: International Association of Asian Crime Investigators.

Hatfield, Larry D. 1989. "Gambling devastates Asia immigrants." *San Francisco Examiner*, August 28: A2.

Hays, Constance L. 1994. "Drug case derails U.S.-China law tie." *New York Times*, February 20: A23.

Henican, Ellis. 1987. "Chinatown hops with the rabbit." *New York Newsday*, January 30: 17.

Hetchman, Michael. 1977. "Chinatown gang foe knifed, ex-'Mayor' stabbed 3 times." *New York Daily News*, July 11: 4.

Hilgartner, Stephen, and Charles Bosk. 1988. "The rise and fall of social problems: A public arenas model." *American Journal of Sociology* 94, no. 1: 53–78.

Hindelang, Michael, and Michael Gottfredson. 1976. "The victim's decision not to invoke the criminal justice process." In William McDonald (Ed.), *Criminal Justice and the Victim*. Beverly Hills: Sage.

Hindelang, Michael, Michael Gottfredson, and James Garofalo. 1987. *Victims of Personal Crime*. Cambridge, Mass.: Ballinger.

Horowitz, Ruth. 1983. *Honor and the American Dream*. New Brunswick, N.J.: Rutgers University Press.

Howe, Charles. 1972. "The growth of gangs in Chinatown." *San Francisco Chronicle*, July 7: 1.

Howe, Charles, and Rose Pak. 1972. "How gangs are terrorizing S.F. Chinatown." *San Francisco Chronicle*, July 5: 1.

Howe, Marvine. 1986. "Chinatown plan is key to dispute." *New York Times*, July 20: 12.

———. 1987. "City's third Chinatown is emerging in Brooklyn." *New York Times*, September 13: 74.

———. 1989. "Drug smuggler pleads guilty in heroin case." *New York Times*, April 15: 31.

Howe, Robert. 1993. "For Asian Crime Task Force, 1st year brings results, criticism." *Washington Post*, June 3: 3.

Hudson, Edward. 1972. "3 in Chinese gang held in shooting of 6." *New York Times*, December 17: 28.

Ibert, Deborah L. 1985. "Gang attacks spread fear in Chinatown." *Bergen Record*, May 27: A27.

James, George. 1991. "Man dies in 5th Ave. restaurant shootout." *New York Times*, November 18: B3.

Jankowski, Martin Sanchez. 1991. *Islands in the Streets*. Berkeley: University of California Press.

Joe, Karen. 1993. "Getting into the gang: Methodological issues in studying ethnic gangs." In M. De La Rosa and J. Adrados (Eds.), *Drug Abuse among Minority Youth: Methodological Issues and Recent Research Advances*. NIDA Monograph Series 130. Washington, D.C.: Government Printing Office.

———. 1994. "The new criminal conspiracy? Asian gangs and organized crime in San Francisco." *Journal of Research in Crime and Delinquency* 31, no. 4: 390–415.

Jones, Robert C. (Ed.) 1984. *Patterns of Unauthorized Migration: Mexico and California*. Totowa, N.J.: Rowman and Allanheld.

Kamen, Al. 1991. "A dark road from China to Chinatown." *Washington Post*, June 17: A1.

———. 1993. "China helping stem flow of illegal immigrants." *Washington Post*, November 1: A6.

Kaplan, David. 1992. *Fires of the Dragon: Politics, Murder, and the Kuomintang*. New York: Atheneum.

Kaplan, David E., Donald Goldberg, and Linda Jue. 1986. "Enter the dragon: How Hong Kong's notorious underworld syndicates are becoming the number one organized crime problem in California." *San Francisco Focus*, December: 68–84.

Kelly, Robert, Ko-lin Chin, and Jeffrey Fagan. 1993. "The dragon breathes fire: Chinese organized crime in New York City." *Contemporary Crises: Law, Crime, and Social Policy* 19: 245–69.

Kerber, Fred, and Don Gentile. 1982. "The tongs' hammer lock: Merchants silent in face of extortion." *New York Daily News*, December 26: 5.

Kerr, Peter. 1987a. "Chinese now dominate New York heroin trade." *New York Times*, August 9: A1.

———. 1987b. "Chasing the heroin from plush hotel to mean streets." *New York Times*, August 11: B1.

Kessel, Jochen, and Peter Hum. 1991. "Crime in Chinatown: Wave of killings hits Toronto as rival gangs battle for lucrative market." *Ottawa Citizen*, March 16: B5.

Key Publications. 1990. *Chinese Business Guide and Directory*. New York: Key Publications.

Kifner, John. 1991. "Abducted Chinese illegal aliens rescued." *New York Times*, January 8: B3.

Kinkead, Gwen. 1992. *Chinatown*. New York: HarperCollins.

Klein, Malcolm. 1971. *Street Gangs and Street Workers*. Englewood Cliffs, N.J.: Prentice-Hall.

Klein, Malcolm, and Cheryl Maxson. 1989. "Street gang violence." In Neil Wiener and Marvin Wolfgang (Eds.), *Violent Crime, Violent Criminals*. Newbury Park, Calif.: Sage.

Klein, Malcolm, Cheryl Maxson, and Lea Cunningham. 1991. "'Crack,' street gangs, and violence." *Criminology* 29, no. 4: 623–50.

Kneeland, Douglas E. 1971. "Young hoodlums, scorning tradition of hard work, plague San Francisco Chinatown." *New York Times*, September 5: U29.

Knox, George. 1992. "Gangs and related problems among Asian students: Preliminary findings from the First National Asian Gang Survey." Unpublished manuscript.

Koziol, Ronald. 1988. "Multimillionaire charged in heroin case." *San Francisco Examiner*, April 27: A7.

Kuo, Chia-Ling. 1977. *Social and Political Change in New York's Chinatown: The Role of Voluntary Associations*. New York: Praeger.

Kwong, Peter. 1979. *Chinatown, N.Y.: Labor and Politics, 1930–1950*. New York: Monthly Review Press.

———. 1987. *The New Chinatown*. New York: Hill and Wang.

Kwong, Peter, and Dusanka Miqsqcevic. 1990. "The year of the horse." *Village Voice*, July 17: 27–34.

Lai, David Chuenyan. 1988. *Chinatowns: Towns within Cities in Canada*. Vancouver: University of British Columbia Press.

Lam, Willy Wo-lap. 1992. "Foreign rings blamed for drugs flood." *South China Morning Post*, June 26: 13.

Lau, Alan Man S. 1993. Statement made by Alan Man S. Lau, Chairman of Fukien American Association, at a press conference held at 125 East Broadway, New York, New York, September 28.

Lavigne, Yves. 1991. *Good Guy, Bad Guy: Drugs and the Changing Face of Organized Crime*. Toronto: Random House of Canada.

Lay, Richard, and Chris Dobson. 1993. "Rise and fall of Machine Gun Johnny." *South China Morning Post Spectrum*, March 14: 4.

Layton, Mary Jo. 1991. "Crimes by Asian gangs growing." *Bergen Record*, November 3: A22.

Lee, Adam. 1992. "Macau drive against illegals." *South China Morning Post*, September 2: 7.

Lee, C. Y. 1974. *Days of the Tong Wars*. New York: Ballantine.

Lee, Henry. 1989. "Blood of the flower." *New York Daily News Magazine*, February 5: 8–9.

Lee, Rose Hum. 1960. *Chinese in the United States*. Hong Kong: Hong Kong University Press.

Leng, Veronica W. F. 1984. "The Oriental Gang Unit in New York City's Chinatown." Unpublished manuscript.

Leong, Gor Yun. 1936. *Chinatown Inside Out*. New York: Barrows Mussey.

Light, Ivan. 1974. "From vice district to tourist attraction: The moral career of American Chinatowns, 1880–1940." *Pacific Historical Review* 43: 367–94.

Lipman, Jonathan, and Stevan Harrell (Eds.). 1990. *Violence in China*. Albany: State University of New York.

Loo, Chalsa. 1991. *Chinatown*. Westport, Conn.: Greenwood.

Lorch, Donatella. 1990a. "Mourners returned fire, police say: Retaliation is expected over cemetery shootout." *New York Times*, July 30: B1.

———. 1990b. "Robber shoots robber as a victim ducks." *New York Times*, August 28: B3.

———. 1991. "Immigrants from China pay dearly to be slaves." *New York Times*, January 3: B1.

———. 1992. "A flood of illegal aliens enters U.S. via Kennedy: Requesting political asylum is usual ploy." *New York Times*, March 18: B2.

Los Angeles County District Attorney. 1992. *Gangs, Crime and Violence in Los Angeles*. Los Angeles: District Attorney's Office.

Louttit, Neil. 1982. "Toronto extortion gang plays on Chinese traditions." *Toronto Star*, February 18: 4.

Lubasch, Arnold H. 1985. "Asian crime group hit by U.S. arrests." *New York Times*, September 17: A1.

———. 1986. "Family accused in Taiwan-U.S. prostitution ring." *New York Times*, April 26: A33.

———. 1992. "7 sentenced to life terms in a gang case." *New York Times*, October 3: 26.

Ludlow, Lynn. 1987. "Golden Dragon massacre: Pain still felt a decade later." *San Francisco Examiner*, May 10: B1.

Lyman, Stanford. 1986. *Chinatown and Little Tokyo*. Millwood, N.Y.: Associated Faculty Press.

Ma, L. Eve Armentrout. 1990. *Revolutionaries, Monarchists, and Chinatowns*. Honolulu: University of Hawaii Press.

Maltz, Michael. 1985. "Toward defining organized crime." In H. E. Alexander and G. Caiden (Eds.), *The Politics and Economics of Organized Crime*. Lexington, Mass.: D. C. Heath.

Mano, D. Keith. 1988. "There's more to Chinatown." *The World of New York*, April 24: 42–46.

Mark, Gregory Yee. 1992. "From Jung Gwok to Gam Saan: Wah Kiu and Yen Shee." Paper presented at the Luodi-Shenggen Conference on Overseas Chinese, San Francisco, November.

Marriott, Michael. 1989. "Heroin seizure at 3 Queens sites is called biggest U.S. drug raid." *New York Times*, February 22: B5.

Marsh, Jon. 1992a. "International heroin task force proposed." *South China Morning Post*, May 31: 4.

———. 1992b. "Sino-US drugs battle stumbles against bizarre 'Goldfish case.'" *South China Morning Post Spectrum*, June 14: 3.

Marshall, Catherine, and Gretchen Rossman. 1989. *Designing Qualitative Research*. Newbury Park, Calif.: Sage.

Martin, Douglas. 1988. "New York's Chinese: Living in 2 worlds." *New York Times*, February 20: 29.

Martin, Mildred Crowl. 1977. *Chinatown's Angry Angel*. Palo Alto, Calif.: Pacific Books.

Maxson, Cheryl, and Malcolm Klein. 1990. "Street gang violence: Twice as great, or half as great?" In Ronald Huff (Ed.), *Gangs in America*, Newbury Park, Calif.: Sage.

McCoy, Alfred W. 1973. *The Politics of Heroin in South-East Asia*. New York: Harper and Row.

McFadden, Robert D. 1988. "A Chinatown businessman is charged in a slaying." *New York Times*, June 12: 34.

———. 1994. "Benny Ong, 87, reputed godfather of Chinatown crime, dies." *New York Times*, August 8: B7.

McLeod, Alexander. 1947. *Pigtails and Gold Dust*. Caldwell, Idaho: Caxton Printers.

McLeod, Jay. 1987. *Ain't No Makin' It: Levelled Aspirations in a Low Income Neighborhood*. Boulder, Colo.: Westview.

Meskil, Paul. 1989. "In the eye of the storm." *New York Daily News Magazine*, February 5: 10–16.

Miller, Stuart Creighton. 1960. *The Unwelcome Immigrant: The American Image of the Chinese, 1785–1881*. Berkeley: University of California Press.

Miller, Walter. 1958. "Lower class culture as a generating milieu of gang delinquency." *Journal of Social Issues* 14 (fall): 5–19.

Millman, Joel. 1985. "Casinos luring Chinese." *New York Times*, February 24: NJ15.

Minke, Pauline. 1974. *Chinese in the Mother Lode (1850–1870)*. 1960. Reprint, Saratoga, Calif.: R & E Research Associates.

Moloney, Paul. 1991. "Bloodbath in Chinatown: More police urged for Chinatown." *Toronto Star*, March 4: A3.

Moore, Joan W. 1978. *Homeboys*. Philadelphia: Temple University Press.

———. 1990. "Gangs, drugs, and violence." In Mario De La Rosa, Elizabeth Lambert, and Bernard Gropper (Eds.), *Drugs and Violence: Causes, Correlates, and Consequences*, NIDA Research Monograph 103. Rockville, Md.: National Institute of Drug Abuse.

———. 1991. *Going Down to the Barrio*. Philadelphia: Temple University Press.

Morain, Dan, and Philip Hager. 1991. "Officials call heroin seizure a major victory." *Los Angeles Times*, June 22: A24.

Morgan, W. P. 1960. *Triad Societies in Hong Kong*. Hong Kong: Government Press.

Mydans, Seth. 1992. "Chinese smugglers' lucrative cargo: Humans." *New York Times*, March 21: 1.

Myers, Willard. 1992. "The United States under siege: Assault on the borders, Chinese smuggling 1983–1992." Unpublished manuscript.

Nadelmann, Ethan. 1993. *Cops across Borders: The Internationalization of U.S. Criminal Law Enforcement*. University Park: Pennsylvania State University Press.

Nee, Victor G., and Brett de Barry Nee. 1986. *Longtime Californ'*. Stanford: Stanford University Press.

New York Times. 1993a. "Voyage to life of shattered dreams." July 23: B1.

———. 1993b. "An increasing sense of vulnerability; Mourning a murder victim, Chinese express frustration with crimes at restaurants." December 3: B1.

Newman, Maria. 1992. "They volunteer to protect and serve." *New York Times*, April 19: 27.

Ng, David, and Paul Tharp. 1983. "Chinese gang war claims new victim." *New York Post*, March 7: 4.

Nieves, Evelyn. 1993. "Chinese immigrants kept padlocked in warehouse." *New York Times*, May 26: B5.

North, Hart H. 1944. "Chinese highbinders societies in California." *California Historical Society Quarterly* 23: 335–47.

O'Callaghan, Sean. 1978. *The Triads: The Mafia of the Far East*. London: W. H. Allen.

O'Kane, James M. 1992. *The Crooked Ladder: Gangsters, Ethnicity, and the American Dream*. New Brunswick, N.J.: Transaction Publishers.

Orrick, Phyllis. 1990. "Chinatown cop." *New York Press* 3 (May 30): 10–12.

Padilla, Felix. 1992. *The Gang as an American Enterprise*. New Brunswick, N.J.: Rutgers University Press.

Pak, Rose. 1972. "Chinatown gangs—ex-member talks." *San Francisco Chronicle*, July 6: 1.

Penn, Stanley. 1980. "Youth gangs plague Chinatown merchants with payoff demands." *Wall Street Journal*, August 18: 1.

———. 1990. "Asian connection: Chinese gangsters fill a narcotics gap left by U.S. drive on Mafia." *Wall Street Journal*, March 22: A1.

Polsky, Carol. 1985. "Feds: Chinatown indictments target modern 'Black Hand.'" *New York Newsday*, February 19: 3.

Posner, Gerald. 1988. *Warlords of Crimes*. New York: McGraw-Hill.

Powell, Michael. 1989. "Tong influence in Chinatown turns to drugs." *New York Newsday*, February 27: 7.

President's Commission on Organized Crime. 1984. *Organized Crime of Asian Origin*, record of hearing III—October 23–25, 1984, New York, N.Y. Washington, D.C.: Government Printing Office.

Raab, Selwyn. 1984. "Asia crime groups held active in U.S." *New York Times*, October 24: A1.

Rabin, Bernard, and Paul Meskil. 1986. "Rubout in a massage parlor." *New York Daily News*, February 20: 7.

Ramirez, Raul, and Larry Hatfield. 1977. "The view from Joe Fong's cell." *San Francisco Chronicle*, September 25: 1.

Reiss, Albert, and Jeffrey Roth. 1993. *Understanding and Preventing Violence*. Washington, D.C.: National Academy Press.

Rice, Berkeley. 1977. "The new gangs of Chinatown." *Psychology Today* 10: 60–69.

Rosario, Ruben, and Mike Santangelo. 1986. "Girl is found strangled." *New York Daily News*, February 19: 5.

Rosenfeld, Seth. 1993. "Alleged gang boss indicted." *San Francisco Examiner*, October 12: A1.

Ruffini, Gene, and Joe Cotter. 1980. "Merchant kills teen gangster." *New York Post*, May 7: 3.

Sanders, William. 1994. *Gangbangs and Drive-bys*. New York: Aldine De Gruyter.

Saxton, Alexander. 1971. *The Indispensable Enemy: Labor and the Anti-Chinese Movement in California*. Berkeley: University of California Press.

Scardino, Albert. 1986. "Commercial rents in Chinatown soar as Hong Kong exodus grows." *New York Times*, December 25: A1.

Schalks, Toon. 1991. *Chinese Organized Crime in the Netherlands*. The Hague: National Criminal Intelligence Service, NCB Interpol.

Schemo, Diana Jean. 1993a. "Survivors tell of voyage of little daylight, little food, and only hope." *New York Times*, June 7: B5.

———. 1993b. "Chinese immigrants tell of Darwinian voyage." *New York Times*, June 12: A1.

Schermerhorn, Jim, and Beth Hughes. 1984. "Pro style marks home robbery, killings of rich S.F. couple." *San Francisco Examiner*, May 25: A1.

Scilla, Susan Servis, and Lila Locksley. 1985. "Chinese restaurateur threatened: 5 charged in extortion." *Bergen Record*, August 27: C1.

Sciolino, Elaine. 1994. "State Dept. report labels Nigeria major trafficker of drugs to U.S." *New York Times*, April 5: A1.

Seagrave, Sterling. 1985. *The Soong Dynasty*. New York: Harper and Row.

Seper, Jerry. 1986. "Chinese gangs and heroin cast lawless shadow." *Washington Times*, January 28: A1.

Seper, Jerry, and Glenn Emery. 1986. "Opium daze and Pink Knights herald the age of the dragon." *Insight*, February 17: 20–24.

Seward, George. 1881. *Chinese Immigration: Its Social and Economic Aspects*. New York: Scribner's.

Shaw, Clifford R., and Henry D. McKay. 1942. *Juvenile Delinquency in Urban Areas*. Chicago: University of Chicago Press.

Shelly, Kevin. 1994. "Asian mob linked to A.C. casinos." *The Press of Atlantic City*, June 5: A1.

Short, James, and Fred Strodtbeck. 1965. *Group Process and Gang Delinquency*. Chicago: University of Chicago Press.

Simmel, Georg. 1955. *Conflict and the Web of Group-Affiliations*. New York: Free Press.

Skogan, Wesley. 1984. "Reporting crimes to the police: The status of world research." *Journal of Research in Crime and Delinquency* 21: 113–37.

Skolnick, Jerome, Teodore Correl, Elizabeth Navarro, and Roger Rabb. 1988. "The social structure of street drug dealing." *BCS Forum*. Bureau of Criminal Statistics. Sacramento, Cal.: Office of the Attorney General.

Smith, Pat. 1988. "B-line to Chinatown." *New York Post*, April 28: 55.

Sollenberger, Richard. 1968. "Chinese-American child-rearing practices and juvenile delinquency." *Journal of Social Psychology* 74: 13–23.

Song, John Huey-long. 1992. "Attitudes of Chinese immigrants and Vietnamese refugees toward law enforcement in the United States." *Justice Quarterly*, 9 no. 4: 703–19.

Song, John Huey-long, and John Dombrink. 1993. "The depiction of Asian criminals: Media, experts and the framing of a criminal event." Paper presented at the 45th annual meeting of the American Society of Criminology, Phoenix.

Song, John Huey-long, John Dombrink, and Gilbert Geis. 1992. "Lost in the melting pot: Asian youth gangs in the United States." *Gang Journal* 1, no. 1: 1–12.

Spataro, Michael F. 1978. "Report on international Chinese street gangs and triad organized criminal activities." Paper presented at the first annual meeting on Chinese Triad Societies, New York Police Academy, New York.

Spector, Malcolm, and John Kitsuse. 1977. *Constructing Social Problems*. Menlo Park, Calif.: Cummings.

Spergel, Irving A. 1964. *Racketville, Slumtown, Haulburg*. Chicago: University of Chicago Press.

———. 1990. "Youth gangs: Continuity and change." In Michael Tonry and Norval Morris (Eds.), *Crime and Justice: A Review of Research*, vol. 12. Chicago: University of Chicago Press.

———. 1995. *The Youth Gang Problem: A Community Approach*. New York: Oxford University Press.

Stalk, Jeffrey. 1993. "Dutch focus on smuggling of Chinese." *International Herald Tribune*, May 7: 1.

State of California, Department of Justice. 1973. "Triads: Mafia of the Far East." Unpublished report.

Steinberg, Jacques. 1991. "Tourist in car killed as she chances upon Chinatown gunfight." *New York Times*, July 6: L23.

———. 1992. "7 in Asian gang are convicted." *New York Times*, March 31: B3.

Strom, Stephanie. 1991. "13 held in kidnapping of illegal aliens." *New York Times*, January 2: B3.

Stutman, Robert M. 1987. "Emerging criminal groups in heroin trafficking." Statement made before the Select Committee on Narcotics Abuse and Control, U.S. House of Representatives, July 10.

Sullivan, Mercer. 1989. *Getting Paid: Youth Crime and Work in the Inner City*. Ithaca: Cornell University Press.

Sullivan, Ronald. 1992. "Five indicted in a robbery at a church." *New York Times*, December 31: B3.

Sung, Betty Lee. 1967. *Mountain of Gold*. New York: Macmillan.

———. 1977. *Gangs in New York's Chinatown*. Monograph No. 6. New York: Department of Asian Studies, City College of New York.

———. 1979. *Transplanted Chinese Children*. New York: Department of Asian Studies, City University of New York.

———. 1987. *The Adjustment Experience of Chinese Immigrant Children in New York City*. New York: Center for Migration Studies.

Surovell, Hariette. 1988. "Chinatown Cosa Nostra." *Penthouse*, June: 41–44, 96–100.

Suttles, Gerald. 1968. *The Social Order of the Slum*. Chicago: University of Chicago Press.

Takagi, Paul, and Tony Platt. 1978. "Behind the gilded ghetto: An analysis of race, class, and crime in Chinatown." *Crime and Social Justice* 9: 2–25.

Tam, Bonny. 1992. "198 illegals arrested in Tin Shui Wai." *South China Morning Post*, September 8: 2.

Taylor, Carl. 1990. *Dangerous Society*. East Lansing: Michigan State University Press.

Thompson, Jennifer. 1976. "Are Chinatown gang wars a cover-up?" *San Francisco Focus Magazine*, February: 20–21.

Thornberry, Terence, Marvin Krohn, Alan Lizotte, and Deborah Chard-Wierschem. 1993. "The role of juvenile gangs in facilitating delinquent behavior." *Journal of Research in Crime and Delinquency* 30, no. 1: 55–87.

Thrasher, Frederic M. 1927. *The Gang: A Study of 1,313 Gangs in Chicago*. Chicago: University of Chicago Press.

Torode, Greg. 1993. "US raid on ship upsets HK police." *South China Morning Post*, July 5: 2.

Torres, Vicki. 1993. "2 men tell of torture at hands of smugglers." *Los Angeles Times*, October 3: B1.

Toy, Calvin. 1992a. "Coming out to play: Reasons to join and participate in Asian gangs." *Gang Journal* 1, no. 1: 13–29.

———. 1992b. "A short history of Asian gangs in San Francisco." *Justice Quarterly* 9, no. 4: 647–65.

Tracy, Paul. 1987. "Subcultural delinquency: A comparison of the incidence and severity of gang and nongang member offenses." Unpublished manuscript.

Treaster, Joseph B. 1991. "U.S. officials seize huge heroin cache." *New York Times*, June 22: A10.

———. 1993a. "Behind immigrants' voyage, long reach of Chinese gang." *New York Times*, June 9: A1.

———. 1993b. "U.S. plans tougher strategy to combat alien smuggling." *New York Times*, June 14: A1.

Tsai, Shih-shan Henry. 1986. *The Chinese Experience in America*. Bloomington: Indiana University Press.

U.S. Department of Justice. 1985. *Oriental Organized Crime: A Report of a Research Project Conducted by the Organized Crime Section.* Federal Bureau of Investigation, Criminal Investigative Division. Washington, D.C.: Government Printing Office.

———. 1988. *Report on Asian Organized Crime.* Criminal Division. Washington, D.C.: Government Printing Office.

U.S. Department of State. 1993. *Narcotics in Burma.* Conference Report. Washington, D.C.: Government Printing Office.

———. 1994. *International Narcotics Control Strategy Report.* Washington, D.C.: Government Printing Office.

U.S. District Court, Eastern District of New York. 1990. *United States of America v. Chen I. Chung, a/k/a 'Tony Chan' et al.* Complaint, Criminal Division, November 21.

———. 1991. *The United States of America v. Chen I. Chung, a/k/a 'Tony Chan' et al.* Indictment, Criminal Division, May 17.

U.S. District Court, Southern District of New York. 1985a. "Government version of the offense" of Ghost Shadows members." Report. New York: U.S. District Court.

———. 1985b. *United States of America v. Yin Poy Louie et al.* Indictment, New York, February 18.

———. 1985c. *The United States of America v. Chang An-lo, a/k/a 'White Wolf' et al.* Complaint, September 16.

U.S. House of Representatives. 1987. *Public Hearings on Emerging Ethnic Crime Group Involvement in Heroin Trafficking.* Select Committee on Narcotics Abuse and Control. JFK International Arrivals Terminal, New York.

U.S. Immigration and Naturalization Service. 1989. *The INS Enforcement Approach to Chinese Organized Crime.* Washington, D.C.: Investigations Division, Immigration and Naturalization Service, U.S. Department of Justice.

———. 1993. "Vessels that are known to have attempted to smuggle PRC nationals into the United States," unpublished report, August 17.

U.S. Senate. [1877] 1978. *Report of the Joint Special Committee to Investigate Chinese Immigration.* Reprint, New York: Arno Press.

———. 1986. *Emerging Criminal Groups.* Hearings before the Permanent Subcommittee on Investigations of the Committee on Governmental Affairs. Washington, D.C.: Government Printing Office.

———. 1992. *Asian Organized Crime.* Hearing before the Permanent Subcommittee on Investigations of the Committee on Governmental Affairs. Washington, D.C.: Government Printing Office.

———. 1993. *Congressional Record.* June 10: S:7093–98.

Vigil, Diego. 1988. *Barrio Gangs.* Austin: University of Texas Press.

Vigil, Diego, and Steve Yun. 1990. "Vietnamese youth gangs in Southern California." In Ronald Huff (Ed.), *Gangs in America.* Newbury, Calif.: Sage.

Wallis, Belinda, and Tommy Lewis. 1993. "East Wood case discussed." *South China Morning Post,* March 15: 2.

Weintraub, Sidney. 1984. "Illegal immigrants in Texas: Impact on social services and related considerations." *International Migration Review* 18, no. 3: 733–47.

Weiss, Murray. 1983. "Chinatown gang leader shot dead." *New York Daily News,* March 14: 5.

Whyte, William Foote. 1943. *Street Corner Society.* Chicago: University of Chicago Press.

Wilson, Carol Green. 1974. *Chinatown Quest.* San Francisco: California Historical Society.

Wolfgang, Marvin, and Franco Ferracuti. 1982. *The Subculture of Violence.* Beverly Hills: Sage.

Wong, Mende. 1978–79. "Prostitution: San Francisco Chinatown, mid- and late-nineteenth century." *Bridge Magazine* 6, no. 4: 23–28.

Wu, Robin. 1977. "What the ***** is goin on?" *Bridge Magazine* 1 (fall): 5–11.
Yablonsky, Lewis. 1970. *The Violent Gang*. Baltimore: Penguin.
Zhou, Min. 1992. *Chinatown: The Socioeconomic Potential of an Urban Enclave*. Philadelphia: Temple University Press.

In Chinese

Centre Daily News. 1985a. "Chinese are the most uncooperative people, Fifth Precinct Chief complained." June 7: 20.
———. 1985b. "Ghost Shadows leader 'Fisheye' captured." November 21: 20.
———. 1986. "Chinatown's largest gambling den shut down by the police." September 18: 20.
Chang, Mung-yen. 1991. "Facts about Hong Kong triad societies." *Wide Angle Magazine*, May: 30–39.
Chi, Zong-xian. 1985. *Gangs, Election, and Violence*. Taipei: Jiao Dian.
China Press. 1992. "The revival of the illegal gambling industry on East Broadway." January 30: 16.
China Tribune. 1976. "Restaurant owners slain by Chinese youth gang members." December 11: 1.
Chou, Ker-ting. 1993. *Ghosts and Spirits in New York City's Chinatown*. New York: People and Events Publisher.
Huang, Yuan-ling. 1988. "The number of Chinese heroin cases increased dramatically in 1987." *World Journal*, January 6: 36.
Li, Chen-dong. 1981. *The Values of Three Classical Novels*. Taipei: Buffalo Book.
Liu, Pei-chi. 1981. *A History of the Chinese in the United States of America, II*. Taipei: Li Min.
Sing Tao Jih Pao. 1989. "Seven Chinese youths robbed a massage parlor; a young woman masseuse was raped." September 25: 24.
———. 1990. "Malaysian young women are becoming active in the sex industry." December 4: 24.
———. 1991a. "Four BTK members arrested after robbing a Chinatown jewelry store." January 22: 28.
———. 1991b. "Asian suspects robbed a group of jewelers in midtown Manhattan," April 25: 24.
———. 1991c. "To fight Asian crime, the FBI is actively recruiting Asians." May 24: 28.
———. 1991d. "Three Chinese gang members were arrested for selling a box of mooncakes for $2,000." September 5: 28.
———. 1992a. "Police chief urge Fujianese immigrants not to be afraid of reporting crime to authorities." May 7: 28.
———. 1992b. "The Morals Division raided a prostitution house on the Lower East Side; 16 women arrested." May 27: 27.
———. 1992c. "The Senate will conduct public hearings on Asian organized crime activities." June 17: 27.
———. 1992d. "Two members of the Golden Star were arrested for home-invasion robbery." November 6: 28.
———. 1993a. "INS district director accused members of the S.F. Chinese community for not reporting alien smuggling activity." January 11: 24.
———. 1993b. "Queens Asian gang unit acclaimed by NYPD Chief Detective." February 5: 32.
———. 1993c. "Two Chinese youths nabbed for extorting merchants along Eighth Avenue." March 10: 28.

———. 1993d. "Four Fujianese youths robbed an apartment and a Fujianese man was shot to death." August 2: 28.

———. 1993e. "New sex businesses in New York City's Chinatown." August 31: 30.

———. 1993f. "Parents of kidnapping victim blame the police for victim's death." September 27: 25.

———. 1994. "Eight Tung On gang members arrested for extorting $100,000 from a restaurant owner." November 12: 28.

World Journal. 1980a. "Gang members assaulted a youth after he refused to join them." November 4: 24.

———. 1980b. "Two masked gunmen shot the manager of a travel agency to death." November 18: 24.

———. 1985a. "All Chinese-speaking police officers in the NYPD are temporarily assigned to Chinatown to prevent gang warfare." May 30: 24.

———. 1985b. "Police in the tri-state area set up roadblocks over the long weekend in an attempt to crack down on highly mobile Chinese gangs." October 16: 16.

———. 1986. "The father of a slain young girl is dissatisfied with police attitudes." February 21: 3.

———. 1988. "A two-year joint operation between the U.S. and Hong Kong authorities resulted in a crackdown on an international drug trafficking organization." April 17: 1.

———. 1990a. "CCBA leader expressed his disappointment with 5th precinct chief." June 1: 28.

———. 1990b. "Senator Biden warned that Chinese mobs' involvement in heroin trafficking will become a disaster for the U.S." August 22: 1.

———. 1991. "The Chinese criticize the U.S. for offering refuge to a criminal." June 27: 3.

———. 1992a. "FBI New York branch active in combating Asian gangs." April 30: 21.

———. 1992b. "Queens Asian Crime Investigation Unit is formed to deal with gang crimes." May 4: 19.

———. 1992c. "The reluctance to testify among Chinese victims causing a police officer to wonder 'Are Chinese people willing to be victimized forever?'" August 12: 22.

———. 1993a. "Officials allege that the number of Asian prostitutes in New York City is increasing; Chinese gangs are believed to be in control." May 18: B1.

———. 1993b. "23 Chinese illegals rescued, members of White Tigers and Flying Dragons arrested." June 19: A3.

———. 1993c. "Human smuggling gangs may be indicted under RICO." June 20: B1.

———. 1993d. "With the increase in Chinese gang members in Brooklyn, the police are actively collecting information about the gangs." July 1: B1.

———. 1993e. "Chinese illegals are forced to commit subway robberies to repay their smuggling debts." August 12: B1.

———. 1994a. "The 5th precinct's Asian Gang Task Force is active in fighting Chinese gangs." August 26: B1

———. 1994b. "Fifth Precinct Officer claimed that victims' tolerance empowers the gangs." October 13: B1.

———. 1994c. "Turn a New Leaf aids young Asians from staying away from gangs." November 1: 30.

Wu, Cheng Hsiung. 1993. *Immigration and Chinese Communities*. Taipei: Ying Chen.

Yang, Wen-yu. 1985. "Chinese commercial sex in New York City." *Rainbow Biweekly*, August 2: 5.

Zhang, Sheng. 1984. *The Activities of Hong Kong Organized Crime Groups*. Hong Kong: Tien Ti.

INDEX